Praise for *Madly in L*

"Loving ourselves is one of the most challeng_____ _____ing, growth, and transformation. *Madly in L_____ ___ ___* is a passionate call for each of us to make peace with who we are and love ourselves unconditionally. As a man, father, and husband, I can think of nothing more important to do for ourselves, our partners, and our children."
— Mike Robbins, author of *Be Yourself, Everyone Else Is Already Taken*

"The greatest relationship we have is with ourselves. Christine Arylo brilliantly shares a pathway for women to fall in love with the essence of who they are. This book is a great gift to all women and their daughters and dares us to love with all our hearts."
— Kristine Carlson, *New York Times* bestselling author
of *Don't Sweat the Small Stuff for Women*
and *Don't Sweat the Small Stuff for Moms*

"For any woman who wants to love herself, not just in theory but in everyday life, Christine Arylo has written the go-to guide on self-love. Christine is a brilliant teacher and catalyst who leaves readers feeling connected and joyful. Fresh, smart, and fun, *Madly in Love with ME* belongs on every woman's nightstand."
— Amy Ahlers, author of *Big Fat Lies Women Tell Themselves*

"Self-love served up on a sparkly silver platter? Sign me up for a heaping helping! While self-love gets a bum rap by those who mistakenly think it's selfish or narcissistic to love yourself, in *Madly in Love with ME*, Christine Arylo reframes self-love as a spiritual practice aimed at increasing your awareness of the divine spark that lies within us all. By learning to love and accept the true nature of who you are, radical transformation — and true healing — naturally follows."
— Lissa Rankin, MD, founder of www.OwningPink.com
and author of *Mind Over Medicine*

"Every woman wants to fall in love with herself and then share that love with the world. Revel in this book and you will. Much more than a self-help book, *Madly in Love with ME* is an illuminated self-love guidebook that shows you exactly how to love yourself well and live your happiest life — no matter what."

— SARK, artist and author of *Glad No Matter What*

"*Madly in Love with ME* is like a magic elixir — just the potion we need to recapture that powerful, transformational force of loving ourselves fully and fiercely. Christine reminds us that loving ourselves is not just a crucial individual act for the quality of our own lives but a radical act of social change for women and girls everywhere. This is a practical, fun, and radiantly clear handbook to meet the love of your life — you!"

— Meggan Watterson, author of
Reveal: A Sacred Manual for Getting Spiritually Naked

"The world is in desperate need of more love, and the fastest path to doing your part is to read this book and begin to love yourself deeply and joyfully. The only 'selfish' thing about self-love is withholding it from yourself and everyone else!"

— Arielle Ford, author of *Wabi Sabi Love*

"*Madly in Love with ME* is a manual for your soul. Christine Arylo teaches the essential practice of self-love in a way that is deeply healing, profoundly transformational, absolutely brilliant, and fun! This book will free you from beliefs and patterns that may be sabotaging your life and crack your heart open to infinite, unconditional love."

— Christine Hassler, author of *20 Something, 20 Everything*

"Christine Arylo is an inspirational guide for anyone on the journey to self-love. Through her personal growth and experience, she has crafted a book for you to release all that blocks you from true freedom and peace. Allow Christine to be your teacher on your miraculous journey inward."

— Gabrielle Bernstein, author of *May Cause Miracles*

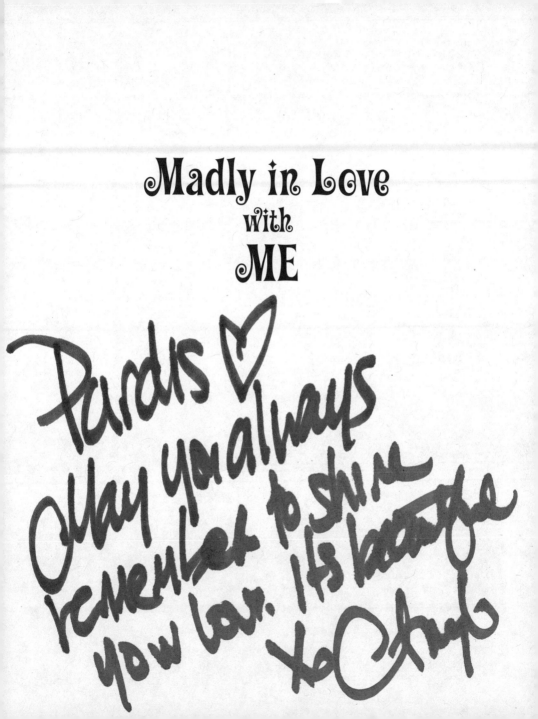

Madly in Love
with
ME

Pardis ♡

May you always
remember to shine
your love. It's beautiful

xo Christine

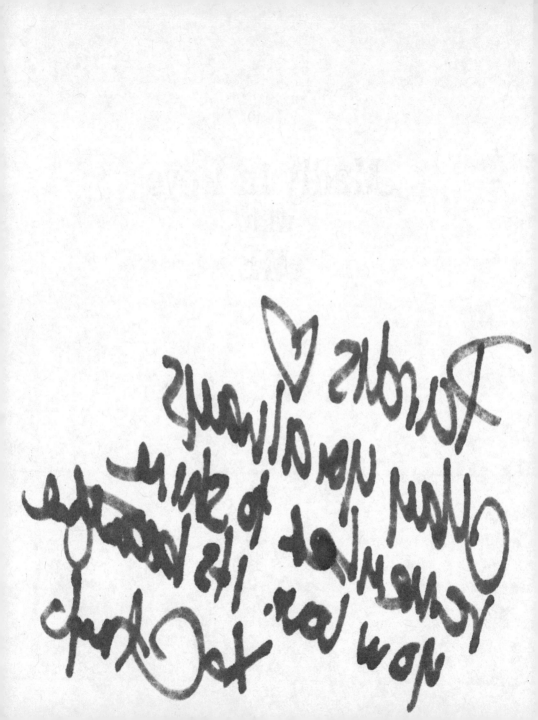

Madly in Love

with

ME

THE DARING ADVENTURE
of becoming your own best friend

CHRISTINE ARYLO

New World Library
Novato, California

New World Library
14 Pamaron Way
Novato, California 94949

Library of Congress Cataloging-in-Publication Data
Arylo, Christine, date.
 Madly in love with me : the daring adventure of becoming your own best friend / Christine Arylo.
    p.   cm.
Includes bibliographical references.
ISBN 978-1-60868-065-8 (pbk. : alk. paper)
1. Self-esteem. 2. Self-acceptance. I. Title.
BF697.5.S46A79 2012
158.1—dc23   2012031886

First printing, November 2012
ISBN 978-1-60868-065-8
Printed in the USA on 100% postconsumer-waste recycled paper

New World Library is proud to be a Gold Certified Environmentally Responsible Publisher. Publisher certification awarded by Green Press Initiative. www.green pressinitiative.org

10 9 8 7 6 5 4 3 2

*To Lucy McIntyre Shapiro and Jane Roberts Wagner —
my two goddess-daughters — and their mother, Anne —
my soul sister — whose love and presence in my life made
it possible for me to devote my life to sharing the message
and teachings of self-love with the world*

Contents

Part 3. AMPLIFY the LOVE!
Secrets to Cultivating a Long-Lasting,
Loving Relationship with Yourself

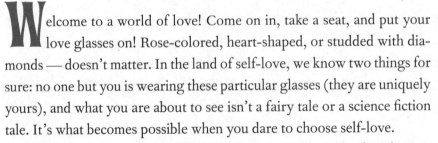

Imagine a World of Love

Welcome to a world of love! Come on in, take a seat, and put your love glasses on! Rose-colored, heart-shaped, or studded with diamonds — doesn't matter. In the land of self-love, we know two things for sure: no one but you is wearing these particular glasses (they are uniquely yours), and what you are about to see isn't a fairy tale or a science fiction tale. It's what becomes possible when you dare to choose self-love.

Imagine, if you will, a *world* in which every girl born on this planet is born in love with, and stays in love with, herself. A world in which every girl, throughout the entire span of her life, never feels disconnected from the thread of love that makes her feel safe, loved, cared for, and special. Instead of learning to measure (and therefore judge) herself by the external images and standards that bombard her daily with the subconscious message "You are not enough," each girl grows up believing that, regardless of her accomplishments, body shape, love-life status, or material possessions, she is *more* than enough, just because she is herself. The thought that her unique soul could be measured against and compared to that of another person or an outside ideal would never occur to her. To commit such an act on oneself would be, in her mind, insane.

Imagine *generations of girls and women* who never suffer from eating disorders, who refuse to tolerate an abusive or toxic relationship in their lives. Women who take care of themselves first, without guilt or obligation, rendering exhaustion and the sense of being overwhelmed obsolete, ancient diseases only read about in textbooks. To them the notion that they should give and give and give until they have nothing left for themselves would be as absurd as placing their hands directly into the flame on a hot stove. The girls in this world would know, without a doubt, that in order to give they must also receive, and self-care would be as natural as breathing and as everyday as eating.

Now, imagine *a girl or woman in your life* whom you love dearly. What if she could go her entire lifetime without comparing, judging, or emotionally beating herself up? What if her first reaction was always to be kind and compassionate to herself, to tell herself that she was doing the best she could? Imagine how much more love and happiness she would feel and, as a result, how much more empowered she would be to live her best possible life, one that would give *her* everything her heart and soul *really* desired — not what she thought she *should* have — a life that would let her do and be whatever she chose.

What a world that would be! And while this world may not currently be the norm for us, this reality is not so far outside of our reach. The possibility of this world already lives inside each of us. This possibility lives inside you.

Imagine if you dare. Put your hand on your heart, close your eyes, take a breath. Now imagine that the girl or woman we just spoke of — the one who loves herself unconditionally, who freely gives her gifts to the max, whose heart is open to receive endless amounts of love and support, who doesn't bother judging herself according to other people's standards or lives, but who instead has an inner compass she trusts implicitly to guide her to her happiness and greatest life — is you.

You are the girl or woman who never drives herself to exhaustion but instead makes it a priority to take care of herself daily, without guilt or worry that everything will fall apart. You're the one who asks for what you need. Imagine that every year as you age, you fall *more* in love with your body, even as cellulite or wrinkles get added to the package. To you, your body is a personal temple, and you adore and serve her and celebrate her for the one-of-a-kind body she is.

Connected securely to the thread of love, you respect yourself so deeply that each of your relationships reflects that same unwavering respect and unconditional love — or you don't remain in that relationship. You know your first loyalty must be to yourself. You'd rather be by yourself than in the type of relationship (whether it's a romance, a friendship, a working relationship with a colleague, or a family relationship with a relative) that keeps you from living your greatest life or being your best self. You're not afraid of being alone, because you know *you* are always with you. As a result, your life has *more* love, not less.

Imagine being as compassionate with yourself as you are with the girls and women you currently love without question. Imagine loving *yourself* without question. Imagine that all this self-love is as natural as breathing, because you always remember and hold sacred the idea that the relationship you have with yourself is *the most important relationship of your life*.

Wherever you are on your self-love journey, today marks your commitment to keeping the thread of self-love alive all year long, an everyday connection to your heart and soul. In the pages that follow, you will take a stand and make sure that from this day forward, your relationship with yourself is as important as every other relationship in your life. This means that, just like in any other relationship that you want to flourish, you'll need to give it love and attention, often. Just like in a relationship with a romantic partner, if you want

> The relationship you have with yourself is the most important relationship of your life.

the relationship to rock, you'll need to communicate, check in, and be committed. And just as you'd do almost anything to make sure your best friend or your child had what he or she needed in order to be, love, and live the magical, fantastical life your friend or child deserved, so will you make sure you get what you need. Today you promise to remember to love yourself every day for the rest of your life. For if you aren't willing to make sure you are happy, loved, and well cared for, then how can you expect anyone else to?

So how do you do *that*? Have no fear! You are in the right place. Because, while you may not have received the "Self-Love Handbook" while growing up, the one that would have shown you how to be and act as your own best friend always and without apology, you hold it in your hands right now.

Why Didn't You Receive
the Self-Love Handbook before Now?

The wisdom of how to love yourself is ancient feminine knowledge, and the permission to do so is an indisputable birthright, both of which could be, and *should* be, passed down from generation to generation, available from the moment we are born and at every moment following that. Imagine how your life might have been different if self-love had been spoken of openly as you grew up. What I am speaking about is not just the "you can do anything" rah-rah talk but also the message of unconditional love that no matter what you accomplished, you were enough and you were loved. Imagine if the women you looked to as role models had been stellar examples of self-care, self-compassion, self-awareness, self-expression, and self-respect because their mothers had passed to them the knowledge of self-love. What if together you became a strong tribe of women bonded through love, each committed first and foremost to being her own best friend, knowing that this promise to herself was what allowed her to be a loving mother, auntie, grandmother, godmother, and big sister who could teach others how to love themselves. An approach like this sure would have saved us all a lot of hefty therapy bills and unnecessary pain and suffering!

Self-love never crossed my mind until the day my life hit rock bottom, when my fiancé decided he didn't want to marry me (on the way to our engagement party) — ouch. It was only after two weeks of begging this man to take me back, and crying so much that I had to stop wearing eye makeup altogether, that I was finally able to gather my self-honor and self-respect and, as a self-empowered woman committed to herself first, leave behind my home and life as I knew it.

Raw, defenses down, and the blueprint for my perfect life ripped to shreds, I found myself face-to-face with a really hard question: "How did a smart woman like me end up in a place like this?" While I didn't expect a verbal response, within seconds a voice within me blared like a radio: "Well, Christine, you don't love yourself! You like yourself a lot, and you've got a ton of self-esteem. Yes, you believe that you can do anything you set your mind to, but you don't love yourself, and frankly you don't even know what that means." Damn! My mouth gaped open. While I didn't like what this voice had to say, she was right. Oh, and wait, now that she had the microphone, there was more: "And while you look like you have this great life — the friends, the traveling, the money, the stuff — and you have achieved lots of success in your career, the truth is, you are settling for less than you deserve. You know it and I know it." Damn, right again.

I was a woman who, if she had stopped being busy long enough to be honest with herself, would have realized that even though she "had it all," the life she was living was never going to lead to her happiness. A woman who, if she had been taught to feel her feelings rather than stuff them down, would have seen that her relationships were never going to give her the loving, respectful, and soulful connections she craved. A woman who knew how to work hard and had tons of self-confidence but who had never considered self-compassion, self-care, or self-acceptance as essential to cultivate as things like success and financial security. I was a woman who had never considered self-love. I found myself realizing how badly I needed to find it, but I had no idea where to start.

My first step was to ask all of my friends, really smart, successful women, "How do you love yourself? What is self-love and how do I get some?" They surely would have the answers, right? Wrong. They were just as dumbfounded and ignorant as I. They too had never considered such questions. None of our studies, advanced degrees, or cultural indoctrination from reality TV shows, romantic movies, and tabloid magazines had provided any clues.

So I asked some of my older female relatives, "Can you tell me how to fall in love with myself?" I assumed that because these women were older, they must know the answer. Their replies were worse, although they sure did explain a lot about how I ended up in my current circumstances. They said things like "Why would you want to know such a thing? Stop asking so many silly questions. Just be happy with your life as it is."

It was then that I realized I, and most every woman I knew, had descended from a long line of "stuffers" and "self-sacrificers" — women who had been taught to stuff their feelings and instincts down (or mistrust them altogether), to put their needs at the bottom of the list (if these made it onto the list at all), and to forge ahead no matter what (preferably with a stiff upper lip and unwavering sense of confidence). Our female predecessors had no Oprah, after-school self-esteem programs, or self-empowerment weekend workshops. All they had was the "Self-Sacrifice Handbook, Extreme Edition," whose main teaching said something like this:

> Give, and then give some more, and then give some more. And even
> if there's nothing left for you, or even when you have nothing left to

give, give more. Suck it up and never complain (at least in public), because it's your duty to give, not receive.

This heavy-burden-promoting handbook never talked about needing to fill yourself up before you give to everyone else. It had no passages about loving and nurturing yourself or ensuring that you always act as your own best friend. No examples of how to give to others without giving away yourself in the process, or how to serve the things and people you love without sacrificing your dreams and needs. Unfortunately, this old handbook taught women to equate our self-worth with how much we give and get done in a day — without regard for our own self-care, self-compassion, self-respect, or self-pleasure (a.k.a. self-love). If we weren't giving everything we had away, keeping ourselves busy, or silently suffering or toiling in some way — oh, the guilt and the feelings of inferiority. Ugh!

Thankfully, a wave of feminism rejected the suppressive model of what and how a woman was *supposed* to be. And, while still influenced by this old message of sadistic self-sacrifice that our overly patriarchal society clung to, we now had access to a new, self-empowering tome, "The Self-Esteem Handbook." With it came new opportunities, more equality, and a permission slip to express ourselves and pursue our desires. Yes!

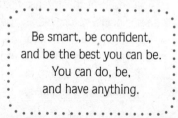

Be smart, be confident, and be the best you can be. You can do, be, and have anything.

Finally we women were empowered by the message of self-esteem. We were liberated to pursue the lives we wanted for ourselves, fully empowered by a new belief: "Be smart, be confident, and be the best you can be. You can do, be, and have anything."

Today girls grow up knowing that they can choose to go to college, get married or not, travel the world, and become anything they can dream of being, without having to rely on a man to get there. We are more empowered and financially independent. And we are free to express ourselves as confident, powerful women. The message that we can do, be, and have anything has taken us far. Thank you to all who fought to make this possible.

And yet there is still more road for us to travel; something is still missing. If you look at the tired faces of women and the stressed-out and overscheduled lives of girls (and ourselves), you can't deny that we have learned to equate strength and success with getting a lot done, staying busy, and having financial success at any cost, even the cost of our own happiness. This fact is backed up by a study conducted by the Rockefeller Foundation and quoted in a *Time* magazine article that compared the level of happiness experienced by women in the 1970s to that of women today. The results are revealing. Yes, women have more opportunity and equality, but we aren't happier. Our happiness levels have stayed the same. Translation: More work and less happiness. Raw deal!

> As a result of this intense focus on our ability to do, be, and have *anything*, we have become a generation of women and girls who feel pressured to do, be, and have *everything*.

Today, from the moment you, as a little girl, learn to read, watch TV, and mimic the women around you, you start feeling the pressure to be, do, and have it all. You grow up striving to attain and maintain the perfect body, the best grades, the successful career, the big bank account, the happy relationship, the ageless face, the perfect family, and on and on — everything that you see outside of you as the "ideal." You're conditioned to believe you must have it all at the same time, and must do and be everything perfectly. So when you begin to realize you don't or can't, instead of asking, "Why the heck am I working so hard to achieve this unrealistic expectation?" you are more likely to ask, "What's wrong with me?"

While there may exist somewhere a superwoman who has the ability to meet all these expectations in a single bound, we mortal women cannot. Instead, full of self-esteem but lacking unapologetic self-care, we drive ourselves harder than ever before, striving to live up to the manufactured images that create our unrealistic expectations, which in turn feed our feelings of never being, doing, or having enough. Lacking a strong sense of self-compassion, we never measure up and instead are extremely hard on ourselves, emotionally bludgeoning ourselves daily. Lacking unwavering self-respect, we ignore the state of our relationships and let our external self-confidence mask the deeper insecurities we can't even admit to ourselves. Lacking self-worth, we never feel like we are enough no matter how much we do or achieve.

We are a generation of women and girls starving for self-love, without the tools to find it and without the permission to keep it...until now.

What Is Madly in Love with ME?

Madly in Love with ME is more than just a book; it is an international social-change movement, a call and an invitation to every woman alive today — including you — to take a stand for every child and woman in this world, including ourselves, and to say, "Enough with the self-criticism, self-hate, self-abuse, and self-neglect. Enough with the unrealistic measures of what a happy and successful woman looks like. Enough with being treated by anyone with anything less than respect and unconditional love." It is a giant permission slip for every single one of us to fall madly in love with ourselves. And yes, I mean *madly*, as in expressing the love you have for yourself without shame, apology, or holding back.

And while this particular book is written by a woman to women and girls, addressing much of the social conditioning that has taken us away from our natural tendency to love ourselves well, men and boys are also invited to participate. As it turns out, every person on this planet can use what self-love has to offer. Love is a human need.

Madly in Love with ME is a challenge to take a stand in your own life to be and act as your own best friend, no matter what. To show up for yourself, to put your self-care first, to remind yourself how fabulous you are, often, and to always be on your own side.

Madly in Love with ME is a huge promise to yourself to always remember what the little girl inside you needs — laughter, joy, play, hugs, unconditional acceptance, and compassion — and to give it to her. At the same time, it's a promise to go for her big-girl dreams and desires, even when they don't make sense to anyone else.

When you say yes to Madly in Love with ME, you say yes! to freely and fully expressing yourself. You also say yes! to treating yourself with love and respect and requiring that you get this same respect and unconditional love from every relationship in your life, without exception. You say yes! to being, loving, and living *you*!

Consider this book your own personal, fantastical, magical handbook of self-love, just like one of those storybooks you'd open with giddy delight when you were a little girl. Remember how you would open the cover, and, in an instant, it was as if you had been transported into a different world, where outside time just seemed to stop? Where you became friends with the characters, and together you traipsed through magnificent new lands, expanded possibilities, and previously unimaginable creations of happiness and splendor? Oh, my! The only difference between this book and those magical storybooks is that this story is all about you. You are the main character. You are the storyline for Madly in Love with ME.

When you open this book and enter these pages, together we *will* imagine and create new magical, fantastical realities for you, guaranteed to fill your life with extraordinary amounts of happiness, love, and freedom. This is your life — you get to decide what it is filled with. It all starts with you. Choose to fill yourself up with love, and you'll create more love in your life. Choose to fill yourself up with care, and you'll be better taken care of. Choose to fill yourself up with compassion, and you'll receive more understanding and kindness from others. See, it's magic! You choose self-love, and more of what you want and need comes to you.

Let the magic of love — directed toward you! — begin....

The Madly in Love with ME Manifesta

We believe that every woman has the right to fall madly in love with herself. To be so in love with who she is, to so deeply honor her body, mind, and spirit, that every choice she makes reflects that same deep honoring. We believe not only that she is *entitled* to love herself but also that she is *empowered* to love herself simply because she is.

In this world, where a woman knows how to fall madly in love with herself, there is no need for her to fit into someone else's image of what a beautiful, intelligent, and successful woman is. She need only be the woman she truly is inside her soul. *She is free to be, fully.*

In this new world, where a woman is *encouraged* to fall madly in love with herself, there are no apologies for who she is (or is not). There is full acceptance and celebration of who she is, right now, in this moment. *She is free to love, fully.*

In this world, where a woman *lives* a life where she falls more madly in love with herself every day, there is no living for tomorrow or sacrificing and settling for less today. There is only the creation of the world that her heart and spirit desire at the very core of her essence. *She is free to live, fully.*

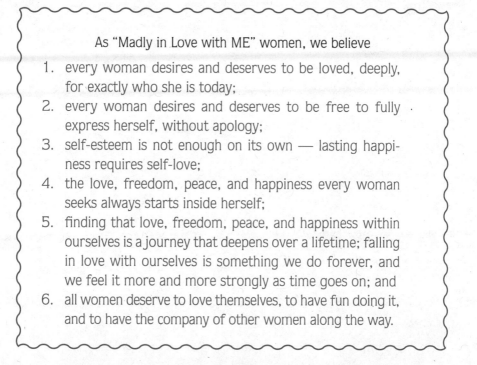

As "Madly in Love with ME" women, we believe

1. every woman desires and deserves to be loved, deeply, for exactly who she is today;

2. every woman desires and deserves to be free to fully express herself, without apology;

3. self-esteem is not enough on its own — lasting happiness requires self-love;

4. the love, freedom, peace, and happiness every woman seeks always starts inside herself;

5. finding that love, freedom, peace, and happiness within ourselves is a journey that deepens over a lifetime; falling in love with ourselves is something we do forever, and we feel it more and more strongly as time goes on; and

6. all women deserve to love themselves, to have fun doing it, and to have the company of other women along the way.

For a guided trip through this fantastical world of love and self-love, go to www.MadlyinLovewithME.com and view the three-minute video *Imagine a World of Love*. This video will guide you on an adventure in imagining a world in which you love yourself unconditionally. After you finish watching the movie, close your eyes, wrap your arms around yourself in a loving embrace, and feel that you are already a beautiful, powerful, and free woman, just because you are you. And get ready, because there is a whole lot more of this magical feeling of love directed at you in the chapters ahead!

PART 1

SEE the LOVE!

The Truth about Self-Love

CHAPTER 1

Why Is It So Hard to Say "I Love You"...to Yourself?

Recently, I was asked to speak at a college conference of sorority girls — the leaders of our future world and the mothers of our future children. From my place up on stage, I could see all of their young, hopeful faces waiting for me to share my secrets on how to be a successful woman in today's world. There was no doubt that these girls were excited to be at this conference, to learn, to continue to excel and work toward their goals. So when I asked for each to turn to her neighbor and say, "I would really like to have tremendous self-esteem!" it was no surprise that every young woman in that room excitedly turned and pronounced her commitment to believing in herself. When I asked these young women to raise their hands to indicate if their proclamations of self-esteem felt good, every hand in the audience went up as if to say, "Of course, I want self-esteem; self-esteem is good." This was a great sign! The message that holding yourself in high regard is something to cultivate had seeped into their consciousness to such a degree that, without apology, they were able to publicly claim their right to high self-esteem.

The next question, however, elicited a much different response. I turned to these future leaders and mothers and posed this question: "How many of you would now turn and say to your friend, 'I would like to love myself'?" Silence. Then squirms. A few giggles pierced the air, but not one hand went up — except for mine and that of my friend in the front row, another author, speaker, teacher, and woman on her own self-love journey. Instead, the girls moved uncomfortably in their seats, dumb-founded at the notion of publicly making such an audacious statement. Embarrassed to say the word *love* in a way that pointed their feelings of love toward themselves rather than toward another, these young women just sat in their seats staring at me. They had no idea how to respond, so they waited to see what I would do and say next.

In an inspired moment, I dropped down to my knees (wearing a dress and heels, mind you) and exclaimed,

Now I invite you to imagine that I am the child you will have some-day. I am your little girl between the age of five and seven. And I come to you and I say, "Mommy, is loving myself a good thing? Should I love myself? Be my own best friend?" What would you say? Would you say, "No, honey, that's selfish. No, child, have self-esteem but not self-love. Self-love is selfish, or something you only do in private"? Of course not! You would never say that to your child. Why? Because you have no doubt in your mind that you want your child to love himself or herself.

Instinctively, you know that loving yourself is crucial to a happy life, and you want your child to be happy. Your instincts are clear — self-love is good. You would say to her, "Yes, child, be your own best friend! Love yourself and treat yourself well. Be proud of who you are; share her with the world. Honor and respect yourself without apology, because if you don't, how can you expect anyone else to? Go for your dreams, regardless of what anyone else says. Take care of yourself, because if you don't, you won't be able to care for anyone else."

"So, all of you beautiful, powerful, intelligent young women," I said to those students that day — and I say this to you too — "if these instructions are so obviously appropriate for a child, then why don't they also apply to you?"

Since leaving my corporate job to teach, speak, and write full-time about self-love, love, and the true power of the feminine, I have talked with thousands of women and have received some of the wildest comments when I voice the term *self-love*. One moment, as we talk about self-esteem, their heads are nodding, their faces are smiling, and all is good. But as soon as I mention *self-love*, heads quirk to the side, defensive walls go up, and comments like these come out of their mouths:

"Loving myself? I don't have time for that."

"Oh, sure, I love myself. I went to the spa last month."

"I think that self-love stuff is all pretty hippie-dippy!"

Then there's the take-my-breath-away, shocker-every-time-I-hear-it line: "Self-love? Do you mean masturbation?" (And they don't mean it in a good way.)

My heart gets so sad at how quickly people link something so sacred, so essential to our basic happiness — love — to behaviors and traits that are frowned upon, hidden, and often a source of shame in our society when the word *self* is added to it. You don't see people walking around proclaiming, "I don't have time for love" or "Love is only for hippies." No, while we may not always be good at loving others, we all know and believe that loving others is a good thing. So why would love, when directed at yourself, be any different? We consider it acceptable, even admirable, to express love by giving to others our energy, time, resources, compassion, and more with little thought for ourselves, and by saying words like "I love you," "I appreciate you," and "I respect you" to friends, family members, and lovers. But saying, "I love myself" out loud? Better keep that under wraps! Or giving to yourself first? Why, that's selfish! And yet, it's the same energy — love — simply pointed in a different direction.

At first I thought the self-love taboo affected only people who had never been introduced to the concept of loving themselves. Just like the college girls in the room that day, I too, at the age of twenty, hadn't yet received the Self-Love Handbook. But when I observed that the women and men who came to the workshops I held at spiritual centers, which are like self-love safe havens, were just as resistant to publicly claiming their love of self, I was floored. One Sunday I asked a group of spiritual seekers I was speaking with, "Who here would stand outside after next Sunday's service with a flag that on one side says, 'I am madly in love with ME,' and on the other side says, 'Love yourself; you deserve it!'?" Surely there would be at least a few bold souls willing to be beacons of love. Yet again, not one person raised a hand, except for the person I had brought with me to the workshop, my soul partner, Noah. Okay, yes, I had upped the ante by asking for a public display of self-love, but these people were used to hearing about self-love and were part of a community that supported love in all forms. Surely they would have no fear about proclaiming their self-love in public. But they did.

What the heck was going on? What was causing the fear surrounding self-love? What I discovered was shocking.

I looked up the definition of *self-love* on Dictionary.com. I've learned over time that the definition of a word can tell you a lot about the current beliefs our society, institutions, and familial tribes — and, therefore, we — deem acceptable, valuable, and either right or wrong. Definitions — because they reflect mainstream thought — influence and inform the ideas and beliefs that run through our subconscious minds and, subsequently, affect our actions and thoughts. And because many of us may be unaware of the meanings of specific words (honestly, how often do you look up words you hear every day?), we often have no clue that we are being influenced by outside forces that may not even align with what we believe to be true in our hearts but that nonetheless affect our actions. Moreover, the definition we give a word today may not even be the original meaning of the word. Words seem to change over time, without explanation. This is the power of words, and once I realized this, I started looking up definitions and the history of words a lot more!

I'm not sure what I expected as I typed the word *self-love* into the white search box on Dictionary.com — maybe something simple about self-love promoting happiness and well-being. What appeared on my screen, however, was quite different. My mouth dropped open; my eyes could not believe what I was reading. *Self-love* was defined as "conceit," "vanity," and "narcissism."

What? My eyes scrolled the page again and again. I had to make sure I wasn't just seeing things. And then, as if a lightbulb went on in my mind, everything began to click. Now I understood the wacky responses and lack of raised hands. By definition, *self-love*, in mainstream society, is considered taboo, scary, and maybe even a little dirty. Which, of course, makes public displays of self-love feel wrong and risky, something to be avoided. Who wants to be called a narcissist, after all?

Merriam-Webster.com was not much better. While it defines *self-love* as "love of self" (which essentially is just the word *self-love* in a reverse order), the first full definition given is "conceit," which it goes on to define as an individual opinion, especially excessive appreciation of one's own worth or virtue, a fancy item, or a trifle. I think it is not a stretch to say that you, and no one you know, wants to be called conceited or excessive. And since when is love a trifle or an opinion instead of a sacred, beautiful, essential act?

What I wanted to know next was who the heck writes these erroneous definitions. Is there some person or council in some city sitting at a desk deciding on a whim what *self-love* means today? If so, they should be fired for bastardizing such a sacred word and then fired for poisoning our minds. When the word *self* is placed in front of the indisputably beautiful and good word *love*, this should not change the beauty and the goodness, only the direction in which it flows.

Maybe you're thinking right now, "Of course I know that self-love isn't all those awful things." And yes, at some level you do know that loving yourself is a good thing, or you wouldn't be reading this book. And yet, you know there are still places in your life where you don't let your self-love flag fly free, where you don't show up as your own best friend or make sure you get what you really need to be happy, healthy, and well-loved. One big reason for this is that you have been influenced, whether you know it or not, by the collective thoughts of a society that says loving others is good, and loving yourself is selfish, vain, narcissistic, and something you may do only in private.

Think about it this way. If you saw a woman loving her child in public, what would you think? That she's a good woman doing a good thing, right? If you witnessed a woman spending her time and energy nurturing others, what would you believe? Good woman doing a good thing. If you heard a woman expressing how much she loves her parents, friends, or partner, what would you say to yourself? Good woman doing a good thing. She is a loving person.

Now let's say that same woman turns the love around and directs it at herself instead of others. Imagine her saying something like "I really love myself." What would you think? Be honest. That she's conceited? Audacious? Full of herself? What if this woman told you she'd made a decision to take care of herself before giving to someone else? Would you think of her as selfish? Narcissistic? You probably wouldn't be thinking, "There goes a good woman doing a good thing; she is a loving person," because your belief system has programmed you to think that openly and fully loving yourself is not acceptable, that taking care of yourself first is selfish.

You live in a society that has made it more comfortable to read a book about the ten ways to get a guy or girl to fall in love with you, or to obsess about your romantic love life, than to share your self-love journey with your friends and family. You're bombarded with images and media, like reality TV shows, whose underlying message tells you it's normal to look to outside sources for confirmation that you are good enough, rather than to unapologetically stand for self-respect and self-worth.

Given the cultural climate, it's no wonder we have such a hard time loving ourselves. I have no doubt that every person at the spiritual center that day believed loving oneself is a fabulous idea. Fear of being seen as selfish, conceited, or vain prohibited them from freely expressing what they had come to receive: self-love. If not for the collective belief that self-love is selfish, the recognition that "self-love lets you love others more not less" would have prevailed. Fear wouldn't have stopped them from expressing the most power-ful force in the world — love — even when that love is directed inward.

> No matter what direction love is pointed — toward others or toward yourself — love is always good.

The rest of this book is dedicated to show-ing you how to give love to and express love for yourself, always — how to *choose* love for your-self in all its forms, again and again, daily, weekly, monthly, yearly for the rest of your life. Choosing self-love is like taking a powerful stand for yourself and saying no! to accepting the energy of hate, abuse, neglect, shame, fear, and guilt, whether that energy comes from yourself or from anyone else. And it's saying yes! to receiving and giving love in its many forms — to receiving love from and giving love to yourself first and, as a result, sharing the overflow of love with those around you.

If you complete the journey this book can take you on, then not only will you be able to say, "I love you!" to yourself out loud without shying away, but also, most important, you will be able to make big life decisions and everyday choices that are congruent with, and aligned with, love.

That is, you will act like a woman who truly does love herself. It's one thing to say, "I love you," but to act on that love is the true test, and it's where the true power lies. Note that *choosing* is an active verb. *To choose* requires you to make a choice to give love to yourself, to express love, or to receive love.

The more you act from self-love, the greater will be your ability to feel love for yourself no matter what is going on in your relationships, the outside world, or your external circumstances. You will become empowered to draw love from within yourself, rather than have to look for it in someone or something else. You will become masterful at filling your mind with loving thoughts, even when self-doubt, fear, and self-criticism are knocking on your mind's door. And as a result, you will find it easy and natural to act with love and kindness toward yourself.

You see, in addition to being one of the best ideas in the world, loving yourself, and making sure that you have the love, care, happiness, joy, and peace you desire, is a necessity. You need love in order to survive and thrive. And while there are many ways to get this love from outside ourselves, it's when we remember how to get it from inside that we come to know the deep levels of love that our heart and soul crave.

The good news is that you already know how to love yourself; you've just forgotten. You were actually born in love with yourself; it's your natural state. Think back to yourself as a little girl, to a moment when you remember being carefree and open to the wonder of the world, a moment when your light was superbright, before anyone told you to dim it down. Even if you can't remember a specific time when you felt this way, this part of you that could fully and freely be, love, and live you still exists.

Close your eyes for a moment, put your hand on your heart, and just see if you can feel this younger self, maybe even see her, sense her. Maybe you can recall a time when you were doing something you loved as a little girl — playing, creating, laughing. Maybe a time when she was all alone, with no one but her "magical" friends (whether imaginary friends, stuffed animals, or a favorite doll). This is the part of you that knows how to love yourself easily and without care for what others may think. As we go through our magical, fantastical journey together, we want to connect with that part of you as much as possible, because she is going to be a huge ally. She will give you permission to be madly in love...with yourself.

If you'd like some assistance in connecting with your little-girl self, I've recorded a meditation for you called "Come Play with ME!" It's a visualization that will reconnect you powerfully and sweetly to your inner little girl. Sometimes our little-girl selves are easy to access, and sometimes they like to stay hidden. Whichever is the case for you, know that it's okay; you can rest assured that she is going to come out to play, to be loved and adored, on this adventure. You can download this visualization at www.SelfLoveMeditations.com.

You should know that self-love, while yummy, fulfilling, and healing, is by nature a daring adventure, one designed not to make you comfortable but instead to bring you more love, which is often uncomfortable. We do what works, regardless of what you may look like in the process or what other people might think. In fact, the farther out of your comfort zone you move, the more likely you are to bust through the blocks standing between you and your ability to love yourself well, unconditionally, and forever.

The other piece of good news I have for you is that there are steps to take, practices to follow, understandings to reach, and choices to make in order to increase your ability to choose self-love — and I will share them with you in the pages that follow. You will be invited to partake in all kinds of interesting, daring, playful, and profoundly shifting opportunities to deepen the relationship you have with yourself, to come to new understandings about yourself, to move out of your comfort zone and into your full-self zone, to bust through blocks that prevent you from acting as your own best friend, and to become better able to choose love for yourself in any situation. I invite you to dive into every single one of these experiences and escapades with the curiosity and carefree spirit of your little-girl self and the commitment and conviction of a woman who knows all too well the consequences of not loving herself enough. Today marks a turning point in your life. Whether you have been on a self-love, self-discovery, or self-healing journey for years or you are just getting started, this adventure holds something for every woman and girl. Because the truth is, loving ourselves is something we need to do for ourselves every day, and something we are always getting better at!

By making the choice to take this daring adventure inside yourself at this time in your life — through your mind, body, heart, spirit, and soul — you have made a commitment to more deeply honor the most essential relationship in your life, the one with yourself.

My promise is to be your guide on this adventure to the best of my ability. As a person who has spent over a decade relearning and remembering how to love herself, I have a pretty good map, some darn cool tools, and a lot of good stories to tell, many of which I have included in the pages of this book.

What to Expect in the Pages That Follow

Throughout this magical experience you will encounter several different types of adventures, most of which I have listed below: daring acts, creative escapades, heartfelt conversations with yourself, and small but mighty spiritual practices. Stop here and try some of these out right now.

Daring Acts of Love

 You offer acts of love to others all the time, daily even, but too often you leave yourself out of the equation, for all the reasons I've already stated. So to help you build up your ability to love yourself, I've created some short but powerful invitations that dare you to get out of your comfort zone and into your love zone, especially when it comes to directing love to yourself! These "Daring Acts of Love" may seem wacky or insignificant, and you may find yourself wondering, "How could *that* have any impact on me?" They may feel like risks, and the fears that currently hold you back will attempt to stop you from taking these dares. Or they may even seem superfun from the get-go. Regardless of the feelings these Daring Acts of Love elicit, they promise to build up your "Self-Love Mojo" — your capacity and strength to love yourself. They also build your "Love Power" — your ability to feel loved, give love, and receive love no matter who or what is or isn't happening outside of you. If you find yourself resisting the dares, call on your little-girl self, who believed that love was always there for her and who didn't care what anyone else thought because, to her, she was just being herself. I *highly* encourage you to take every single one of the dares. In fact, I dare you!

ME Art

ME Art Regardless of how you feel about your creative abilities today, your little-girl self wasn't afraid to pick up a crayon and draw. All children can draw, until someone tells them they can't. And taking things from mental concept to something you can see with your eyes or feel in your body will shift you to an entirely new level — and these are the levels you need to open up access to in order to increase your capacity to choose love for yourself and your mastery of that love. If what you were already doing was working, you wouldn't be here on this adventure. So be adventurous! And here's the good news: All ME Art will be created by your inner little girl, the one who didn't worry about coloring outside the lines. In fact, daring girl that she is, she kind of likes it. You don't have to be an artist, don't have to be technically good at drawing; you just need to be willing to express yourself. Okay? Are you willing?

Great! Then to give you a taste of what you will experience throughout our adventure together, let's have some fun by combining a Daring Act of Love with some ME Art.

Daring Act of Love
Write a Secret Love Note to Yourself and Wear It All Day Long

As we begin your Madly in Love with ME journey, keeping your self-love as a special secret between you and you is A-OK. For now, the secrecy keeps the pact and bond special, just like a secret between best friends. There will be a point when you fly your self-love flag where all can see, but for now this dare is just for you.

On the palm of your hand, write yourself a love note in ME Art fashion, meaning: give it a little girlie flair. Write the words "I love you!" and then draw a heart underneath it. Just like you were in seventh grade. Now, throughout the day, look at your palm to remind yourself that you have indeed said yes! to taking a fantastical adventure with yourself.

Love Mantras

These short but superpowered phrases are really just words repeated to invoke a particular kind of energy and intention, in this case love for you. They have the power to instantly change your thoughts and feelings — from fear to love, criticism to compassion, doubt to courage, hate to love, anxiety to peace. They also have the ability to plant seeds in the form of new, self-loving beliefs and feelings. When used regularly, these new beliefs and feelings will get you thinking, feeling, and acting differently, in ways that are rooted in love for yourself.

If you've never used a mantra, rest assured that the process is simple. In moments when you find yourself disconnected from love — feeling afraid, ashamed, or anxious — say the mantra out loud again and again for as long as it takes, until the unloving feeling dissipates and you generate love for yourself. As you repeat this powerful and specific string of words, you will eventually feel a shift, often in your body and in your emotional field, as your heart opens itself to love and relaxes. Ahhh!

Why do mantras work? It's not voodoo, just simple science with a dash of spirituality. When words come out of your mouth, they create sound. Sound is vibration. Your body and spirit are already attuned to the vibration of your thoughts and surroundings, so when you say words attuned to love, you take away the power of thoughts attuned to fear. The more you use the Love Mantras, the more your self-love will grow. I like to carry a mantra or two in my mind always, just as I always make sure I have a pack of mints in my purse. Why? Because just as bad breath needs a superquick freshening up, you don't want to be caught without a way to shift your thoughts and feelings when some yuck-filled energy has overtaken your mind.

To get started with your Love Mantras right now, let's add on to the Daring Act of Love you just took. On the hand where you've written the words "I love you," add your name, so that it reads, "I love you, <<insert your name>>." Say these words out loud over and over again, looking at your palm, until you feel a shift in your body or heart. Love Mantra Power! Oh, yeah!

ME Moments

Imagine sitting down to have a loving heart-to-heart with your best friend. Just as a wise friend always starts by asking you questions instead of trying to give you advice or opinions, ME Moments will guide you through a series of short but powerful questions to help you find answers inside yourself. Sometimes, just a like a friend who reflects back to you your beauty, perfection, and brilliance, the ME Moment will lead you through a visualization, meditation, or set of questions that connects you back to the truth of who you are — a beautiful, powerful, and free woman who knows who she is and what she needs, as long as she remembers to ask herself. In fact, let's stop here for a moment.

ME Moment *Why Are You Here? What Do You Desire?*

Close your eyes, put your hand on your heart, and take a deep breath. (Don't skip that part. These three physical steps attune your mind, body, and spirit to your heart, which is where your wisest answers and unwavering sense of self-love live.) Then open your eyes, and ask yourself the questions on the next page.

You always have the choice to answer ME Moment questions in one of three ways:

1. Mentally: think the words to yourself.
2. Verbally: speak your answers out loud so you can hear them.
3. Visually: write or draw the answers so you can see the words.

Depending on how deep you want to go with yourself, and how much power you want the ME Moment to pack, decide which action is most appropriate. Answering mentally will have the lightest touch. You will just begin to entertain a new awareness. Speaking words out loud will add more power as you force the sound of the words (a vibration of love) to pass through your lips, which will affect your body and brain at a deeper level, a feeling level. Writing the words will add a visual imprint, as well as activate deeper parts of your subconscious, where love is needed most. For maximum benefit and lasting impact, take all three actions — think, speak, and write or draw.

1. Why are you here? **What brought you here to this book, at this time?** What's happening in your life or in your relationship with yourself that you want to no longer be true? List three things, using the words "I no longer wish <<insert situation>>." For example: "I no longer wish to put myself last all the time. I no longer wish to have toxic or unhealthy relationships. I no longer wish to neglect my body and her needs."

2. What do you desire to be true instead? **What would you like to be different in your relationship with yourself and, as a result, in your life** after completing the adventures contained in this book? Begin with the words "As I remember how to love myself more, I will choose <<insert shift>>," and list three things. For example: "As I remember to how to love myself more, I will choose relationships that are healthy and happy. As I remember how to love myself more, I will choose to make myself as important as everything and everyone else. As I remember how to love myself more, I will choose to give my body what she needs to thrive."

3. What self-sabotaging blocks or habits have prevented, or will prevent, you from giving yourself this love? And are you willing to release them? It's okay, we all have blocks. Often these are formed by the crazy beliefs we've acquired from what we've witnessed about love and self-love or from what we've been told by the media, our families, our societal institutions, and our social circles. The beliefs become blocks against love — we've learned to put up walls to protect ourselves from the very love we want. Or they become self-sabotaging habits that drive us to make choices that send us farther from love. The good news is, these beliefs have power over us only when we keep them in the dark. Bring your blocks about self-love into the light by honestly

admitting to yourself — without judgment — any blocks you have that are likely to stop you from completely following this path of self-love you have chosen for yourself.

Use this sentence and process if it's helpful: "In the past, I've sabotaged myself by choosing <<insert self-sabotaging choice>> over choosing <<insert self-loving choice>> for myself." For example: "In the past, I've sabotaged myself by choosing to keep working over choosing to take care of my body. My self-sabotaging habit is caring for my work more than I do for myself."

Once you have identified the habit, proclaim, "I am willing to release the self-sabotaging habit of <<insert habit>>. I choose self-love." The first step in any shift is awareness and willingness; you don't need to know the how — that's what this book is for!

For some of the ME Moment and ME Art adventures, I've created magical, hand-illustrated, colorful templates to help you through the process in a powerful and fun way. I like to call these Loveplates! To gain access to and download these Loveplates, go to www.ChooseSelfLove.com.

Way to go! You've claimed what you desire, and you've been honest with yourself about how you sabotage yourself — how you prevent yourself from getting what you need and desire. Self-honesty is one of the major parts of self-love, because where truth is admitted, even when it's hard to look at, there is always love right behind it waiting to give you a big hug. So let's keep the momentum going and get rid of any other blocks that may be keeping you from choosing love again and again for your very best friend, yourself.

CHAPTER 2

Self-Love Isn't a Dirty Word, and You Can't Catch Narcissism

Are you ready to clear the way for big l-o-v-e? Ready to throw out the guilt-laden and shame-creating beliefs that stop you from flying your self-love flag, or that get in the way of your acts of self-love? Ready to release the belief that you must not think too much of yourself, put yourself first, or express your love for yourself in public? Then wave good-bye to words like *selfish*, *vain*, and *narcissistic*. They bear no relation to self-love. Say hello to knowing that, without a doubt, no matter what anyone else says, self-love can only be a good thing. With your self-love mind-set in place, you'll be free and clear to love yourself openly without apology. Fearless self-love!

Over the next several pages, you will come face-to-face with some of the biggest misunderstandings and lies about self-love, beliefs that may have taken up residence in your conscious or subconscious mind, causing you to create habits and beliefs that don't serve you. When this "dirt" about self-love is present in your psyche, you cannot do right by yourself and love yourself well, no matter how much you want to. But once you can see the dirty beliefs and mucked-up misunderstandings more clearly, you'll gain the power to clean them up, get them out of your mind, and replace them with the truth about love. With the truth in place, you will find it easier to make self-loving choices.

This clean-up is essential. Your mind is tricky. If it doesn't believe it's safe for you to love yourself, and that only good can come from loving yourself, it will sabotage even your best intentions. Your heart, however, is wise and courageous, and it always knows the truth. Your mission is to put your mind at ease and in the backseat, and to rev up your heart so it can take control. Your heart instinctively knows the path to love. It has been waiting for you to give it permission to override the misunderstandings that clutter up your mind. Of course, we will do this in Madly in Love with ME style — in a way that is powerful yet playful, and daring yet practical. You, my dear, are about to take a Love Bath.

We are going to dive into four of the most common misconceptions and misunderstandings about self-love. As you come upon each one, follow these four steps:

1. Read the misunderstanding about self-love.
2. Pause for a ME Moment and answer the questions provided. Spot-check yourself to see if this mucky belief has stuck itself to your mind. Answer the questions to determine whether you need to do some cleanup. If you answer no to the questions listed, you are clear and can move

on to the next misunderstanding. But if you answer yes to any of the questions, you are in need of a Love Bath, so proceed to step 3.

3. Take a Love Bath. Get your love loofah out and stop to take a Love Bath — superfun, supereasy, and superpowerful; directions below.

4. Bonus: Accept a Daring Act of Love. To get the love soaking into an even deeper level (we don't want to leave space for that dirt to seep back in!), I recommend that after each Love Bath, you indulge yourself with a Daring Act of Love for yourself. Think of this as wrapping yourself in the most luscious bathrobe or blanket after a refreshing bath and enveloping yourself in love. Take the Daring Act of Love immediately if you can, or schedule it on your calendar — you know, make a date with yourself. After all, who better to have a date with?

ME Moment *The Love Bath*

Step 1. Scrub off the dirty belief.

With gusto and conviction, speak aloud while wiping off your arms, from your shoulders down to your fingertips, as if you were giving yourself a brisk loofah scrub: "I release the belief that loving myself is <<insert misunderstanding>>." For example, say, "I release the belief that loving myself is selfish."

Imagine, as you literally rub your hands up and down your arms, a love loofah wiping off any dirt in your mind and body cells that gets in the way of your giving yourself love in all its forms. Keep rubbing and repeating the words until you feel a release. Imagine this misbelief being scrubbed right out of your system. Rub everywhere and anywhere. Stand up and move around; get your body into it. Then blow out the belief with a huge exhale!

Step 2. Rub in the love!

Now, as if you were rubbing the most luxurious, silky, aromatic lotion onto your chest, slow down, close your eyes, breathe, and move your hand in clockwise circles right over your heart, touching your skin, repeating the new belief as a Love Mantra using what I've written below (or your own words) three times.

When you add a physical component to Love Mantras, they connect you to your heart through movement and touch, which gives you double the love power. When you slowly rub your hand in circles over your heart so that you can feel your hand moving over your skin, it is as if you were rubbing the truth about love right into your heart. Go ahead and test it out right now. Rub these words into your mind, body, heart, and spirit by saying the Love Mantra out loud while rubbing your hand in a circular motion over your heart:

> "Only good can come to me and others from my choosing to love myself..."
> "Only good can come to me and others from my choosing to love myself..."
> "Only good can come to me and others from my choosing to love myself."

Then stop, keeping your hand on your heart, and feel the words and their superlove vibe sink in. Notice any shifts in your feelings and body sensations. This is what giving love to yourself feels like. It's good, isn't it?

Love Note: I'd never ask you to do something I haven't done myself! I always experiment with myself (and with other daring souls) before recommending a Daring Act of Love. If you'd like to see a live video demo of me in this Daring Act of Love, check out Self-Love TV, which I created just for people like you who make the daring choice to choose self-love. Go to www.SelfLoveTV.com to access these videos, where you'll be welcomed into a playground of self-love — seriously, it's a self-love candy land!

As you move forward, challenge yourself to dive into each misunderstanding and find what's there for you to release, so that you can rewire your mind with a new self-loving truth. Answer the questions honestly, take the Love Baths when needed, and engage in the Daring Acts of Love. Just reading the words won't work. You need the combination of the power of the mantra (spoken word), movement, and brain science, with a twist of good old-fashioned fun and comfort-zone-pushing, to get results.

The impact? Liberation to love, baby. Liberation to love!

Note: If you still can't get past feeling silly about taking this Love Bath, ask your inner seven-year-old to do it for you. Remember that little girl you invited to take this journey with you? She doesn't care what anyone, including you, thinks about how silly she looks!

Misunderstanding #1. Self-Love Means Masturbation

When I made the announcement that I was leaving my corporate job to go out into the world to teach self-love, I'll never forget what one of my male clients said to me. As if stating some undeniable truth that I was totally oblivious to, he said, "Christine, you can't go out into the world and talk about self-love. Everyone will think you are some kind of crazy sex lady talking about masturbation!" He was dead serious. Now, I won't even get into why people think talking about sex and masturbation is crazy (I'm pretty sure that sex is meant to be a natural part of our adult lives), but the fact that people's minds go directly and narrowly to this place is just wrong.

Love Truth
Love requires intimacy, not sex. Self-love is nothing to be ashamed of.

Regardless of your beliefs about masturbation, whether you're pro, con, or neutral, linking self-love immediately to masturbation, as if the two were one and the same, is like saying one drop of water makes up the entire ocean. Masturbation could surely be categorized as part of self-pleasure, and self-pleasure is certainly an aspect of self-love, but self-love is a vast concept and a deep reality that encompasses much more than physical self-pleasure. Not to mention the fact that there are lots of ways to create pleasure for ourselves that have nothing to do with sex — long walks in nature, ice cream, spending all day in bed reading a good book, yummy food, cashmere everything, shoe shopping, and anything that makes you laugh. And truth be told, we could all use a lot more of the joy that self-pleasure can bring us when we are not operating under the misunderstanding that self-pleasure, and therefore self-love, is taboo. Just imagine if your life were bursting with pleasure — how fulfilled, happy, and cared for you would feel. Nothing wrong with that at all!

Let's clear the air and clear the way for more self-love for you, shall we, by releasing this misunderstanding and giving you new love-generating information to operate from. What masturbation and self-love do have in common is that they are both taboo words in our culture. Not taboo because masturbating or loving yourself is inherently wrong, but taboo because we are a people bred to be *extremely* uncomfortable with being intimate, both with ourselves and with others. Just mentioning the word *intimate* (another misunderstood word) can freak people out and make them squirm. I remember once telling my sister that I wanted to have a more intimate relationship with her. Imagine my reaction when, in reply, she jumped off the couch, her face completely contorted in horror, and she said to me, "What? You mean have sex with me?" Of course that's not what I meant! But because the words *intimacy* and *sex* have become so interlinked, although wrongly so, people confuse sex with intimacy all the time. But in fact, intimacy has nothing to do with whether your clothes are on or off your body.

The best definition I've heard for *intimacy* is "into-me-see," as in letting someone see the truth of who you are, see deeply into your heart and soul. And while this may feel scary — expressing and sharing your true self with another, or with yourself for that matter — it does not require removing your clothes. But it does require letting someone past your protective walls, where they can see the truth of who you are. But before you can experience the deep levels of love you desire from another, you must into-me-see with yourself first, which is exactly why self-love is such a positive act.

Masturbation and self-love also have another unfortunate trait in common. Just as we've been taught to be ashamed of our sexuality, we've also been taught to hide our full brilliance and abstain from too much pleasure. As a result, we tamp down both, and then we act out our repressed sexuality, self-expression, and need for pleasure in all sorts of unhealthy ways — addiction, codependency, and dishonoring our bodies (to name a few), all while lacking awareness of our impact on others. The world would be such a better place if our beliefs liberated us to instead embrace and express our sexuality and brilliance and receive great pleasure in both empowering and sacred ways. Owning and becoming comfortable with expressing your sexuality and full brilliance, and making self-pleasure an everyday requirement, are musts for any woman on a self-love journey.

ME Moment *Spot-Check Yourself for the Misunderstanding That Self-Love Means Masturbation, and Take a Love Bath*

Answer each question, yes or no:

1. Do you think that masturbation and self-love are the same or closely related?
2. Would you choose not to speak about loving yourself for fear that people would think you were talking about masturbation or something else that "should" be talked about only in private?
3. Are you uncomfortable with the idea of being intimate with yourself?
4. Do you lack emotional and physical intimacy with yourself? If you don't know what that means, the answer is yes.

If you answered yes to any of these questions, then this reflects a misbelief that's influencing you. Stop here so you can take a Love Bath and scrub off the dirt and rub in the love. If you answered no to all four, move on to misunderstanding #2.

Love Bath Step 1. Scrub off the dirt.

Refer to the Love Bath directions (page 22) to get the full instructions. Choose from one of the three release statements listed below, or use all three. Don't think too much; just go with what feels right.

"I release the belief that self-love is the same thing as masturbation."
"I release the belief that loving myself should be done only in private."
"I release the belief that loving myself is something to be ashamed of."

Say your release statement(s) out loud, over and over, for at least a minute (setting a timer is a great idea) while wiping your body with your love loofah. Keep going until you feel some kind of physical release in your body. If you feel a little weird and have a hard time getting into it, put some energizing, nonvocal music on in the background to help get you moving, or stomp your feet up and down while you vigorously love-loofah yourself.

Love Bath Step 2: Rub in the love!

Now slow down, close your eyes, breathe, and move your hand in clockwise circles right over your heart, touching your skin, repeating the new belief, this Love Mantra, until you feel the love sink in. Rub the truth about love right into your heart, body, mind, and spirit:

"The more I love myself, the more I know myself.
This can only be good."

Pause, and feel the truth of this Love Mantra seep into your cells.

Daring Act of Love
Date Yourself, and Include Romance!

A romantic table for one, please! That is the reservation you will be making this week. You are taking yourself out for a romantic date, the most romantic excursion you can imagine. Invite yourself out for a night of intimate connection. Make choices — from the dress to the dinner to the nightcap — that lend themselves to intimate conversation and experiences with yourself. Don't pick the loud, trendy restaurant. Dare to go to where all the couples go. Wear your most flirty dress and sexy shoes. Buy yourself flowers. Have a warm robe ready and romantic music playing when you get home.

On this date, make a real effort to get to know yourself better. Bring a journal, turn your phone and all electronic devices off (I mean completely powered off, not on vibrate), and let go of caring about what anyone but you thinks. Put all your attention on yourself, and see what she reveals.

Double Dare: Take yourself on a romantic weekend getaway.

Misunderstanding #2. Self-Love Is Narcissistic and Selfish

I've actually met a few real true-blooded narcissists in my day. I've dated them, my friends have married them, and I've even had them living under my roof. And while, yes, they were self-absorbed and self-centered to a fault, they did not love themselves. In fact, I would say they didn't know love at all.

According to the Mayo Clinic, "Narcissistic personality disorder is a mental disorder in which people have an inflated sense of their own importance and a deep need for admiration. Those with narcissistic personality disorder believe that they're superior to others and have little regard for other people's feelings." The narcissist is excessively preoccupied with issues of personal adequacy, power, prestige and vanity, "but behind this mask of ultra-confidence lies a fragile self-esteem, vulnerable to the slightest criticism." Hmmm. While I am not a person trained to analyze and help such people, it seems to me that this isn't self-love. This is self-loathing.

Love Truth

The more you love yourself, the more you will love others.

Loving yourself is not something you do *instead* of loving others. *Loving yourself is the prerequisite to loving others.* In order to give love to others, you must have love to give. How can you give what you do not have? You cannot. Just as you cannot lend money you don't have, you cannot give unconditional love if you don't first feel unconditional love for yourself. Most of us, until we consciously choose to commit to loving ourselves, spend our lives giving love to others based on conditions, and so we also learn to give love to ourselves based on conditions. In either case, both we and those we love lose out.

You see, love is not an either-or choice; it's a both-and circumstance. Self-love doesn't exclude others; it includes others. The more love you generate for yourself, the more love you have to give, because, as a rule, *love always creates more love.* Although our mainstream society has been blind to this love truth for centuries, spiritual teachers who live by the rules of love have known it forever. Consider what some of them have written or spoken about it:

> *"You yourself as much as anybody in the entire universe deserves your love and affection."* — *Buddha*

> *"I love myself . . . I love you. I love you . . . I love myself."* — *Rumi*

> *"No matter how much we give love, if we don't give it to ourselves, nobody can love us enough."* — *Louise Hay*

> *"If enough of us embrace love, the world will eventually be saturated with love. The love in the world begins with the love within ourselves."* — *Deepak Chopra*

> *"I have an everyday religion that works for me. Love yourself first, and everything else falls into line."* — *Lucille Ball*

Love Truth

Sometimes you will be self-absorbed and self-centered, because that is what will be required of you as your own best friend.

When you need to take care of yourself, to go for your dreams, or to set healthy boundaries in relationships, you have to be willing to take a stand for yourself — without apology, guilt, or fear of being called a narcissist. Here's the good news: If you aren't already a full-blown narcissist, you're not going to become one. Narcissism isn't contagious. Honestly, you are more likely to be too selfless than too selfish. So you really have nothing to worry about.

Deep down, you know that choosing *me* before *we* is often required for your own health, sanity, and happiness. Your best friend would never say to you, "How dare you be so selfish! You are such a narcissist." She'd tell you, "Love yourself enough to take care of yourself. You can't give what you don't have. The best thing you can do for those you love is to love yourself."

ME Moment Spot-Check Yourself for the Misunderstanding That Self-Love Is Narcissistic and Selfish, and Take a Love Bath

1. Do you believe you must love others before loving yourself?
2. Are you afraid you will become or be called self-absorbed if you put yourself first?
3. Imagine telling your friends or family that you have made a promise to fall in love with yourself. Does this bring up fear?
4. Do you feel uncomfortable putting your needs and wants before other people's — at home or at work — even when doing so is exactly what you need in order to take care of your physical, emotional, spiritual, or financial well-being?

If you answered yes to any of these questions, jump into the bathtub! If you answered no to all, move on to misunderstanding #3.

Scrub Off the Dirt — Get Your Love Loofah and Go to It!

"I release the belief that loving myself means I love others less."

Rub in the Love — Imprint This Love Mantra into Your Heart, Body, Mind, and Spirit

"The better I love myself, the better I can love others. This can only be good."

Daring Act of Love
Mirror, Mirror, on the Wall...

According to myth, Narcissus met his fate when he stared at his reflection for so long that he fell in love with his image, and he died staring at it. He was infatuated with himself. But unlike Narcissus, you intend to engage in self-love, not self-infatuation. Self-love is rooted in seeing yourself through the eyes of love, and it makes you better able to do the same with others — "both/and," remember! Surviving this self-love dare will prove that you never have to be afraid of being a narcissist! Every morning after showering or washing your face, head straight to the mirror and get really close, so close you can see the color of your eyes. Keep staring into your eyes until you can see yourself. Look deeply until you feel something inside you stir. That's when you'll know you've broken through the layer that masks your heart and soul.

Now challenge yourself to look even deeper, to connect to the spirit that is you. See into your Self. Once you feel the connection — a flutter in your heart or stomach, or a grounded sense, even if it's just a glimmer — inhale and say out loud to yourself:

"I love you, <<insert your name>>." Repeat the Love Mantra at least ten times, making a real effort to see yourself as you say the words.

Double Dare: For extra love throughout the day, sneak a peek in any mirror and, instead of checking your hair, whisper to yourself, "<<insert name>>, I see you; I love you."

Misunderstanding #3.
People Who Love Themselves Are Conceited and Vain

These words are deadly to anyone who wants to freely express love for herself! Being a braggart is right up there with being a leper in our society. No one likes a boastful, "hey-look-at-me-I-am-so-great" person. But being a braggart — someone no one likes to be around — is very different from being a person who truly loves herself and is unafraid to express that love. How can you tell the difference? It's all in the come-from. Are your words coming from lack or from love? There is a big difference between being "full of yourself" and being "full of love *for* yourself."

Love Truth

Bragging is not the same as letting your brilliance shine. One is an effort to fill a lack of love, the other is a gift of love.

Recall times when you have been with people who went on and on about how great they were or who were so into themselves that there was no room for you. What did their energy feel like? Did their vibes feel welcoming? Did they seem as if they were present, as if they connected with you? Unlikely. More likely you felt distant from them, pushed away. As if each had created a giant force field that let in only adoration and accolades and that kept intimacy and authentic connection out. Just like narcissists, people who brag and become overly obsessed with their looks and status are usually overcompensating for the feeling that they lack something in another area of their lives. All the bravado, props, and primping are signs of deep insecurity. This is not self-love. This is undiscovered, often undetectable, self-hate — a result of a severe lack of love.

Compare one of these people to a person you know who is confident, unafraid to shine. A person who expresses himself or herself fully without shrinking back, yet who is fully present, welcoming, and genuinely interested in connecting heart to heart with other people. This could be someone you personally know, or someone you've admired from afar. What do you notice about his or her energy? Is this person open or closed to connection? Does he or she generate more love and connection or less? I bet more. People like that don't need to brag; they just shine. And they do so because they love themselves. They also know that their shine gives others permission to shine too.

Love Truth

The brighter you shine, the more love you create.

The brighter you shine, the more clearly you give permission to others to share their gifts to their fullest extent. Imagine if all people on the planet were unafraid to share their divine gifts! Nothing vain about that. Many of the world's problems would be quickly solved, and I'll bet that people would be less crabby and way happier.

When people truly do love who they are, they can, without apology, be themselves without holding back. They don't have to prove something or protect their deep insecurity from being seen. They don't need to brag, and yet they are unafraid to own their greatness, often because they know their greatness is an expression of the divine within them. The last time I checked, no one thought the divine was a conceited braggart!

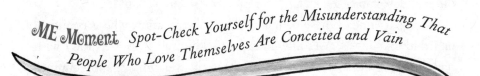

ME Moment Spot-Check Yourself for the Misunderstanding That People Who Love Themselves Are Conceited and Vain

1. Do you feel shy expressing the real and full you? In the moments when you could shine, do you tend to pull back?

2. Are you humble to a fault? Do you believe that giving yourself kudos or expressing your pride is negative, taboo, or uncouth?

3. Do you have a hard time receiving compliments? Do you discount a compliment by saying things like, "Oh, that's not such a big deal," or "This old thing? I've had it forever," and so on?

4. Do you ever hold yourself back from shining, either because you don't want others to feel bad or because you're afraid they will judge or reject you?

If you answered yes to any of these questions, it's scrub-a-dub-dub time! If you answered no to all, move on to misunderstanding #4.

Scrub Off the Dirt — Grab Your Love Loofah and Go to It!

"I release the belief that expressing love for myself is conceited and vain."

Rub in the Love — Melt This Love Mantra into Your Heart,
Body, Mind, and Spirit

> "I know that when I express my brilliance, I am expressing love. This can only be good."

Daring Act of Love
Make a Public Display of Love for Yourself

Time to come out of the closet about loving yourself. Don't fear, we'll start small. No need to get out the "I am Madly in Love with ME!" flag yet (although if you're inspired, go for it). Think of a person in your life who'd clearly support your love for yourself, someone you can trust who can give you unconditional love. Pick up the phone and call that person (no emailing) and tell him or her that you are taking a vow to love yourself, just as people who get married take vows. Share the vow and tell this person why you are excited about keeping it.

Start by saying, "I am taking a vow to love myself no matter what, and..." or "I am taking a vow to become my own best friend, and..." Explain that you are making this public display of love for yourself because, by going public, you're more likely to keep the promise.

Double Dare: Ask your friend to help you stick to your promise. Give your friend permission to tell you when she or he sees you breaking it. Accountability with love makes success a gazillion times more likely.

Misunderstanding #4. If You Pamper Yourself, You Love Yourself

If I could remove the word *pamper* from the dictionary, I would. Not because I don't enjoy the activities that are often associated with the word *pamper*, which means "to overindulge" — such as a combo manicure and pedicure or a spendy lunch or weekend spa visit. It's because the notion of taking specific days during the year — which are usually few and far between — to pamper ourselves has created the notion that it's acceptable to nurture and treat ourselves well only on "special" days, not every day. To make fabulous self-care or delicious self-pleasure part of every day — why, that would be selfish. To focus on yourself every day — why, that would be narcissistic. Well, who says?

The truth is that self-love is not something you do only on vacation or at the spa. You don't schedule it for Wednesdays and then spend the other six days of the week running yourself ragged, engaging in toxic relationships, or hating your body. Loving yourself is something you do every day, in every moment, for the rest of your life. Self-love is a way of living, a practice, and an awareness that you carry with you as a compass and a decision guide to how to live your life. It has nothing to do with how big your spa bill is, how many days you work out, or how often you get your nails done or buy yourself a nice outfit, but everything to do with how you nurture your mind, body, heart, and soul every day. In fact, some of the people who pamper themselves the most love themselves the least — overindulging in pampering just provides a good-looking mask for the lack of self-love.

Love Truth

Self-love is a choice made in every moment, every day, not something you do only on special days.

Self-love is a moment-by-moment, everyday practice. It's one you start your morning with, live your day with, and go to bed with. And like anything you practice, the more you practice it, the better you become. The best thing about practicing self-love is that unlike many things you were forced to practice as a kid, practicing self-love every day is fun and ridiculously rewarding!

ME Moment Spot-Check Yourself for the Misunderstanding That Pampering Yourself Means You Love Yourself, and Take a Love Bath

1. Do you start your day by jumping out of bed and rushing around serving others or taking on your to-do list before either taking care of yourself or connecting with yourself?

2. Do you go for days without nurturing your body, mind, and spirit? And then realize you have run yourself down to zero?

3. Do you take good care of your body — get your nails done, get massages, take vacations, and the like — and make it a priority to give yourself what you need, yet find you're not really happy inside?

If you answered yes to any of these questions, it's scrub-a-dub-dub time! If you answered no to all, you are clean, so continue on.

Scrub Off the Dirt — Get Your Love Loofah and Get to It

If you answered yes to question 1 or 2, then say:

"I release the belief that loving myself is an indulgent, frivolous act."

If you answered yes to question 3, then say:

"I release the belief that spending money on pampering myself is enough to make me feel loved, happy, and cared for."

Rub in the Love — Melt This Love Mantra into Your Heart, Body, Mind, and Spirit

> "Loving myself is something I get to do every day. And that can only be good."

Daring Act of Love
Take a Self-Love Soak Every Day!

At first waking, before rising from your bed, open your eyes and then close them right away. Keeping your eyes closed, wrap your arms around your body, and tell yourself (either in a soft whisper or silently inside), "<<insert name>>, I love you." Say these words over and over again, and, so that you can literally feel the self-love soaking into your cells, add a hug — just as you would hug your partner, child, or four-legged companion in the morning. In this case, the being you are directing love to is you. Lie there in that hug, feel your heart open, and imagine pink light enveloping you, infusing your cells with love. Keep the soak going until you feel some love soak in. When the love is activated within you, open your eyes.

At first you may feel nothing; it may take you a few days, even weeks, to open up to receiving love in this way. So fake it until you make it, knowing that eventually the love will get through.

To complete this Love Bath, you need to look in one more set of places — your private places. No, not your private parts — lol! Your private *places*.

I shared with you four of the biggest misunderstandings about self-love, but unfortunately there are many more. As we grow up, they come to us from so many directions — the media, our parents, relatives, friends, school, religious institutions, and our communities. I'd have to write an entire encyclopedia on misunderstandings to list them all — and given that you haven't been afflicted by them all, that'd be a poor use of time that could be better spent on where we are going. We're going to *grow* your self-love!

So what I've done is come up with a superspeedy self-love adventure using some powerful transformative ME Art that will help you identify the misunderstandings about self-love that you picked up from early childhood to today, so that you can see them, scrub them off, and then rub in some love. Create this ME Art and use it to evoke the self-love mind shifts you need to make, and then take a Love Bath to release each one. And, of course, I've created a full-color Loveplate that you can download at www.ChooseSelfLove.com! The entire excursion can take you less than an hour. I'll be waiting for you on the other side!

ME Art My Self-Love Imprint

This adventure was inspired by a combination of powerful techniques I learned from two self-love superstars — Pele Rouge Chadima, one of my spiritual mentors, and Christine Hassler, my self-love sister and cocreator of the Choosing ME before WE 40-Day Self-Love Practice.

Supplies:

♥   A few sheets of paper and some markers

♥   Permission to let the little girl inside you pick up a pencil or marker without judgment of her creative abilities, including the permission to draw and color outside the lines

♥   Optional: "Self-Love Imprint" Loveplate at www.ChooseSelfLove.com

Mission:

Restructure your mind's understanding of self-love and uncover the subconscious beliefs that you absorbed from the big influences in your life as a result of what you saw, heard, experienced, and witnessed while growing up. Then, you get to take back your Love Power and scrub off these dirty beliefs and rub in the good Love Mantras that a woman committed to loving herself lives by.

How-to:

Step 1. Sketch out your Self-Love Imprint.

In the middle of the paper, draw a small heart and write the word *Self-Love* inside it. Then draw lines to split the entire paper into four quadrants, and draw four small circles, one in each quadrant. Draw four spokes coming off each circle. Name the four circles Media and Society, Friends and Peers, Parents and Relatives, Education and Religion.

Step 2. Write up to four beliefs about self-love that each of these groups of people told you, showed you, or seemed to believe based on how they lived or spoke.

Go through each group, one by one, thinking to yourself, "What examples, habits, or beliefs about self-love did I see, hear, or otherwise observe…?" Use the following list as thought starters to help you uncover the beliefs about self-love that you learned, both pro–loving yourself and anti–giving love to yourself. Keep in mind that the terms *self-love* and *loving yourself* probably weren't often used, but that people likely expressed judgments about the attitudes and opinions that self-love and loving yourself include, which you unknowingly picked up in your subconscious. Write the beliefs on the spokes.

- ♥ taking care of oneself and one's needs
- ♥ accepting, forgiving, or being kind to oneself
- ♥ giving oneself pleasure
- ♥ expressing oneself fully
- ♥ saying good things about oneself

- ♥ being in romantic relationships
- ♥ having relationships with friends and relatives
- ♥ trusting your inner wisdom
- ♥ going for your dreams
- ♥ having high self-esteem and self-worth

Step 3. Take a ME Moment and just notice what you see.

1. What beliefs do you find here that you didn't realize you had, that you no longer want to keep? Which ones are you not surprised by but don't want to keep around either? Circle or underline those — these are the beliefs you will take to your Love Bath.

2. How have these beliefs affected your ability to love yourself well? To make good decisions for yourself? To choose unconditional love and respect, no matter what?

3. What have these beliefs cost you?

4. What would you like to believe instead? Write a new belief for each of the old beliefs as powerful self-loving statements on your Self-Love Imprint. They will become the basis for your new Love Mantras.

Step 4. Clean up your beliefs and take your love power back.

For each dirty belief, take a Love Bath!

Scrub off the dirt and then, on a clean piece of paper, write out a new Love Mantra that you can use when you rub in the love. You can also use the second page of the Loveplate on www.ChooseSelfLove.com as a template to guide you through releasing the dirty beliefs and claiming the new love-based ones. Create an entire set of new Love Mantras that you can start using on a regular basis to restructure your beliefs in support of you loving yourself.

And here's a small but mighty Love Boost for the road, a short love poem to help you always remember that love is good, even when — especially when — it's directed at you:

> Where there is love, there is nothing to fear.
> People may misunderstand.
> But that is their business.
> As long as you are aligned with love,
> you can create no harm.
> Step forward from here knowing that choosing to love yourself —
> in all the ways that will come to light —
> can only be a good thing,
> for when you act from love,
> everything in your life aligns just right.

CHAPTER 3

What Is Self-Love...and How Can You Receive More?

Someday I will petition Dictionary.com to change its definition of *self-love*. But I'm not willing to wait for that to happen before I set the record — and your mind — straight about what self-love really is. Especially not after all the work you just did to clear yourself of those big misunderstandings and ridiculous beliefs about self-love. However, I do admit I dream of millions of us, self-loving women and girls, mailing letter upon letter to the office where this council of definition-makers resides. But for right now, we need to evoke your individual love power to put your self-love mind-set in place for good, so that nothing holds you back from expressing love for yourself without apology.

First, I took it upon myself to write a new definition for self-love that we can all rally around and embrace. One that you can input into your memory banks. A definition that will make you think, "Choosing self-love is good! Do that! Often." Here goes. Open your mind, heart, and spirit for the real definition of self-love.

> Self-love is the unconditional love and respect
> that you have for yourself
> that is so deep,
> so solid,
> so unwavering
> that you choose only situations and relationships —
> including the one you have with yourself —
> that reflect that same unconditional love and respect.

Okay, let's pause here for a moment. You want this to sink in deep. Put your hand on your heart and read the definition out loud. Really get the vibration of love passing through your lips and seeping into your heart. Feel the love in your body as you speak this truth. Yum, huh?

Now, let's make it personal. Reread the definition again, this time transforming it into a belief that you can hold and come back to again and again. Read the definition aloud, *slowly*, replacing the "you" and "yourself" with "I" and "myself," making this about your love for you.

> Self-love is the unconditional love and respect
> that I have for myself
> that is so deep,
> so solid,
> so unwavering
> that I choose only situations and relationships —
> including the one I have with myself —
> that reflect that same unconditional love and respect.

Reread the entire definition out loud three times for maximum benefit. (Don't ask why three times; this is one of those magic-inducing things that just is — vows, mantras, and anything you want to stick in your heart and mind need to be repeated out loud at least three times.) Read at a pace that allows you to feel the words sink into your body, as if they were penetrating your cells. Close your eyes, take a deep breath, open your eyes, and read, listening with your heart, as if your heart were soaking the words in. Keep your hand on your chest right over your heart for extra love power (this is the place on your body that you can always touch to activate your connection to your best-friend self). After you finish reading this self-love definition, pause for a few moments, eyes still closed, and let your heart consider this version of self-love to be a reality for you.

> What would it be and feel like to have such unconditional love and respect for yourself that only situations and relationships that reflect that same unconditional love and respect would be acceptable to you?

What would it be like to love yourself so much that you, as your best friend, would be willing to take that kind of stand for yourself? To stand for yourself and your right to unconditional love and respect before anything or anyone else?

Unconditional love and respect is a powerful and purposeful choice of words. It means that, without exception, parameters, rules, or expectation, you commit to giving yourself love and respect. That the love and respect you have for yourself is just there, even when you screw up, make bad choices, or don't show up as your best self. You are human, and to be human means that you will make mistakes, fail, and fall down. Your job as your very best friend is to always reach out your hand to help yourself up, just as you would an innocent child. If you witnessed a child fall down or stumble while learning to walk, you wouldn't say, "Get up, you loser! What's your problem? You can do better than that!" No, you would likely reach out your hand, help the child up, and say, "It's okay, keep trying. You are doing great!" Your job is to do the same for yourself, to always choose to give yourself a hug and remind yourself that you're still growing and learning. That's what a best friend or a loving parent would do, and that's what you will learn to do as choosing self-love becomes your natural go-to state.

We've all had relationships in which people didn't love us unconditionally, but instead used love as a reward, a punishment, or a manipulation tactic. In my own experience, the times that a person I trusted and loved — whether a parent, friend, or lover — took love away were some of the most damaging and painful times I've ever known. Perhaps you too have experienced love being taken away or used against you — it hurts! So do yourself a favor and make the relationship with yourself different. Make it better. Make it so that love is always given and always present, no matter what.

> Make your relationship with yourself the best relationship in your life.

ME Moment *Check In on Your Relationship...with Yourself*

When's the last time you sat down and checked in with yourself, and asked, "How is our relationship going? Are you getting the love and respect you need from me?" Ha! I wish we had been taught as young girls to have this conversation with ourselves on a regular basis. But alas, the majority of us were taught the opposite. Here's the good news: Throughout this entire book I'll show you how to check in with yourself to make sure you are getting what you need and desire in every way. Not in ways that add another to-do to your list, but in a manner that adds joy, happiness, peace, and a sense of unwavering connection and unconditional love to your life. Sound good? Let's take a practice run just to get a sense of where you are in your relationship to yourself — a kind of quick check-in that reveals the strength of the relationship between you and yourself.

Read each of the descriptions on pages 51–53 and choose the one that most represents your current relationship with yourself. Then record the corresponding number in the space provided at the end of the list. Base your decision on your ability to choose unconditional love and respect for yourself, rather than all those other things — doubt, shame, guilt, hate, neglect, and judgment — that you've been programmed to default to, and that, in the process, cause you to make self-sabotaging, self-critical, self-abusive choices instead.

But here's the thing about this check-in: It is not a test. This is not an invitation to judge yourself (that is so not self-loving). And this is not like one of those magazine quizzes you take and then lie about to make your score higher so you can feel better about your life (it's okay, we've all cheated on those). This is a communication between you and yourself, a way for you to compassionately notice where you are in your relationship with yourself and in your ability to choose love for yourself. So honesty is actually required. Let your inner guidance lead you to where your current relationship stands — because here is the good news: You can only go up from here! And the more honest you are now, the less likely you will be to judge yourself later. Being where you are, and being okay with that, is an act of self-love. In fact, just think of this as taking a quick pulse check of your love for yourself.

Which of the following best describes your current relationship to self-love and your ability to choose love for yourself?

1 — Sure, I choose self-love; what is self-love again? Honestly, up until now or very recently, I hadn't ever considered that loving myself would be a good idea, or that love was something that I had to choose for, and give to, myself. So I probably haven't been the best friend to myself. I've mostly been going through my life doing the best I could, unaware that my relationship with myself affects everything else around me. I feel like I am just waking up to the idea that I am having a relationship with myself. I am open to it, though, and ready to explore this. I like the idea of being a best friend to myself.

2 — I choose self-love but not very often. I have a hard time directing love instead of hate, shame, guilt, judgment, and doubt toward myself. I want to be a better friend to myself and make choices that lead to my taking care of myself, believing in myself, and being kinder to myself, but I am not sure exactly how to do that. I haven't yet really made a commitment to loving myself, which I suppose is why I can't seem to follow through for myself in ways that a best friend would. I don't have a strong line of communication with myself, although there have been times I have listened to an inner voice, and the results have been good. I am ready to listen more. I am ready to be, love, and live *me* more. I just don't know the way.

3 — I choose self-love sometimes. I want to choose self-love over self-neglect, self-judgment, self-hate, and self-doubt, but I am still learning — I mean remembering — how to do this. Honestly, I am so-so at making the choices for myself that a best friend would. And the truth is that I am hard on myself. But I have made a commitment to myself to create a better relationship with me, to make choices that are good for me, to consider changing relationships that are not loving and respectful, and to stop being so hard on myself. I am beginning to check in more with myself, to trust myself, and to listen for what I need. So I'm on my way. It's as if I'm on self-love training wheels.

4 — I choose self-love often. I do a really good job at showing up as a best friend for myself, although sometimes I am hard on myself or have trouble giving myself what I really need. But I am pretty good at noticing when self-judgment or self-neglect creep in, and I can get myself back to unconditional love and respect fairly quickly. I've established an open line of communication with myself. And while sometimes I may struggle to be kind to myself or take care of myself, what I can proudly say is that I have taken a solid stand to ensure that all of my relationships with others are based on love and respect, or I drop or transform them. And I really do love myself in many ways! I love who I am, and I love sharing her with the world. And every day I become freer to do so.

5 — I choose self-love always. I am my own best friend. I am always on my side. Unconditional love and respect is my come-from, and I expect and require it from every person in my life, which is probably why I have so many loving, spectacular relationships with others too. While I am certainly not perfect at always choosing self-love (that's an unrealistic

expectation), I rarely have negative thoughts about myself. When I do, I know exactly how to listen to what's going on inside so I can take care of myself. I see these thoughts as indicators that I need to listen more closely to myself. I ask myself what I need, almost on a daily basis, and I make sure I receive it on all levels — physical, mental, emotional, and spiritual. I am committed to making sure that my life is full of happiness and love, and that I give my full self to the world, and in return am open to receiving tons of love and joy. I am actively creating that reality for myself.

My Current Self-Love Pulse _____

Note: You may also fall somewhere in between these five levels, which is totally okay. In that case, your self-love pulse might be 2.75 or 3.5 or whatever number feels right. This score is just an indicator of your self-love pulse right now — a quick mini-check-in to see how much consistent, unconditional love you're giving to yourself. There will be time for more extensive pulse checks, and I'll discuss ways to raise your self-love pulse as we go on. This book is full of ways to increase your power to choose love for yourself in any situation you face.

What Is Self-Love?

In our culture, there are a lot of words other than *self-love* that people are much more comfortable using, words that many people mistakenly believe mean the same as *self-love*, such as the following:

Self-acceptance   Self-appreciation
Self-acknowledgment   Self-awareness

Self-care	Self-honesty
Self-compassion	Self-honor
Self-confidence	Self-pleasure
Self-empowerment	Self-respect
Self-esteem	Self-trust
Self-expression	Self-worth
Self-forgiveness	

While all the ideas expressed by these words are components of self-love, none alone is a synonym for *self-love*. Love is a specific, unparalleled, and all-powerful vibration. And none of these words on its own has the power, depth, or vastness to communicate or transmit the life force that the word *love* can and does. But put them together, and wow!

Each of these aspects of self-love relates to and supports the others, just as a tree's branches rely on each other to grow, be healthy, and keep the tree balanced and strong. When you practice self-care, you increase your self-compassion. When you build your self-awareness, you increase your self-esteem. When you improve your self-esteem, you more fully feel your self-worth. When you practice self-trust, you base decisions on self-respect. When you take actions that reflect a deep self-respect, you honor yourself. When you express yourself fully, you increase your self-pleasure. And when you exude self-compassion, you create self-acceptance. Each branch supports the other branches, and as one grows, so do the others.

So how does self-love fit into this? Self-love is the tree itself. Self-love is the whole; it encompasses all of these sacred and loving qualities and actions, which is why it is the most powerful of them all.

To really love yourself and have the ability to choose love in your daily actions, decisions, and thoughts over the course of your lifetime, all ten branches of self-love must be taken care of, acknowledged, and grown. Stop for a moment and take a look at each of these ten branches, reading the words written on them out loud or to yourself. Notice that each branch comes from the shared trunk, where they all connect at the heart, signifying your connection to love, both self-love and the "big love" — you know, love from the universe, the divine, spirit, or whatever you call that source.

You'll also notice that some of the branches include multiple aspects of self-love. For example, self-respect and self-honor are part of the same branch, just as self-compassion and self-forgiveness share a branch. This is because they are so similar that to differentiate between them would be less powerful than marrying them together to create one superstrong branch. You know how, on some trees, some branches never quite grow thick and strong but remain twigs or branches that couldn't support you? Well, you don't want branches like that on your self-love tree — no way! So I've married the elements of self-love together when appropriate to form a profound, superstrong union of self-love, giving you even more support and strength as you grow your love for yourself.

Every one of your branches must be tended to in order for you to thrive. If you focus too much on one branch and ignore the others, an imbalance occurs, and then your self-love tree becomes unstable and may even topple over. Ever wonder why you can't seem to find balance? Well, you can stop doing more downward dogs to address the problem, and instead take a good look at where your self-love tree is lacking. Remember moments in your life when you've been super-unhappy or stressed-out? You can bet some branches on your tree were close to dying. Stuck in patterns of self-sabotage, neglect, or abuse that you can't shake? Likely one of your branches got too much attention while you ignored the other essential parts of your relationship with yourself. That one branch became overgrown and stole light and nourishment from the ignored branches, which began to wither away or, worse, rot! Leaving you unbalanced, unhealthy, and unhappy. See if any of the following examples and symptoms of an unbalanced, unhealthy, unhappy self-love tree are familiar to you:

♥ You focus on growing self-confidence, but you fail to tend to your self-compassion or self-care. You become a high achiever who works really hard and usually falls over in a heap of exhaustion. Why? Because you silently beat yourself up emotionally and mentally by seeing only what you failed at, didn't achieve, or could have done better. Without self-care you never give yourself a break, and without self-compassion you don't give yourself the chance to learn. Your unrealistic expectations keep you busy, striving, driving, and pursuing happiness but never feeling happy for too long.

♥ You have tons of self-esteem but lack self-respect. You show up as smart in your career, but you sabotage yourself in your relationships. You may not put up with mediocrity or disrespect at work, but you choose mediocre relationships or, worse, relationships with people who don't respect you and who do treat you poorly. Sure, you are successful, but you are also self-destructive.

♥ You have self-awareness but lack a strong branch of self-trust. You gain knowledge about what you want out of life, and you know who you are, but you find it difficult to act on your gifts or pursue your real dreams. Without self-trust, your self-doubt keeps you paralyzed. You need strong self-trust to lean on when you start expressing your talents, taking risks, and generally moving out of your comfort zone.

♥ You go wild on growing self-pleasure without self-honesty and self-honor. You may have a ton of fun, but you either end up broke or alone or in situations that don't honor you, because you aren't being honest about the emotional holes you are trying to stuff all the pleasure into.

Whether you knew it or not before setting eyes on this self-love tree, for your entire life you have been in charge of making sure this tree is well cared for and fed. The question today is not "How good a job have I done?" That question would just lead you down a road of non-self-loving judgment. The only question you need to ask and answer right now is "Am I willing to love myself enough to care for this beautiful, precious, sacred tree of life that flows with unconditional love for me?"

Fed by the heavens above and by the earth below, the tree, and its health — which you can feel at the core of your heart and soul when you stop to listen — directly reflect the condition of your life and your state of happiness, peace, joy, and love at any given time. The Self-Esteem and Self-Sacrifice Handbooks left out mention of this tree, this very important "glyph of love," which means that without the Self-Love Handbook, you couldn't have understood how intricate and connected your internal system of love is. But now that you have this Self-Love Handbook in your hands, you will begin to see how everything is connected to everything else. And when one part of your self-love suffers, the entire system is affected, just like in a living tree.

You'll notice that in addition to having ten branches, this vibrant, healthy, and happy tree of love also has strong roots that keep it grounded during a storm, and fed and watered so it can grow straight and tall for many years. This root system is your self-worth. You need strong roots planted deeply and firmly in healthy soil — full of unwavering, unconditional love — that nurtures you with love always, independently of happenings or relationships outside of your relationship to yourself and your connection to the divine. When your tree is rooted in this love-filled soil, no matter what and how you appear according to external standards, your sense of self-worth remains intact, able to support all the branches of your self-love tree.

Unfortunately, over the years, you've assimilated to life in a society that promotes dependence on external systems — on other people, the popular culture, and educational and social institutions — that decide what is or isn't valued. As you assimilated, the roots of your self-love tree grew into a soil full of toxic, non-self-loving beliefs like "You are not enough unless you do, become, and have it all," "You are not worthy of love unless you give first or sacrifice yourself," and "You are lovable only if someone else loves you."

This has made your self-love tree unstable, even shaky. Dependent on whatever the society's unattainable "all" happens to be and your ability to meet its value standards, or how much external validation, adoration, or love you receive, your sense of self-worth becomes a series of skyrocket highs and superlow plummets, with the occasional stop in the middle, sane place. And as you know all too well — as a woman who may feel confident and secure one day, and like an absolute failure the next — living this way is no good. It's like tying your happiness, worthiness, and security — really your entire sense of self — to a stock market of conditional, external love that lies in someone else's control, changes at a whim, and makes you crazy.

The good news is, this is not your natural state. You were born believing in your inherent self-worth. Your value was not originally determined by conditional, external variables or standards. And, over the course of this self-love journey, you will remember again how to value yourself, regardless of what you have done, achieved, or amassed. Regardless of what other people say, do, or feel about you. Your sense of self-worth, and therefore every branch on your self-love tree, will become stronger and healthier, and you will begin to feel more loved, happier, freer, and more peaceful on a more consistent basis. While the occasional storm of comparison, self-judgment, or self-neglect may sweep in and cause your love and care for yourself to waver, the storm won't last long. With the roots of your self-love tree planted in the soil of unconditional love and unwavering connection to the divine, your tree won't topple over, and you won't ever completely lose your center, because your self-worth will be strong.

Now let me be clear: This doesn't mean that you have to be perfect or that you will never have moments of doubt. Fear, doubt, shame, obligation, neglect — all these polluters of self-love will undoubtedly try to creep into your soil and attempt to rot away your self-worth roots and cause your self-love branches to wither. But as your soil receives more unconditional love and respect and your self-worth strengthens, and as you nurture all the branches on your self-love tree, you will again find your way back to self-love in spite of doubt, fear, or external circumstances.

It is challenging to grow strong roots of self-worth in a world that constantly bombards you with the messages "You are not enough" and

"It's better to give than receive," and which is obsessed with codependent romantic love, finding a mate, and being "chosen." I won't lie to you. But it is possible to grow strong roots over time. With all the bad programming by our externally driven, comparison-ridden culture, and by those two handbooks that emphasize lack, it may take years of personal discovery and spiritual recovery work to get back to your original starting place, where you not only remember but also truly *believe* that you are enough. It is from this deep connection to unwavering love for yourself that you will remember without a doubt that you are worthy of love in all its forms no matter what you do or don't do, that you are worthy to receive regardless of whether you give first or not, and that you don't need anyone else to tell you that you are inherently, unconditionally, undeniably loved and lovable.

In the meanwhile, don't despair. Here's the great news! Every day that you make an emotional, mental, and spiritual effort to cultivate a loving, respectful relationship with yourself — a sort of investment in the health of your self-love tree — you will feel more loved and will receive more love, and you will become happier, freer, and more peaceful. Best of all, you can start feeling and experiencing these shifts right away! This self-love adventure is designed to give you big shifts, midsized shifts, and small but mighty shifts all along the way. You are ready to experience self-love at a higher level today, yes? You are ready to regain the power to choose love in every situation you face — tomorrow, and the next day, and the day after that, forever, yes? I thought so.

Great! If you continue on this adventure, take the dares, deepen your relationship with yourself, and take a stand for having only love and respect in your life, then every day you will become stronger and more centered. And one day you will just notice that your tree has its roots firmly planted in unconditional self-love soil, guaranteed!

Every chapter that follows will support you in your effort to nurture the branches of your self-love tree, get your self-worth roots growing firmly and deeply again in good soil, and feed those roots with unconditional love. Hold on to your self-love flag as we go an adventure to and through each of the ten branches of self-love. You'll engage in powerful Daring Acts of Love, answer ME Moment questions, do meditations, and use magical self-love tools, which will lead to choosing, living, and feeling love for yourself, every day. As your experience of love for yourself in all its forms — care, respect, forgiveness, and so on — expands, all the branches of your self-love tree will grow. Your self-worth will automatically increase, helping you to always remain firm in your commitment to love yourself.

How Do You Get More Self-Love?

Much like anything natural, self-love grows over time. The more water, love, and light your self-love tree gets, the more abundant it becomes and the more strongly the love force runs through its roots and branches. As the force of love that you direct at yourself spreads through you, you will become more vibrant and more alive. You will experience happiness, peace, and a sense of being loved and cared for more often than not.

Regardless of what state your self-love tree is currently in, the good news is that the tree of self-love offers you a great gift. You just have to accept it and use it: the power to make big shifts in your habits, thought patterns, and life situations; the power to adopt new ones that lead you to the love and life you desire. The self-love tree gives you the context to understand which parts of your relationship with yourself are super-healthy and vibrant, and which ones are not, so that you can be clear about what you really need in order to shift in your relationship with yourself. Remember, everything in your life starts and ends with the relationship you have with you.

Shift happens in four stages, beginning with *awareness*. You cannot change what you do not see. Which is why so many of us get stuck in ruts, making the same choices and bad decisions over and over again. This tree is your ticket out of the insanity that has kept you looping through self-sabotaging, self-neglecting,

> Making the Shift to Love
>
> Stage 1. Awareness
> Stage 2. Reflection
> Stage 3. Change in the Moment
> Stage 4. Integration

self-abusive behaviors, choices, and thoughts. Once you're aware of the non-self-loving ways you treat yourself, you can begin to clearly see what needs your attention. Without awareness, you are blind.

Once you become aware, you can move to the second stage of the shift, which is *reflection* — where you still act on the same beliefs and in the same patterns, but afterward you are able to look back at your actions and see that you could have done things differently. With the tree of self-love supporting you from within, you will find the real answers to many of the questions you haven't been able to solve, such as "How do I find balance? What will make me happy? How do I find love?"

With this new wisdom, you'll move to the third stage of the shift, to *changing in the moment*. This is where you will catch yourself in the midst of conditioned behaviors or thoughts and switch gears. This tree will support you as you become a person who chooses love for herself in every moment of every day, who makes choices that lead her to happiness, peace, and love even when it's hard and even when she doesn't make perfect choices.

Over time, as you increase your ability to choose self-love, and as your branches and roots of self-love strengthen, you'll find yourself at the final stage of the shift — *integration* — where a new self-loving pattern of thought or action exists in place of the old self-sabotaging one, leaving you a new woman whose first instinct is to choose self-love.

What this tree — and the chapters that follow — offers you is a context in which to understand where you lack love and where you are already bursting with love. You'll receive tools and practices that will help you grow even more love for yourself and, as a result, love everyone else around you. You will develop daring, fun, and powerful ways to maintain your relationship with yourself, so that choosing love for yourself becomes both first nature and second nature — really the most natural choice you could ever make. Remember, you were born in love with yourself. You were born knowing exactly how to love yourself and others well, how to source the love you need. Now it's all about giving yourself permission to do what you were born to do — *love*!

In this next part of our adventure together, part 2 of the book, you will have the opportunity to closely examine each branch of your self-love tree one by one. At the beginning of each chapter, you will take a Self-Love Pulse Check to get a sense of how healthy, happy, and vibrant that chapter's branch is. This will give you an indication of how easy or hard it is for you to choose self-love and give yourself what you need and desire for each particular branch. Each pulse check consists of ten statements that you will rate according to how true each statement is for you. You'll combine your responses to the first five questions to create your LOVE number, which will measure how much love is currently flowing through the branch, indicating how strong and healthy the branch is. You'll combine your responses to the remaining five questions to create your LACK number, which will measure how your actions, beliefs, and habits are taking love from you. This will indicate how weak and unhealthy the branch is. Subtract your LACK number from your LOVE number to determine your overall self-love pulse for any given branch. This pulse check will tell you where you are today in regard to this aspect of self-love. Together, the pulse checks will reveal which branches need the most love from you now, and which ones are doing mighty fine already.

You'll also learn loads of daring, fun, and powerful ways to grow each branch and, as a result, increase your ability to make choices, take action, and think in ways that bring you vastly more love, happiness, and inner peace.

Then, in the last section of our magical adventure, after you have taken a good look at each of your branches, we'll meet by your self-love tree and I'll share with you three of the most powerful — and absolutely happy-making — ways in which you can ensure that from this day forward, love is what you always choose for yourself. And as we close the last chapter together, you'll leave with your own clear set of instructions for growing love in your life and choosing love for yourself forever.

Oh, yes. Let me not forget to tell you about a totally awesome side effect of choosing self-love. In the process of sending all this love to yourself, you will create a bountiful, vibrant tree of self-love. It will bloom with such beauty that not only will it make you happier inside but you will also begin to attract more magical relationships and situations that bring you more happiness and love than you can imagine today. This is the miracle behind the statement "Everything in your life begins with your relationship with yourself."

Think about it. What person, whether friend, lover, or family member, and what situation — whether a great opportunity or a magical invitation — would ever want to stop by a tree with overgrown self-esteem and self-empowerment branches, but which has eight withering, dinky branches underneath? Or whose self-respect and self-acceptance branches appear to be rotting? No one and not much would be stopping by! And certainly not the kind of people and situations your heart and soul really want to connect with. But if you clear out the debris and the "dis-ease" and fill up with love and nourishment, then — wow! — you will have a self-love tree with such an alluring scent, vivacious vibe, and blooming beauty that fantastic people and opportunities will flock to you.

ME Moment Connect with Your Current Tree of Self-Love

Before you get started on part 2 of our adventure together, zooming in on each of the self-love branches, let's pause for a moment to get a clear picture of what you know and don't know about the state of your entire tree of self-love. It's kind of like taking a snapshot of your capacity for choosing self-love as you understand it today. Using the illustration of the self-love tree on page 55 as a guide, put your hand on your heart to get connected with your best-friend self and imagine that this is *your self-love tree*. That the branches you see are *your branches*, that the heart on the tree has *your name* on it. Have an honest heart-to-heart, and ask yourself the following three questions:

♥ Which branches on my self-love tree are blooming with love? **Draw a** heart next to each of those to signify that your heart is full of love in these areas of your relationship with yourself.

♥ Which branches on my self-love tree need to grow or heal with love? **Draw** a star next to those to signify your desire to create more love in these areas of your relationship with yourself.

♥ Which branches am I unfamiliar with — that is, which ones represent aspects of self-love that I'm not sure I can even grow? **Draw a question** mark next to each of those branches to signify your desire to discover more about these branches of self-love (Note: these may also have a heart or a star.)

If you would like a full-color print of the Tree of Self-Love that you can write on and look back to after you finish this journey, then today love is abundant for you! I've created a print of the tree that you can download, along with other goodies, in honor of your commitment to choose self-love! Go to www.ChooseSelfLove.com, where you will find not only the full-color print but also the hand-illustrated Self-Love Kit.

GROW the LOVE!

The Self-Love Tree and the
Ten Branches of Self-Love

CHAPTER 4

Self-Awareness & Self-Honesty

A deep understanding of who you are and who you aren't, with an unwavering commitment to truth about how your actions, thoughts, and choices affect your reality and the people and world around you.

Self-Love Pulse Check

Take your self-love pulse by rating each statement on a scale of one to five according to how true that statement is for you. Five indicates the statement is totally true, and one indicates that it is not at all true. Add up your first five ratings to get your LOVE # and the second set of five ratings to get your LACK #. Subtract your LACK # from your LOVE # to get your current self-awareness and self-honesty pulse.

____ I know who I am, and who I am not. I see myself outside of the story of my past and the confines of the society and family I grew up in.

____ I know what makes me happy and what matters to me and what doesn't. I have a good barometer that tells me if my choices lead to my happiness.

____ I take responsibility for my impact. I am aware of how my choices, actions, and words affect others.

____ I feel my feelings, even when they are hard. I don't shy away from how I feel; instead I delve into the discomfort to discover what's going on inside me.

____ I am honest with myself, always. I am willing to be honest even when it's hard. I check in with myself regularly.

LOVE # _____

____ I define myself in relation to my past, my family, or my societal expectations. A big part of my identity comes from these things.

____ I am out of tune with my feelings. I don't cry, feel sad, disappointed, ashamed, or scared often. I don't like to admit my feelings.

____ I overindulge often in activities or substances that numb me out. I overuse alcohol, TV, smoking, food, sex, shopping, giving advice, or work.

____ I am out of tune with what is really important to me. I go from one experience to another, or drive hard to get to the next place, without pausing to make sure this is the life I really want.

____ I become self-absorbed and unaware of my actions and words and their impact. I don't always notice how I am affecting others.

LACK # _____

Now, subtract your LACK # from your LOVE # to get your full self-love pulse for this branch.

My Self-Awareness and Self-Honesty Pulse _____

People often ask me, "What is the first step in loving yourself?" And while the execution isn't always simple, the answer to the question actually is. Once you have made the choice to love yourself, the next step is knowing who you *really* are behind all the ideas, masks, personas, ideals, layers of protection, and societal and familial baggage. Not who you think you are, not who you were told to be, and not who you think you ought to be, but who you really are in your heart and soul.

Think of yourself as a brilliant machine that has many intricacies and idiosyncrasies. Your job is to know how you work, to know your "owner's manual" inside and out so that you can see your weaknesses, strengths, blind spots, and zones of brilliance. And as the chief operator of this brilliant machine called "you," it's your role to be diligent in discovering how and from where you are operating in all moments. It's your duty to be aware and awake.

Imagine trying to operate a machine while sleeping — you can't. And you can't sleepwalk through life — although many of us do. Then one day, we choose to wake up (or get shaken up and woken up by the universe), we become self-aware and, we hope, remain awake. And in the process we realize that if we are to remain awake, we must also be honest with ourselves about who we are — about how we show up in and affect the world and the people in it, about the choices we make and have made, and about the reality of our lives, even if that means we don't always like what we see.

One essential cornerstone of any great relationship is honesty, and your relationship with yourself is no different. How long would you stay in a relationship with a romantic partner or friend who lied to you? Or a person who pretended to be someone other than who he or she really was? Not long (if you loved yourself). How happy would you be in a relationship with someone you didn't communicate openly with? Or who didn't take responsibility for his or her actions, words, and choices? Maybe you've had a relationship or two like that, so you know the answer very well: not happy! Your relationship with yourself is no different.

It's kind of crazy to think that we would go more than a day without having a constructive conversation with ourselves — although most of us live that way for years before we realize how much we can

> If you can't be honest and open with yourself, you can't expect others to be honest and open with you.

actually help and guide ourselves, if only we pause to ask ourselves what we need. When was the last time you sat down for a talk with yourself, to check in? It's okay if it's been a while; this self-love journey is going to give you plenty of opportunities. And I invite you to take them all.

It's even crazier to think that we would lie to the person who most needs us to be honest — ourselves. But we choose self-deceit, shame, and self-sabotage over self-love all the time. The truth is scary, right? Well, yes, sometimes it is, but as the saying goes, the truth will set you free. There is great liberation in just being willing to tell the truth to yourself no matter what. We both know that avoiding the truth doesn't mean it's any less true.

One woman who had just started reading my book *Choosing ME before WE*, which is about putting you and your dreams first when it comes to choosing your romantic relationships and only choosing respectful, loving partnerships, wrote me and said she was scared to know who she was.

What if she didn't like what she found? She was afraid to look that deeply at her life. What if she didn't like what she saw? I think we have all been there, knowing there is something for us to see, but doing everything in our power to turn the other way. And how well has that worked out for you? Not very. The truth always surfaces to bite you in the ass if you don't pay attention to it. But you can make the wise choice to grow a strong self-awareness and self-honesty branch and listen to what you have to tell and show yourself.

When you realize that hiding from yourself is a bad idea, you begin giving this branch all kinds of attention. And if you're smart, you never stop taking care of it, you never cease asking yourself the hard questions, because you realize that if you can't accept the truth of who you are and what's happening in your life, then no one can. In fact, as you love yourself more, you become addicted (in a healthy way) to asking yourself questions, talking to yourself, and checking in. You begin to create a strong connection, an open and honest line of communication, and, as a result, an intimate relationship with yourself. Who better to get to know than yourself?

ME Moment *Hold an Honesty Hearing*

Honesty hearings are like going to the dentist. The visits can be painful, but wow, do they leave you feeling clean. And regular checkups are essential for long-lasting health. The dentist in this case is you, and your job is to bust through the buildup of stories, illusions, lies, fears, misperceptions, attachments, and judgments you've been collecting. Now, you don't let just anyone put his or her fingers into your mouth, so you want to be just as cautious about allowing someone into your heart. This means it's essential that you also promise to act as a best friend would in this situation — no judging the buildup, berating yourself for the state of your life, or making yourself feel guilty or ashamed. Yes, what you may uncover during your honesty hearing could sting, but you don't have to scrape the sensitive areas harshly. Apply unconditional love instead.

The following five steps will lead you through your honesty hearing. All you have to do is grab a piece of paper and a mirror and go for it. Remember to keep your commitments: point out the buildup and remove it with love! Give yourself about an hour.

Step 1. State the obvious.

On a piece of paper, draw two lines that divide the paper in four quadrants. At the intersection of these two lines, in the middle of the paper, draw a heart. At the top of each quadrant, write one of the following phrases representing a key area of your life (and a potential place where self-honesty can fall by the wayside).

♥ My Career
♥ My Relationships with Others
♥ My Health
♥ My Money

And in the heart, write:

♥ My Relationship with Myself

Go through each area, one by one, while looking in a mirror for added impact, and tell yourself all the ways you *think* you haven't been honest with yourself. Share your thoughts openly with yourself, seeing your reflection as a best friend who is listening to — not judging — what you have to say. After you finish speaking about each of the four areas, write down on your paper what you said about each.

Step 2. Go deeper.

Go back to the mirror, look into your eyes, and get really intimate with yourself, as if you can see directly into your heart and soul. No mask, just you and you. Now ask this reflection looking back at you — the part of you who loves you unconditionally and has no fear of being honest — to dig deeper to answer the question "How am I really *not* being honest with myself?" Then, either by speaking the answer out loud or by closing your eyes and listening to that wise voice inside you, reveal the truth. No shame, no self-judgment, just honesty in service of love. Remember, you are on your side. After you have finished speaking, write down what you heard. Use the other side of the paper you used in step 1, beginning with the sentence starter "I have not been honest about..."

Step 3. Be grateful, not defensive.

Look into your eyes again and say, "Thank you. Thank you for loving me enough to help me see the truth."

Step 4. Soak the truth in.

Look back at everything you wrote. Challenge yourself to try on the truth. If you find yourself resisting the truth, ask yourself these questions:

"What *consequence* am I afraid of? If I accept this as the truth, what reality will I have to face that I might not want to?" Usually it's not the truth that makes you afraid; it's dealing with the consequences of admitting the truth that freaks you out. When you can face the consequence, you gain the power to move from fear into love, which is exactly the result you are after.

Step 5. Make a new choice.

Using your power of self-awareness, address each of the areas you've tended not to be honest in. Ask yourself the following questions:

♥ What has been the result – the cost – of this lack of self-honesty and self-awareness?
♥ What reality would I like to create instead?
♥ What is one action I can take to create the reality I want this week?

Then commit to taking this action by actually writing down, on each of the four sections of your paper, what you will do and by when.

Note: Just like regular checkups at the dentist, this self-love practice can be scheduled with yourself twice a year. Or do it whenever you feel something in your heart and soul aching or irritating you.

Daring Act of Love
Ask a Friend to Hold an Honesty Hearing for You

Sometimes we cannot see what others can see for us, which is probably why we don't do our own dental work. Sure, we can use a piece of floss to get out something that's stuck in our teeth, but to discover the cracks and cavities-in-the-making, we need someone to show us what we can't see. Ask a person in your life, a wise someone who cares, to help you love yourself more. Choose someone you can count on to listen and reflect back to you the truth that she or he hears in what you are saying, someone who won't give you personal opinions unless you ask. Tell this friend that you'd like him or her to help you see the places where you are not being honest with yourself. If this person agrees to help, use the following modified four-step process, which is modeled on the one previously outlined, to hold the hearing.

Step 1. Open up communication.

Tell your wise friend in what ways, or where in your life, you *think* you are not being honest with yourself about your life. Share your thoughts and any questions that have been percolating inside you. Ask your friend just to *listen.* This is important. Until you move to step 2, you want him or her only to listen.

Step 2. Request reflection.

Ask your wise friend this question: "Tell me what you see: how am I being honest, and how am I *not* being honest with myself?" Now *you* listen. No response, no defensiveness. Just listen and say "thank you" if you need to say anything at all. Remember, your friend is on your side.

Step 3. Get curious to gain clarity.

If you want more information to help you gain clarity, you may thank your friend and then ask only one question. But you must ask it from a place of curiosity, not judgment or defensiveness. Ask, "Can you tell me more about...?" Then listen.

Step 4. Be grateful, not defensive.

Look into your friend's eyes and say, "Thank you. Thank you for loving me enough to help me see the truth." This will make sure you complete the honesty hearing with your friend. You don't want to leave this with your heart and soul still wide open after receiving this kind of deep honesty. Once you do the eye-to-eye thank-you, no more talking about what you just talked about. *Finito*. In fact, best to get up and go do something fun and not too deep together. Later, after your friend leaves, you can sit with what you learned and contemplate it.

Double Dare: Hold the honesty hearing, film yourself, and watch the video. Make a date with yourself to watch it again thirty days later as a way to hold yourself accountable for the shifts you said you would make, and then erase the hearing. Love yourself for being willing to be so honest with yourself as you watch yourself tell the truth.

Love Story: From Ugly Duckling to Proud Peacock

Over the course of my self-love journey, I've heard the following modified and modernized rendition of the classic ugly duckling story, a true self-love story, about the bird who didn't fit in with the family of ducks he found himself in. And I've seen it come to life in the experiences of many of my clients, so I share it with you now so you too can benefit. From his earliest memory, this poor duck was outcast, judged, and compared to others, over and over again by all the birds and people he encountered. He tried everything to fit in, but never did. And so in turn, this poor bird judged himself harshly for being odd, different, and wrong — and felt the torment of not belonging.

Then one day, this bird finally stopped looking to others to determine who he was, and so was able to see his reflection in a pond. And what he discovered was that he was not an ugly duckling at all, but instead a beautiful swan. The truth was, there had never been anything wrong with him. This poor bird had tried to be accepted as a duck when he was really a swan. He hadn't known just how beautiful and perfect he actually was, because he hadn't known the truth of who he was. No wonder he was so unhappy!

One of the women in my spiritual breakthrough programs came to me at the start of the program feeling frustrated, alone, and misunderstood. She was experiencing a ton of pressure from her family and culture to fit the mold of what they thought a woman of her age and stature should be. They expected her to get her MBA, find a husband, and then get ready to, very soon, have children. The pressure of their expectations, along with their relentless judgments about how she was living her life, was causing her severe stress, making her second-guess her own instincts and desires, and filling her head with all kinds of beliefs that weren't hers.

Disconnected from herself and distrusting her own Inner Wisdom, she tried to fit in with her family and community in order to keep their love and approval. And where she couldn't fit in, she kept secrets. She made the choice to get an MBA, even though deep inside she wanted to use her gifts and talents to create social change. She believed she wouldn't be happy until she found a man to marry, and spent endless hours worrying about finding the right one. And she kept trying to fit into the social circles that kept rejecting her, exacerbating her feelings of isolation.

In our initial conversations, I listened intently to all that she told me about who she was, but also about who she couldn't yet see — independent, courageous, bold. As she spoke about herself, I could see a changer of social systems, a seeker, a spiritual warrior, a woman who appreciated beauty, an intelligent woman, and a deep and wise soul (she did not yet know these things, however). I also listened to everything she said that told me who she *wasn't* — meek, traditional, subservient, a maintainer of the status quo, a play-by-the-rules person who let fear stop her (again, she had no awareness about herself in these ways). As our conversation went on, I started to reflect all of what I heard about who she was and wasn't. I took the time to see her and reflect back to her what was already living and breathing inside of her. And then I told her the story of the ugly duckling. But instead of ducks and swans, I talked about turkeys and peacocks.

Neela was a vibrant, independent peacock who loved to create change and reject the status quo (peacocks are spiritually known for their transformational abilities). The trouble was that she grew up in a family of play-it-by-the-book turkeys, good turkeys, turkeys who were hardworking and good-natured with their own kind, but who were fiercely adamant about tradition and nasty bullies to anyone who did not do things the way they were "supposed to be done." To keep the love of her tribe, Neela worked hard to hide her beautiful rainbow-colored feathers, to make herself fit into the society her family was a part of so she could make her family happy. But in the process, she was making herself miserable and crazy and eventually had to move halfway around the world to live, just to escape the pressure.

As we continued talking about her as a peacock who loved transformation, and about her tribe as this proud and stubborn flock who loved the traditional course, she began to see that she wasn't wrong, defective, or defiant just for the sake of defiance; she was simply *different*. Not because she was flawed, but because of who she was in her heart and soul. Her increased self-awareness gave her the permission she needed to begin accepting, being, and expressing more of herself. She was able to begin healing the relationship with her birth family by realizing they were just being good turkeys, and that she was just being herself, a peacock. In seeing who she was, she was able to find and join other peacocks, other circles of support and friendship made up of people who could see who she truly was. When she arrived at our group retreat and walked into a room full of bustling peacocks, phoenixes, herons, hawks, eagles — other women who were committed to soaring as their truest selves — her entire face softened, her chest released a sigh of relief, and her heart opened to being accepted and received for exactly who she was.

Within three days, as she became aware of who she truly was, her deep sense of loneliness began to dissipate. She took a stand for marrying for love instead of in response to familial pressure, and she loosened up her obsessive time frame for finding a man. She settled in to finish her MBA but reached out to social innovators for mentorship. And she dove deep into her own spiritual transformation, learning to trust, to surrender control more often, and to overthink less often. All because she dared to admit who she wasn't, accept who she was, and take a stand for unconditional love, especially for herself.

You are an ugly duckling too, your own version of a beautiful swan, transformational peacock, majestic hawk, soaring eagle, magical phoenix, dancing dove, or whatever bird tribe you hail from. When you can distinguish yourself from the bird tribe you grew up in or currently live in, you can learn a lot about yourself and free yourself to accept and express more of who you truly are.

Birds are one of the ultimate symbols of freedom, and this self-love branch is all about your freedom, about you liberating your heart and soul to fly free. Animal guides are great companions for your self-love journey because their spir-

> When you *know* who you really are, it is so much easier to *be* who you really are.

its can teach you about your spirit — they reflect something that lives in you. Animal totems are happy to let you tap into their natural powers too. When you connect with your bird totem, you gain access to double power — the freedom to fly free as yourself, plus the energy of what that bird represents.

Ready to find your bird tribe? Use the following ME Moment, Daring Act of Love, and ME Art adventures to tap into your superpower bird and discover more about who you are and are not.

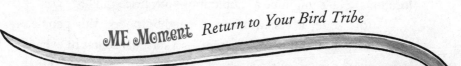

ME Moment *Return to Your Bird Tribe*

From what bird tribe do you hail? Take a trip with your spirit to find your beautiful bird tribe using these questions.

1. If you were a bird, what kind of bird would you want to be? (If you need ideas, do a quick search for images on the Internet.)

2. What kind of bird(s) would you definitely not want to be?
3. What kind of bird tribe are most of your birth family? Your coworkers? Your friends?
4. How is your bird tribe different from theirs?
5. Close your eyes and ask your Inner Wisdom, "What kind of bird am I?" **Write down all that come, and use the Daring Act of Love to try them out.**

To download a recorded version of the full "Finding My Bird Tribe" visualization, go to www.SelfLoveMeditations.com.

Daring Act of Love
Take Your Bird Self Out for a Flight

Make a date with yourself for an afternoon flight and check out new bird tribes. Visit places that have piqued your interest but that you've never gone to because you've been too scared, busy, or judgmental (about yourself or the people who frequent those locations). This might be a shop out of your price range or comfort zone, a restaurant in a neighborhood with people who seem different from you, or a spiritual center or event you've been curious about but too shy to swoop into. You could fly to a museum, gallery, or musical festival with people and art that may or may not be of your tribe. You won't know until you check it out. Make at least three trips to three different locations to have three completely different experiences. Challenge yourself to have a judgment-free self-discovery experience, where you try different energies on and see how they fit or don't fit. Take yourself to dinner afterward and record in your journal what you learned about who you are and who you are not. Remember, there are no bad birds, only different birds.

ME Art Make "I AM" and "I AM NOT" Manifestos

Invite your three-year-old self on a playdate to create a piece of ME Art. Remember, your three-year-old self creates this art. You don't need to be Picasso or perfect in any way. Just be your little-girl self, before anyone told her how to do art the "right" way. I'll give you some suggestions, but at the end of the day the ME Art is all about your way, because each piece is a reflection of your deepening love of you! And if you're a busy superwoman or supergirl who doesn't think she has time to stop and play and create art with her little-girl self, then what I can honestly tell you is that even thirty minutes of ME Art will fill you up with happiness, love, and inner peace equivalent to a day at the spa. And this is a lot less spendy! Have fun and fill up on love.

Supplies:

♥ Two pieces of paper — one for each manifesto
♥ Your color medium of choice (crayons, markers, colored pencils, colored pens, paints, and so on)
♥ Optional: Get the templates for the "I AM" Manifesto and the "I AM NOT" Manifesto Loveplates at www.ChooseSelfLove.com

Mission:

To uncover the truth of who you are and who you are not, and to claim both by creating two ME manifestos: the "I AM..." Manifesto and the "I AM NOT..." Manifesto.

How-to:

Step 1. Make your "I AM..." Manifesto.

On the paper write the words "I AM..." in the center, in a way that feels superjuicy to you. Big and bold. Flowing and cursive. Multicolored.  One color. Whatever feels like you! Then fill the paper with words, phrases, and symbols that express a piece of who you are. As you write the words themselves, choose colors, sizes, fonts, and so on that reflect the meaning of each word, in order to really juice up your ME Art with love. For example, if your word is *vibrant*, write that word in bright colors. If it's *courageous*, use big bold letters. For *funny*, you might draw each letter with a smiley face at the end of it. Let the words reflect who you are, just as the pond reflected the swan who saw himself in it.

Step 2. Make your "I AM NOT..." Manifesto.

On a separate piece of paper, or on the reverse side of the first one, write the words "I AM NOT..." and then fill the paper with words, phrases, and symbols that do *not* express the truth of you. If it's fun for you, then do the same thing with the words: write them in the colors, shapes, sizes, and so on that reflect the energy of what you are describing.

Step 3. Proclaim the manifestos.

After you finish the two manifestos, read both out loud, starting with "I AM NOT..." For an amplified effect, do this in front of a mirror so you can see yourself. Or read them somewhere in nature, such as in a forest or by the ocean. Or somewhere that has a stage, so you can really project your voice and feel like you are being witnessed. At the end of each manifesto proclamation, put your hand on your heart to connect with yourself and say the words "I am myself." Then write the phrase "I am myself" at the bottom of each piece of ME Art, as if you were stamping them with your own imprint. Put these pieces where you can see them or return to them, and if you find a new word along the way that reflects the truth of who you are, and you can squeeze it onto your paper, go ahead and add it.

Love Mantra for Self-Awareness and Self-Honesty

I deserve the truth.
I am ready for the truth.
I embrace the truth.
I am *my* truth.
I am *myself.*

CHAPTER 5

Self-Acceptance

The choice to actively like who you are, without exception, judgment, or wishing you could be someone other than you. In fact, *truth* be told, you adore and appreciate who you are and wouldn't trade places with anyone else for the world (at least for more than a few moments!). You consistently acknowledge yourself for all the ways in which you are imperfectly, perfectly you.

Self-Love Pulse Check

SELF-LOVE
PULSE CHECK

Take your self-love pulse by rating each statement on a scale of one to five according to how true that statement is for you. Five indicates the statement is totally true, and one indicates that it is not at all true. Add up your first five ratings to get your LOVE # and the second set of five ratings to get your LACK #. Subtract your LACK # from your LOVE # to get your current self-acceptance pulse.

____ I love being me. I wouldn't want to be anyone else but me. Being me is grand.

____ I love all of me, even the stuff that's hard to love. I'm committed to loving my seeming flaws, darkness, and shortcomings.

____ I rarely if ever compare myself to others or to external standards. There is only one me, and to compare myself to someone else is insane.

____ I accept and love my body for who she is. I may not like every single body part, but I do love them all. I don't talk badly about any part of my body.

____ I lovingly appreciate and acknowledge myself, often. I give myself kudos, as well as adoration and affection consistently.

LOVE # _____

____ I wish I could be someone other than who I am. I obsess about what I could or should look like, or who I could or should be. And then judge myself for not being that.

____ I am mean to my body. I get upset that my body is not different. When I look in the mirror, I see what I don't like, not what I do like.

____ I see other people as perfect or put together and me as flawed. I look at other people, and think that I am wrong, imperfect, or damaged goods.

____ I compare myself to others. I measure my success or my body based on external ideals or other people.

____ I spend more time being hard on myself than I do on appreciating and acknowledging myself. I find it hard to see what's good about me and celebrate it.

LACK # _____

Now, subtract your LACK # from your LOVE # to get your full self-love pulse for this branch.

My Self-Acceptance Pulse _____

Do you like yourself — really, truly like yourself for exactly who you are? Like what you stand for, how you look, sound, and even taste, lol? Like how you move and groove through life as a one-of-a-kind imprint of divine love sculpted into human form? In fact, if you could send a telegram to the great creator in the sky who minted you, would you write something like the following?

> Thank you for making me, me! I couldn't be happier with the results. In fact, I won't be trading me in for a new model anytime this lifetime. Yes, I know she's not perfect and seemingly has a few flaws, but I adore and appreciate this version. I love being so perfectly me.

If your answer is not a resounding "Yes, of course, I adore and appreciate who I am!" — not just in theory, but as in: you can feel in your cells your appreciation, acknowledgment, and adoration of and affection for the being you are — then this branch needs love, and you are the only person who has the power to provide the deep level of self-acceptance needed. To accept yourself is to liberally apply all four of these love-sourced energies to your relationship with you. Think of this branch as the "Fantastical Four," because when you've got all four A's flowing toward you, wow! Not only will you cultivate unconditional self-acceptance, but all this loving energy — this appreciation, acknowledgment, adoration, and affection — directed at yourself will make you feel simply fantastical!

> Just as you give appreciation, acknowledgment, adoration, and affection to others, you must also give this same kind of love to yourself.

Love becomes tremendously powerful — as do you —when you treat it as a verb, as something you *do*, instead of treating it like a noun, as something you have or don't have. You gain the ability to direct one of the most healing and magical energies on this planet to exactly where you need it most.

What do you suppose would happen if you directed this mighty love power to all the places inside you and qualities about you that you don't like, haven't liked, or have even hated? The places that you take for granted, don't value much, or have forgotten about? The pieces of you that have been starved for affection and adoring kisses and hugs? What would happen to the self-judgment, self-neglect, and self-hatred that have been infecting your self-love tree, and your heart and soul, if you applied love to a less-than-perfect you? If you remembered to tell yourself how much you appreciated and adored the unique being of divine love you are?

I will tell you what would happen, because I've seen it happen again and again. This self-directed and self-generated unconditional love would instantly transform your love-lacking, downer vibes, such as shame, hate, disgust, fear, regret, and wishful thinking, into a feeling of being loved and accepted. How does this happen? By powerfully turning you away from the mirror you've been using to judge, compare, and abuse yourself in response to external standards — the ones that lead you to feel you continually fall short — and turning you toward unconditional self-acceptance instead. And with that turn, you would see that inside you resides an indisputable knowing that you are a perfect, one-of-a-kind imprint of divine love — an imperfectly perfect human you!

There is only one you out there in the world, you know. There's no one else exactly like you. The great creator in the sky broke the mold after you were minted. It knew that you were so thoroughly enough that there didn't need to be another imprint of divine love in human form just like you in this world. Just as no two thumbprints are the same, no two humans — each a unique imprint of divine love — are exactly the same. This is stupendous news! Because if there is only one you, then there is absolutely no benefit in comparing yourself to anyone or anything else. Doing so would be an act of insanity. Comparing yourself to another human imprint of divine love makes no sense. It's like comparing a bird to a rock. What would be the point? No value is created, it's a waste of energy, and you can bet that neither the bird nor the rock would have any interest. The bird would be too busy being a bird, flying and soaring in the sky. And the rock would be content with hanging out on the ground, helping to keep the earth matter stuck together. Everything has its part, and every person is different, just as you are.

Which means that judging yourself according to standards set by some external force — who arbitrarily said you should do, be, or have this thing or that thing in order to be enough, to fit in, or to be perfect — makes no sense either. You know, the standards we all believe we should strive for — the perfect body, home, career, family, lifestyle, and so on — were made up by people. People trying to sell us stuff, make themselves feel better, and deal with their own lack of love — they too are caught up in a system that feeds on making us feel we are not good enough. Gadzooks! Do you see the craziness? Do you see how you've been trained to give your power to feel and be acceptable — to be enough — to others, who create arbitrary, subjective standards?

This is why Madly in Love with ME is a "mad revolution of self-love." You are engaging in a daring act by saying *no* to all b.s. (that's shorthand for bullshit standards!) that have you confused about who you are: perfect and beautiful in your brilliance and in your imperfections.

You are being courageous enough to say yes to something different from what this society has been feeding on for way too long.

ME Moment What's Stopping You from Loving Yourself Just as You Are?

What do you say? Are you willing to stop holding yourself up to, and judging yourself by, someone else's external b.s.? To give up the toxic habit of comparison? If you are *willing* to choose self-love over these self-abusive habits, then the divine will rise up to meet you. That great creator in the sky — the divine Superpower of Love — will take note and reach out to help you in all kinds of ways. Pause here and go deeper to remove the blocks that keep you from being willing and able to release toxic, self-hating habits like comparison and judgment. Asking yourself, and honestly answering, the following questions will help you do this:

♥ What's the benefit of comparing and judging myself? How does it serve me? (Note: there is always a benefit, or you wouldn't do it.)

♥ What's the cost of comparing and judging myself? What's it keeping me from or taking from me?

♥ What's the truth about why I compare and judge myself? What am I afraid will happen if I stop comparing myself to, and judging myself according to, external standards, other people, and my own internal expectations about the person I think I should be?

♥ What do I need to say no to so that I can stop comparing and judging myself? What actions, thoughts, habits, situations, and maybe even relationships keep me in the insane loop of comparing or judging my divine, unique imprint of love?

♥   What do I need to say yes to? What loving habits, thoughts, actions, situations, and relationships will steer me toward choosing self-acceptance, and giving myself appreciation, acknowledgment, adoration, and affection?

Daring Act of Love
Surrender to the Person You Are

Now that you are willing to stop the insanity of comparison and self-judgment, you're definitely clearing the way for love to move and groove through your self-acceptance branch so you can receive the benefit of the Fantastical Four A's. Let's turn the flow up another notch, shall we? There is a profound piece of wisdom that you may have heard of called the Serenity Prayer, which is often used in twelve-step programs. And while there may not yet be a twelve-step program to help stop self-hate, self-abuse, self-neglect, and the like, when you apply this prayer to yourself you'll become able to surrender to the person you are and release the comparison and judgment from your mind. Self-acceptance is an act of surrender.

To engage in this Daring Act of Love, get yourself in front of a mirror pronto. Look into those beautiful eyes of yours — the gateway to the truth of your heart and soul, which reflects your unique imprint of divine love — and repeat the following version of the Serenity Prayer three times. I've modified it to send a big boost of love to this branch of your self-love tree.

> Grant me the serenity to accept the things I cannot change about myself, the courage to change the things I can about myself, and the wisdom to know the difference.

Here's the warmhearted, honest truth: we all have things about ourselves that we have wished were different. You may still be making such a wish about yourself. But wishing you could change things that will never be different, or wishing for changes that would require massive interruption, destruction, and construction, is a bad habit that no self-loving woman can afford. Just imagine the energy and money you would save if you simply accepted your body, your history, your traits, and gifts...your imperfect, perfect self, your one-of-a-kind divine imprint of love.

Where Do You Lack Self-Acceptance?

Maybe for you it's a part of your body you hate on, or it's the circumstances in which you were born that you wish were different. Could be a choice from the past you regret. My heart has broken time and time again while I've watched beautiful, smart women and girls tear themselves apart because of something about themselves they simply cannot accept. Suffering from a lack of love, not understanding that until they can unconditionally accept themselves, without attachment to some preconceived notion of who they should be, they won't feel the appreciation, acknowledgment, adoration, or affection they crave.

I am sure your heart has broken too as you've witnessed the women and girls in your life seeking but not finding self-acceptance, witnessed them not feeling adored, appreciated, or acknowledged, craving affection, looking to the outside for what has to be found on the inside first. Maybe you've watched your gorgeous and intelligent friend who's five foot two with athletic thighs, instead of five foot seven with emaciated-supermodel legs, who obsessively hates her body to the point that she has developed bulimia and body dysmorphic disorder. Instead of adoring and appreciating her beauty and intelligence, she spews disgust and hate for herself, unable to stop thinking about this "flaw" in her appearance that's taken over her mind and skewed her mental pictures of her body.

Perhaps it's your sister, mother, or best friend who drives herself hard because she is trying to become someone else's ideal of who she should be. She can't relax into and accept who she is. Every time she compares herself, she unknowingly rejects herself. Maybe the woman or girl you've been witnessing is you — suffering because you have been looking for acceptance out there, instead of cultivating that acceptance in here, inside your own mind, heart, and spirit.

We've all been there. Trying to be something we are not. Wishing to become, comparing ourselves to, or judging ourselves according to that something, and doing so because we are motivated to reach some external goal that will elevate our self-worth, if only for a moment. But eventually, even if we do reach our goal and win appreciation, adoration, acknowledgment, or affection from the outside, without unconditional self-acceptance, the dis-ease (read: lack of ease) that lives in the core of our self-acceptance branch will resurface.

This dis-ease brings us feelings of sadness and loneliness, and it stems from some of the most harmful forms of self-hate on this planet: self-rejection, self-disgust, and self-judgment. And while the word *hate* may feel too strong, make no mistake: when you choose to judge, reject, dislike, or become disgusted by any piece of or place in yourself, then you are in fact hating yourself. And you already know that it isn't good to direct the energy of hate at anyone. This includes yourself. What you direct at yourself is what you will attract in return.

> If you can't love all the pieces of and places in yourself, how can you expect anyone else to? You can't.

As the one who tends this branch of self-love, you have the job of choosing to fully love all the pieces of and places in yourself. This is a lifelong duty. Your past choices, actions, decisions, lifestyles, and disappointments must be accepted and loved. And you must love who you are today, how you live today, what you look like, what you have or don't have — really, the truth of your one-of-a-kind divine imprint of love. And be prepared to love all your future pieces and places. You can count on the fact that your body and circumstances are going to change year after year, not always in the direction you would like. You will need to accept yourself, not in spite of these changes, but because of these changes. You see, when this branch is strong, you know without a doubt that your human expression, as a divine imprint of love, was made to be imperfectly, perfectly you, and you wouldn't have it any other way.

ME Moment *What about You Has Been Hard to Love?*

Time for an honest heart-to-heart with your b.f.f. about all the things about yourself that you have rejected and hated on. This conversation may not be the easiest one you've ever had, but if you can be honest with yourself, you'll get more clarity about all the ways you do not accept yourself. As a result, a huge space will open for love to come flowing through. Finish the following nine statements with as much detail as you can, without holding back on the words you choose. (Be real and raw, and tap into the energy of hate and rejection that has been bubbling underneath and that now needs to be released.) Give yourself the gift of freedom by really supporting yourself to speak out by writing and writing all that needs to be said until there is no more to write.

1. "I wish that my body wasn't so..."
2. "I wish that my body were more..."
3. "Sometimes I hate that my body is..."
4. "I wish that my past didn't include..."
5. "I wish that my past did include..."

6. "Sometimes I hate that I..."
7. "I wish that I..."
8. "I wish that I didn't..."
9. "Sometimes I hate that I can't..."

Next, take a look at your answers, and notice all the ways in which you wish for yourself to be something other than you are. What is the impact of that wishing on you? And what would it be like if you transformed that wishing into acceptance? What would it be like to turn all those sentence starters around and ferret out all the ways you could affectionately appreciate, acknowledge, and adore yourself right now? Use the following ME Art exercise and Daring Act of Love to transform that self-hate into self-love.

ME Art Make a Love Mirror

Imagine possessing a mirror that always reflects the truth of how beautiful you are — not according to some external standard of beauty, but according to the truth of the beauty you possess by loving yourself for exactly who you are, right now. Imagine further that upon looking into this mirror when you need acceptance, adoration, affection, appreciation, or acknowledgment, you receive it from this mirror. The mirror is just a reflection of how you ultimately feel about yourself. It doesn't have power: your love, reflecting through the mirror, does. This is the mirror you are about to create for yourself — your own Love Mirror. But first you have to come clean about the other mirror, the one you've been using to compare, reject, and hate on yourself.

Supplies:
- ♥ Two pieces of paper
- ♥ Two to three different colored markers or pens
- ♥ Optional: "Mirrors of Transmutation: From Self-Hate to Self-Acceptance" Loveplate, which you can retrieve and print out from www.ChooseSelfLove.com

Mission:

Create two mirrors to give yourself the power to transmute self-hate in any of its forms — rejection, disgust, judgment, and so on — into self-love simply by choosing to face a different mirror. You will use both mirrors in the final Daring Act of Love in this chapter, which will get you practicing self-acceptance every day. Our purpose here is to rewire your mind to see and accept, no matter what, the beautiful, imperfectly perfect imprint of divine love that is you.

How-to:

Step 1. Expose the "Mirror of Dislike and Disgust."

This is the mirror you've been using to compare yourself to others, judge and reject who you are, and make yourself feel bad for being you. It's okay to admit you look into this mirror; we all do it   until the day we take our Love Power back and make a different, self-loving choice. Today is that day for you! To expose this nasty mirror, take the first sheet of paper and, at the top of the page, use a dark color or one you don't like — could be black or brown — to write the following three lines:

THE MIRROR OF DISLIKE AND DISGUST
"I'M LOOKING OUT THERE"
I feel bad about myself — I hate what I see.

Then list all the pieces of and places in yourself that you don't like, wish were different, hate, are disgusted by or ashamed of, the parts that you compare to those of others, or that you judge yourself harshly for having. On the left-hand side of the paper (leave room for one column of writing on the right), write out all the ways you reflect hate at yourself. Include all of what you uncovered in the ME Moment in which you admitted what's been hard to love about yourself, plus whatever else surfaces. Let's call these your "I hate" statements. For maximum impact, use the following three statement starters:

"I hate that my body..."
"I hate that I am not more..."
"I hate that I am..."

For example:

"I hate that my thighs have cellulite."
"I hate that my stomach isn't flat."
"I hate that my boobs aren't bigger."
"I hate that I am not more outgoing."
"I hate that I am not more successful."
"I hate that I am always the person who is single and alone."

Using the words *hate* and *my* together, and the words *hate* and *I am* together, is an essential part of this, because, by looking into this mirror, you see how you have connected the energy of hate to your very being. Give yourself permission to go into these hard feelings and tap into these hidden dislikes and feelings of disgust. Keep writing until you can't think of anything else to add.

Once you have a good number of statements written down on the left-hand side of your paper, pause and take a look at this mirror you have created and which you've been looking into for far too long. This mirror, a reflection of your darkest thoughts and judgments about your very self, is showing you the words and feelings you transmit to yourself daily. Is it any wonder that your self-love tree has been shaky, given the energy of dislike and disgust coming at you? Can you imagine saying these same words to a woman or child you love? Yet you say these words to yourself all the time, even if you don't say them out loud. Now it's time for you to see and feel the damage you are doing to yourself — and to your self-love tree. It's okay to let yourself feel this. We won't leave you here.

Step 2. Get the Big Uglies into the light.

But you are not yet finished with this Mirror of Dislike and Disgust. We've got to get as many of the uglies out into the light as we can, so that we can bring them, and you, back into alignment with love, with unconditional acceptance. Your next step is to look at each "I hate" statement and write out the words that actually run through your mind, heart, and body every time you feel this hate for yourself. Write these statements directly to the right of the "I hate" statements, as if you were disgustedly saying them to yourself. Be blunt. Don't shy away from the brutal language you secretly throw at yourself all the time. But don't worry — like I said, we aren't going to leave you here. We will transform this, and you, into love!

Go ahead and write your statements now. Here are some real examples from real women:

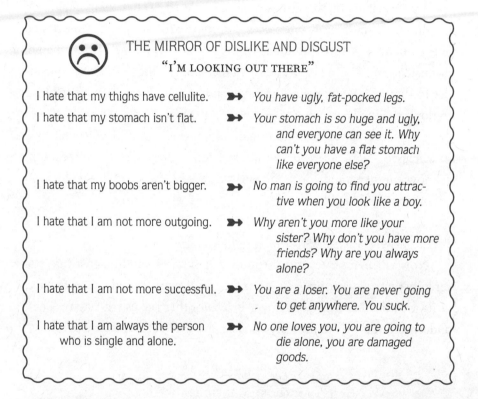

THE MIRROR OF DISLIKE AND DISGUST
"I'M LOOKING OUT THERE"

I hate that my thighs have cellulite. ➡	*You have ugly, fat-pocked legs.*
I hate that my stomach isn't flat. ➡	*Your stomach is so huge and ugly, and everyone can see it. Why can't you have a flat stomach like everyone else?*
I hate that my boobs aren't bigger. ➡	*No man is going to find you attractive when you look like a boy.*
I hate that I am not more outgoing. ➡	*Why aren't you more like your sister? Why don't you have more friends? Why are you always alone?*
I hate that I am not more successful. ➡	*You are a loser. You are never going to get anywhere. You suck.*
I hate that I am always the person who is single and alone. ➡	*No one loves you, you are going to die alone, you are damaged goods.*

Ouch! Right? Go ahead and read your statements out loud to yourself. The words sting, don't they? But isn't this exactly the kind of energy you've been directing at yourself, even if you haven't put it in words until now? It's okay, we all do it. We just don't talk about the hate, disgust, and rejection we throw at ourselves — not even to ourselves! Until now.

The good news is that once you bring all this self-directed ugliness into the light, you can absolutely transform its destructive energy and let go of your self-hating habits. You just completed the first step — shining a light on all the pieces and places you find hard to love. The next step is even better — applying loads of love! Once you wipe off the shame, disgust, and fear, you also let go of all the hate and judgment, you surrender to that which you cannot change, and *presto*! There is space for love to flow in. Finally you can give yourself the gift of self-acceptance! Not grudging acceptance or conditional acceptance, but unconditional love in which you return to your natural state and give yourself appreciation, acknowledgment, and adoration every day, with the same sweet affection a mother would her child.

Step 3. Make your Love Mirror.

Now is the time to transform all that self-hate and disgust into the serenity that comes from l-o-v-e. At the top of your second piece of paper, write the title "My Mirror of Love" in a color that makes you happy. Then underneath that, write these five lines in another color that you love:

MY MIRROR OF LOVE

"I'M LOOKING INSIDE NOW"

I accept myself unconditionally —

I affectionately appreciate, acknowledge, and adore myself.

I love what I see.

Now go back to each of those statements of disgust and dislike and create a mirror for yourself that reflects love. Do this by turning each of the statements into love-powered statements. Your mission is to transform the energy of hate into love for every piece of and place within yourself that you've found hard to love, by writing out a statement or set of statements that reflect self-acceptance — in the fantastical form of appreciation, adoration, acknowledgment, and affection.

Use these statement starters and "I love" statements until you have successfully transformed everything you wrote on the other mirror:

I love you <<insert body part>>.　　▶▶　*You are so <<insert the words your heart wants to say>>.*

I love that I am <<insert the quality and truth of who you are>>.　▶▶　*I love you, <<insert your name>>.*

For example:

MY MIRROR OF LOVE
"I'M LOOKING INSIDE NOW"

I love you, legs. I love you, thighs.　▶▶　*You are so beautiful and strong.*

I love you, tummy. I love you, waist.　▶▶　*You are so sexy and sensual.*

I love you, breasts.　▶▶　*You are so perky and supple.*

I love that I am thoughtful, intelligent, and introspective.　▶▶　*I love you, <<insert your name>>.*

I love that I am exactly where I am today.　▶▶　*I love you, <<insert your name>>.*

I love that I am so lovable and that I always have my own company.　▶▶　*I love you, <<insert your name>>.*

Step 4. Destroy the Dislike and Disgust Mirror, lavish love on yourself, and display your Love Mirror.

Since you won't be hating on yourself anymore, you don't need that old Mirror of Dislike and Disgust. Thank the mirror for the lessons it's given you and let it know its job is done. And just as you would break a mirror whose reflection you no longer wished to see, rip this mirror into tiny pieces (while feeling acceptance in your heart) and then flush it down the toilet or bury it in your yard — sending it back to the earth to be recycled.

Now, your Love Mirror is a different story. Put this mirror in a place where you can see it often, or that you can get to easily when you need a reflection of just how beautiful you are. Visit this mirror whenever you need a dose of appreciation, acknowledgment, adoration, or affection. But first, be sure to engage in the following Daring Act of Love!

Daring Act of Love
Make Love with Yourself

After you finish making your Mirror of Love, stop, stand up, and get ready to ooze good love for yourself. You deserve it! Hold your Mirror of Love in front of you with one hand, or post it on a wall where you can read it as you go. Say your love statements to yourself, one by one, out loud. Yes, out loud. If you have a physical full-length mirror that you can do this in front of, all the better (but it's not necessary).

First read each of the statements related to body parts; touch that body part and feel yourself sending love to it. Feel yourself transforming from a body hater to a body lover, and notice the difference in this energy when compared to what you might have said or done in the past. Feel your body feeling you accepting her for who she is. If you don't yet feel the truth of these words 100 percent, that's okay. Fake it 'til you make it — you have to start somewhere! Your love power will build.

Second, read aloud each statement about the unique and beautiful human that is you, then put your hand on your heart, close your eyes, and imagine yourself this way (or if you are in front of a mirror, look into your eyes). Again, feel the words permeate you and, this time, go straight into your heart and soul. Let your little-girl self and big-girl self feel you accept them just as they are.

Feels good, yes? Now the question is, how do you keep that love coming even in the moments when what and who you see are not exactly what you would have ordered from the universe when it minted your imprint of divine love in human form? Have no fear! Where there is a willingness, there is a way. First, I will tell you a love story, and then I'll help you live your own.

A Love Story: A Woman and Her Cellulite Unite

I used to hate myself every day by hating the cellulite that had become part of the backs of my thighs. Every day I *hated* it. Just think of that for a moment. I hated something that was part of me. Every day I unknowingly sent hateful energy to the person who needed my love the most: me.

My body hate would start in the morning when I'd get out of the shower, look in the mirror, and see myself as one big walking, talking piece of cellulite. I'd walk away in disgust. Or at a summer baseball game, when I'd sit down, cross my legs, and check neurotically to make sure no unsightly cellulite appeared. I was twenty-five, five foot six, and 125 pounds, but I was embarrassed about my body. Afraid someone was going to see the pockets that had taken up residence on my legs and think me fat, unattractive, or just plain gross.

This went on for more than a decade, until I decided to stop creating dis-ease for and disgust about myself and start sending love to myself. Determined to become a body lover instead of a body hater, I made it my self-love practice for one year to pour as much love as I could into the area into which I had formerly poured hate. Every morning, after getting out of the shower, I'd look at my cellulite in the mirror and say to it, "I love you." Then I'd rub lotion all over my thighs while repeating the Love Mantra "I love you." I'd meditate every morning, imagining the pockets of cellulite filling up with pink light and love, one by one, until my entire leg was completely smooth from the inside out.

What happened was nothing short of a miracle. The cellulite disappeared! No, I didn't start training as a triathlete or go on some starvation diet. I simply turned my body hate into body love, and as a result, I stopped *seeing* the cellulite. For a girl who had been obsessed with this body part for more than a decade, this was a welcome relief and a spectacular shift in reality. When I'd get out of the shower, I'd simply see my body as she had always been. When I'd sit down, I wouldn't feel compelled to check my legs. When I'd see pictures of myself in my bathing suit, I'd see a beautiful woman.

The best part of becoming a body lover is gaining the power to turn your inner self-talk from hate to love when you notice something about your body you don't like. On the occasions when my cellulite would reveal itself to me — whether I'd see it in the mirror or a photo, or directly on my body while sitting down — instead of hating my body and getting down on myself, I'd look at it and use it as an opportunity to apply love to my body, saying, "Time to make sure I am caring for my body and remembering to move her every day." Or, "Yeah, got my period today. I'm probably retaining water. That happens. Shrug. Next." Or, "Hmmm ...have I been eating more sugar than usual? What is going on for me? What's the sugar substituting for, and what do I need to let myself feel instead of filling up with sugar?"

You can use this same love strategy for any of the pieces of or places in you that you find hard to love and accept. The transformation will take time, just as it did for me and all the clients I have shared this with. But if you stick with it, directing love instead of disgust and dislike to your body and your interior, you can create miracles for yourself.

Daring Act of Love
Love the Part of Yourself That Is Hardest to Love

Choose one part or piece of yourself that you dislike the most. This is the body part, quality, or truth about yourself that you find the hardest to be with. The one you obsess about the most. Complain and compare the most. Hate on the most. Your Daring Act of Love is to spend the next seven days loving that part of you — applying appreciation, adoration, acknowledgment, and affection — following the same process I used. Each morning after showering or brushing your teeth, look at that part in the mirror — if it's a body part — and beam a series of "I love you's" at it. Rub lotion, oil, or love into it while repeating the same words. Meditate for at least three minutes daily and imagine it being filled with, wrapped in, or wiped clean with pink love. Feel the energy of accepting it as a mother would accept her child unconditionally.

If it's a quality or truth about yourself, then each morning after showering or brushing your teeth, look in the mirror and beam into your eyes these words: "I love you for exactly who you are. I love you because you are <<insert the statement from the disgust mirror>>, because that means you are also <<insert the statement from the Love Mirror>>."

Spend at least three minutes of quiet time, eyes closed, imagining your heart filling up with pink love in the places that you formerly despised. Then throughout the day, practice shifting from hate to love in the moment. At the end of seven days — mark this date on your calendar — ask yourself, "What do I notice about the pieces of and places in me that have been hard to love?" Remember, awareness is the first step in making shifts. See if you can move to reflection by asking yourself, "What action could I take in the moment to accept myself when this comes up for me?" Take note of this and use it to change hate to love in the moment when disgust, dislike, judgment, or hate for yourself next shows up. Or use one of the following Love Boosts, short actions and thought-shifters that have the power to shift you into love.

Love Boost

Whenever you feel down about a part or piece of or place in yourself, try boosting yourself in one of these ways:

♥ Say words of love. Be kind, gentle, and compassionate with yourself by saying nice things out loud to yourself.

♥ Send feelings of love. Put your hands on that part of your body or on your heart and send pink love vibes.

♥ Talk to your body and your heart. Ask, "What can I do to take better care of you?"

♥ Sing yourself a song. Burst into a self-love ditty about that body part or place in yourself and all the reasons you love it. Go country or try super-rock, a Motown soul jam, a pop hit — have fun and make yourself laugh.

One final note about self-acceptance: When you accept yourself, you will feel it. Acceptance is active. You are literally welcoming yourself, acknowledging that you are good and enough, enveloping yourself with affection and adoration. Self-acceptance is you surrendering to yourself — to being who you are, as the universe made you. This includes accepting your body, your qualities, and your essence, the unique imprint of divine love that you are, believing you are perfectly you, even though you are not "perfect" by the idealized standards set by our society. When you activate the love force of self-acceptance, you will feel like you are falling in love with yourself.

Love Mantra for Self-Acceptance

I love who I am,
exactly as I am.
I am myself.
And that is enough.

CHAPTER 6

Self-Care

Choosing to make sure that you get what you need on all levels — physically, spiritually, emotionally, and mentally — every day.

Self-Love Pulse Check

SELF-LOVE
PULSE CHECK

Take your self-love pulse by rating each statement on a scale of one to five according to how true that statement is for you. Five indicates the statement is totally true, and one indicates that it is not at all true. Add up your first five ratings to get your LOVE # and the second set of five ratings to get your LACK #. Subtract your LACK # from your LOVE # to get your current self-care pulse.

____ I feel replenished, nourished, and fulfilled. My body gets good food, my mind good sleep, and I feel happy.

____ I am supported and well taken care of. I have what I need to take care of myself well.

____ I feel full of energy, vibrant, and alive. I am healthy. I wake up feeling energized and stay that way throughout the day. I am rarely sick.

____ I have no problem taking a break to stop and recharge. No matter how much is going on, I take care of myself.

____ I have a balanced life. I feel like all areas of my life — physical, mental, emotional, and spiritual — are well cared for.

LOVE # _____

____ I experience emotional swings and dips in my energy. My emotions and energy seem to go up and down.

____ I feel frustrated, stressed, and sometimes depressed. I get upset easily. I feel anxious and stressed out more than at peace and ease.

____ I feel overwhelmed or exhausted. I am tired. I wake up and go to bed thinking about my to-do list.

____ I feel like the world is on my shoulders. I feel like I have to do everything, or it won't get done.

____ I am out of balance. I give a lot of my energy to one or two specific areas of my life, and other areas suffer because of it.

LACK # _____

Now, subtract your LACK # from your LOVE # to get your full self-love pulse for this branch.

My Self-Care Pulse _____

There isn't a woman alive who doesn't *want* to take care of herself. We all know *how* to take care of ourselves. We read the books and magazines, learn the yoga poses, and eat our green veggies. We set intentions, make New Year's resolutions, and even make promises to ourselves, yet we have *all* struggled with self-care. And most of us still do. Think of the women you know. If you had to guess their self-love pulse rates for self-care, how many do you think would have a strong pulse? You could probably count these self-care enigmas on one hand. The other 90 percent are more likely to experience frequent blips up and big blips down in their self-care pulse. Most of us do a great job of self-care *sometimes* — a vacation here and there; a groove of eating healthy; a stint of getting enough rest, physical exercise, and mental downtime; and a good dose of spiritual fulfillment. But more frequently, we find ourselves just holding on, trying to maintain some semblance of self-care in the midst of the busyness of our overwhelming lives, trying to also deal with the needs of everyone and everything else.

The reason we struggle so, even when we so clearly *want* to take care of ourselves, can be boiled down to two things: bad programming and a screwed-up value system. Bad programming from the world around you rerouted your natural self-loving beliefs, making you think that you have to choose between giving to yourself and to others (as if there isn't enough for everyone), that giving to yourself is selfish (instead of self-loving), and that you have to give before you can receive (hello conditional love). Add to that a societal system that values a drive-'til-you-drop lifestyle of doing, busyness, and outward displays of confidence over the nourishing qualities of being, caring, and nurturing, and no wonder your self-care branch is suffering.

Of course it's been hard for you to consistently follow through on taking care of yourself. The world and your mind have been working against you! If your mind tells you that resting, relaxing, and playing aren't valuable, or that you deserve these things only after working really hard, then of course you won't choose self-care over doing more. Instead, your mind will send bolts of fear and resistance through your body and heart in the form of excuses and rants like "People will think you're selfish if you do this for yourself," or "You don't have time to take care of yourself; you have too much to do," or "If you stop doing things, you will fall behind, fail, or starve." So of course you choose self-neglect over self-love almost every time. But the truth is, you don't have to choose between taking care of others and taking care of yourself. You can do both.

> The more you take care of yourself, the more you can take care of the people and things you love.

The more you take care of yourself, the more you can take care of the people and things you love. Just stop for a moment and read the previous sentence out loud. And then read it aloud again, this time replacing the *you* and *yourself* with *I* and *myself*: *The more I take care of myself, the more I can take care of the people and things I love.* Isn't that so much better than "I have to take care of everyone and everything else before I can take care of me"? Nod your head up and down. Yes. You know it is! Now, what if you really believed it and acted on it?

ME Moment *Will You Believe You Can Take Care of Yourself and Everything Else?*

You may not know how you can have a life in which you get everything you need in order to take care of yourself while still taking care of all the people and things that depend on you — and that's okay. You need only be willing to believe it is possible. Can you do that? And are you willing to take one step at a time toward that reality? Great! Then let's take a ride to the magical land of ME, where you hear what you need, and where you discover great joy in giving it to yourself!

Close your eyes and take a ride through these six steps.

1. Imagine what your life would be like if, the more you took care of yourself, the more love you could give and the more you could accomplish in the world. See yourself on your mind's movie screen, going through your life and making a bigger impact because you choose to care for yourself and fill yourself up first.

2. Repeat softly to yourself a few times, "The more I take care of me, the more I can take care of what I love." Notice how saying these words feels in your body.

3. Answer the following questions. If I really believed this was possible, what would that give me that I don't have today? How would having this be a benefit to me?

4. Close your eyes again, place your hand on your heart, and ask yourself, "<<insert your name>>, what is one thing you really need right now that

I could give you?" Then listen. You are literally asking yourself what you need. When's the last time you did that? This is a good self-care act to turn into a habit starting right now. Whatever bubbles up — in a feeling, some words, an inner knowing, or a visual — is your Inner Wisdom speaking to you. Repeat the answer you receive out loud to help it sink in. Good. This is the self-care action you need to take for yourself pronto.

5. Keeping your hand on your heart and your eyes closed, envision giving yourself that one thing. As if you were leaning in to hand yourself a gift, say out loud, "You deserve to take care of yourself. You deserve <<insert this one thing>>."

6. Seal the deal with a promise. Promise yourself that you will make sure you get what you need. Say out loud (with your hand on your heart) what your Inner Wisdom told you, and then write this promise down: "<<insert your name>>, I promise that I will make sure you <<insert the one thing>>. You can count on me to take care of you."

Breathe and soak that in. Take that action within the next forty-eight hours. If you'd like a guided meditation to help you connect to what you want and need to receive, at multiple levels — so you can be fully cared for — use the self-care meditation at www.SelfLoveMeditations.com.

How Do You Keep Getting What You Need?

If you wanted to take good care of other people you loved, what's the first action you would take? Ask them what they need, of course! There is no way to know what a person needs or wants if you don't ask, and while mind reading may work sometimes, over the long run it doesn't yield the best results. So retire right now from trying to read your own mind, and instead start to get to know what your heart, soul, body, and spirit need — by asking them, as you just practiced doing. It's time to increase the number of open lines of communication between you and you.

> The ability to care for yourself requires an intimate knowledge of and concern for what you need at any given time, and an unapologetic determination to give it to yourself.

You just experienced a taste of what it feels like to take a ME Moment and ask yourself what you need. And that was a great start. Now let's apply it to your everyday life. Self-care cannot be something you do just on vacation, during a spa visit, or on the weekends. It's a 24/7 job, but the benefit is that it is all about you being in service to yourself. And wouldn't it be nice to have someone who was intensely committed to serving you? Well, now you do. You!

Serving yourself and making sure you get what you need is simpler than you think. The execution may be tough at first, but if you apply the following basic principles, self-care will, over time, once again become a natural state of being and doing for you.

Guidelines for Good Self-Service

1. Good communication: I check in with myself. I listen to myself.
2. Follow-through: I do what I say I will do.
3. Consistency and frequency: From morning through night, on a daily basis, I am here for myself.

4. Loyalty and flexibility: I am willing to drop everything, rearrange my schedule, and make sure the person I am serving — that's me! — gets what she needs.

What I've found to be true about self-love in general, but especially about self-care, is that the small things we do over and over again make the biggest difference. We often think we have to have a lot of money to take good care of ourselves, or a lot of time on our hands. But really, self-care starts and succeeds with changing your mind-set and creating new, very simple self-care beliefs and habits that when practiced daily, make mighty differences without breaking your bank or sucking up all your time. What follows are two of the best and most effective. Try them out for yourself using the self-love adventures I've included — all of which I've tried myself, with fabulous results.

Self-Care Belief and Habit #1

NEW BELIEF: "If I start my day by taking care of me, I will feel better taken care of."

DAILY LOVE HABIT: Ask yourself what you need first thing every day...and then give it to yourself, without question and without fail.

How many times after waking up in the morning have you checked your email, voicemail, or electronic device before you peed? Thought about your to-do list before you thought about how you were feeling? Dialed into the Internet before dialing into the divine? Started your day startled by your buzzing alarm clock? How many times have you input and ingested stress-producing thoughts and energies that remind you of how much you have to do, how much you didn't get done yesterday, and how little time there is to get it all done? Or started your day time-deficient, love-starved, and disconnected, feeling like you've already failed and fallen behind, focusing on everything and everyone except yourself?

I was talking with Kristine Carlson, author of *Don't Sweat the Small Stuff for Moms* and *Don't Sweat the Small Stuff for Women*, and she summed up the power of this new self-care belief and habit up the best: "How you start your day is how you live your day."

Start in stress, live in stress. Start feeling like there's so much to do, and live feeling like you never get enough done. Start disconnected from yourself, and live the entire day unaware of what you need. But start your day connected to yourself, and you're way more likely to make sure that your needs get taken care of as well as everyone else's. Start your day connected to your breath and your body, and you're likely to stay connected to your body and its needs. Start your day connected to the divine, and you'll feel supported all day long and maintain a stronger sense of inner peace throughout the day.

> The reason you don't take care of yourself has nothing to do with time, but everything to do with the belief that you don't really deserve to be taken care of and your unwillingness to make the commitment to give yourself that care.

Have excuses started rolling through your mind? "I don't have time to meditate for thirty minutes; my children need me." Or, "I'm just not a morning person. I don't have time...I don't have time..." While all these things may be true, they are never the real reason why we can't. We just don't *believe* that we can.

You don't have to spend thirty minutes on a cushion, teach your kids how to make their own breakfast, or start waking up at 4 AM for exercise. You need to shift your mind-set and assign top priority to your own mental, spiritual, emotional, and physical health. And then watch the miracles occur! When you start to value yourself by spending your time on you, and by choosing how you start your day, your entire day will shift. Try the following two simple but mighty Daring Acts of Love. One takes less than three minutes, and the other requires no extra time at all. Then notice how they change your self-care pulse.

Daring Act of Love
Start Your Day by Taking Care of Your Needs

Upon waking, open your eyes and then close your eyes immediately. Put one hand on your belly and one on your heart. Take three deep breaths and ask yourself this question: "What do I need in order to take care of me today?" Listen for your best friend's answer (that is the voice of your Inner Wisdom). She will tell you. Whatever she says, make sure you get it. Make a commitment every morning to give yourself what your Inner Wisdom says you need. This may be a actual thing, an action to take, or who knows! Do this ritual for seven days and notice the impact. Become aware of which of your unconscious anti-self-care beliefs get revealed, and which of your habitual patterns get pushed out of your comfort zone. Challenge yourself to go beyond comfort into radical self-care.

For extra support, keep a journal close to your bed and write down what your Inner Wisdom says and the commitment you make — on behalf of yourself as your own b.f.f. — each morning. Use it as a big permission slip that says, "You can <<insert self-care commitment>> today." Rip the page out of the journal and take it with you as you go about your day. When the time comes to take action, read the permission slip to yourself and engage in the radical act of believing you are worth spending your time on.

Daring Act of Love
Love-Start Your Day

This dare will take a few days, but it's so worth it. This dare is one of people's favorites, and they always report big shifts after taking it on. For the next three days, notice what energy you start your day with, and then notice how that affects the rest of your day. Notice the "toxic starts" and the "love starts." Toxic starts are ways you start your day that are not full of pure love, happiness, or peace. They are the effect of things like loud alarm clocks; stress-inducing activities; mind food like emails, television, and the Internet; not-so-healthy foods and habits like sugar, smoking, and skipping breakfast altogether; and emotions like worry, anger, and frustration. After three days of observation, switch to allowing only the energy of love, peace, and joy to be what comes into you first thing in the morning.

Each morning for three days:

1. Notice the first three things you *do* each morning.
2. Notice the first three things you *consume* or otherwise put into your body each morning.
3. Observe how your habitual actions and consumption patterns affect the rest of your day. What is the link between what you always do and consume and how you feel and act the rest of the day?

Then, on day 4, make the big shift to love starts only.

4. After three days' time, begin your mornings only with love starts; no toxic starts allowed. The rule is that the first six blasts of energy — whether they're actions or things you consume — must come from and generate love, peace, or joy. Count them. One through six. And keep counting every morning until you return to your first nature, automatically surrounding yourself with love, happiness, and peace.

Seven of My Favorite Love Starts

1. Hot lemon water. This flushes toxins out of your body. Body happy!
2. Breath. For thirty seconds or three minutes, just breathe. Connect yourself to your body and spirit. Presto!
3. Gratitude. Out loud, list five things you're grateful for. Do

this with your partner or pet for extra good juju. Your heart instantly opens to love, and you feel cared for.

4. Saying good morning to the earth. **Walk outside or open a window and say out loud with glee, "Hello, sun! Good morning, plants and animals!" Connect to nature; feel peace and the sense of being supported.**

5. Kisses or hugs with someone you love, even if that someone is you! **Generate the feeling of being loved.**

6. The soothing sound of beautiful music. **Replace your buzzing alarm clock with a CD alarm clock and wake up to soothing morning music. I recommend Deva Premal or Karen Drucker. Music opens your heart and spirit to love and happiness.**

7. Incense or flowers. **Burn Nag Champa incense, use a rosewater spritz, or put a bouquet of flowers next to your bed — heck, do all three! You'll wake up with a sense of beauty, which is naturally calming.**

Self-Care Belief and Habit #2

NEW BELIEF: "I give only what I can afford to give."

DAILY LOVE HABIT: Check your energy tank daily. Retain and replenish your energy.

I am about to share with you with one of most magical tools of self-care I have ever come across. It will give you the superpower to do what you need to get done in a day, without draining all your energy or spending all your time on everything and everyone else. But first a love story.

Love Story: Ancient Chinese Secrets for Modern-Day Superwomen

Before I had a consistent self-care practice, I got a lot done, and I mean *a lot*. I was a human doing machine. And then every three months or so, almost without fail, I'd have an emotional, physical, and spiritual meltdown. I'd experience a big bout of exhaustion usually accompanied by some kind of physical malady, and, as screwed up as it sounds, I would find myself happy to be sick so I could rest! And, honestly, also mad as hell that I was sick and unable to attend to what I wanted to get done. When the exhaustion was really bad, I'd also suffer a bout of mild depression, where I'd start asking myself things like "What's this all for? Is what I am doing really enough? Does anyone really care? Maybe it would be better if I just moved to Tahiti and started selling coconuts for a living." Perhaps you can relate?

My Superwoman battery pack could keep going for a long time before it would run out and I'd reach this point. But as I grew my self-love, I grew tired of this pattern and sought help. The universe brought me a very wise man, a Taoist master and acupuncturist named Dr. Alex Feng. He took one look at me, put his hand on my belly, and smiled as if he knew the ancient Chinese secret I should have known all along. The words he spoke pierced my workhorse skin and changed my life. He said, "Retain. Retain. Retain."

That's when it hit me. Our bodies and spirits are like gas tanks that hold energy. Most of us women employ the system of drive, drive, drive until our tank says "Empty," and even then we keep driving because we know there are still a few gallons in reserve. So we push it, then run on fumes and pray we get to our destination before the fumes run out. Of course, because we roll through life like Superwoman, we almost always get to our destination, but at a cost — often a big one. I call the outcome the "Crash and Crumble Effect," because not only do we deplete our standard energy tanks, but we also spend our *reserves*, and we crash in a heap, emotionally, mentally, physically, and spiritually in pieces.

Self-Care Rules for Replenishing and Retaining

Here are a few simple but powerful self-care rules that I invite you to begin adhering to right away. Do this as an act of self-love for yourself and as an act of love for those you serve — including yourself.

Self-Care Rule #1. Always Keep Your Tank at Least Half Full

After your energy tank level dips below half, it seems to run out faster. And it takes a lot more time and energy to recharge, just like your cell phone. Never let your energy tank go below 50 percent.

Self-Care Rule #2. Never Serve from Your Reserves

Your reserves are never to be spent on anyone else. They are made up of energy that takes way too much to replenish and, in some cases, can't be replaced. Ask any woman who has suffered from chronic fatigue syndrome or adrenal gland fatigue and failure, and she'll tell you she got wiped out because she spent her reserves.

Daring Act of Love
Check Your Energy Tank Daily

One of the best ways to make sure your energy level doesn't dip below the halfway point, and to stop spending your reserves, is to check in with yourself on where your energy level is, daily! Every morning, drop a dipstick into your energy tank and ask your Inner Wisdom how full your tank is. And then take self-care action accordingly. Here's a handy guide:

75–100 percent full: All's good. **Keep doing what you're doing, and keep filling up daily.**

50–74 percent full: Alert. Need energy. **Ask yourself what you need in order to refill. Take whatever self-care action necessary and fill up.**

25–49 percent full: Warning! Stop. Drop. Get support now. **Do not pass go. Do not take on more. Do not keep pushing through. On all self-care levels — physical, emotional, mental, and spiritual — get yourself what you need in order to move past half full.**

0–24 percent full: Stop everything and check yourself into self-care rehab! **You are about to spend energy you may never regain. Clear your calendar. Ask for help. Whatever you need. It will save you time in the long run.**

Daring Act of Love
Say No, and Keep Your Time and Energy for Yourself

When someone asks you to do something for him or her that would cause you to spend time or energy you don't want to spend, or don't have, say no. Even if you really want to do it, when your plate is already full or your energy is already allocated, say no.

Even if you feel like you *should* do it, say no. Even if you don't want to be left out, say no. Make yourself sit in the uncomfortable position of saying no, and then actively spend your time and energy on what you know in your heart is right for you at that time. Take notice of the impact of the decision on all levels, and look for an insight into what you value and how you value yourself and your time and energy.

ME Art Create an "I Care for Me" Proclamation

Time to make these new beliefs, habits, commitments, and rules into art and write down in ink your promise to care for yourself well.

Supplies:
- ♥ A piece of blank paper
- ♥ Your Self-Love Imprint from chapter 2
- ♥ Two different colored markers or pens (or more colors if you like)
- ♥ A mirror or other proclamation-worthy place
- ♥ Optional: Printout of the "I Care for ME Proclamation" Loveplate, found at www.ChooseSelfLove.com

Mission:

Choose three new self-care beliefs — beliefs you are going to live by — and make a written proclamation of these new ways of being and believing. This proclamation is for you, to see as proof of your self-care choices, as well as reinforcement over the course of your upcoming new mornings and days of self-care. When you not only make a commitment to something — in this case yourself — but you also write and proclaim it, you are a gazillion times more likely to keep your promises to yourself.

How-to:

Step 1. Choose your three new self-care beliefs.

There are a few sources where you can go to find the three new beliefs that you want to program into your mind and belief system. Try choosing from the following:

♥ The self-care beliefs and habits that we just went through together.
♥ Beliefs mentioned in this chapter. Take them as they are or rewrite in your words.
♥ Your Self-Love Imprint from chapter 2. Look at the beliefs that have stopped you from taking care of yourself and rewrite them as beliefs that actually support you.
♥ Here are a few more to choose from:
  • "I can get what I need even if I don't work hard."
  • "I ask and listen to my body because she tells me what I need."
  • "I deserve to receive what I need, regardless of what I give."
  • "I can take care of myself before I take care of others."
  • "I will be supported when I choose to support myself first."
  • "I have plenty of time to take care of myself."
  • "I have plenty of money to take care of myself."

Step 2. Begin the proclamation page.

Down the middle of the paper, draw a line of three hearts, spacing them so they go from the top to the bottom of the page, but leaving some room at the top for a headline. On the top of the page above the hearts, write, "I Care for ME." Number the hearts by placing the number 1 in the top heart, 2 in the middle heart, and 3 in the bottom heart. These three hearts signify the three promises you are about to make to care for yourself; they also convey the expression of love that comes from the statement "I care for me." Say those words — "I care for me" — out loud to get a sense for what that feels like.

With the hearts dividing the paper down the center, you now have two columns — one to the left of the hearts and one to the right — to write in. Above the left-hand column, write, "I believe…" This is where your new beliefs will go. Above the right-hand column, write, "I choose to…" This is where you will write your new self-care habits.

Step 3. Claim your new beliefs and habits.

On the left side of the paper, next to each of the three hearts — your self-love symbols of choosing self-care — write one of the three new beliefs in your own words. Now, to actually claim this belief, there is one more step. Read each belief out loud — "I believe…" — while drawing an arrow to the heart, to the right. Drawing the arrow is an action that signifies your choice and commitment to take this new belief as yours, saying yes to believing that it will lead you to self-love in the form of self-care.

Next, on the right-hand side of the paper, under the words "I choose to…," write the specific new habit you will develop or the action you promise to take as follow-through to your commitment to this new belief and your self-care. Self-care is an active choice made up of small but mighty actions, so you need to take a specific action, or make a specific choice, for this belief to become a reality. The more you practice self-care with positive results, the more you will reinforce this new belief and the more it will become your natural way of being and living. For example, if your new belief is "The more time I take care of me, the more I can take care of those I love," then your action may be to ask yourself every morning what you need and to do that for yourself no matter what. For each habit written next to the corresponding belief and heart, draw an arrow back to the heart to signify your promise to take this action on your behalf.

Step 4. Proclaim your proclamation.

Take this beautiful work of self-love art, stand tall, and read it out loud. "I <<insert belief #1>> and therefore I choose to <<insert habit #1>>." Repeat for each of the three beliefs and new habits. For extra love power, make your proclamation in front of a mirror, where you can witness yourself, or in a place in nature, where you can feel the earth responding to and witnessing your proclamation.

Step 5. Do something caring for yourself.

As a seal-the-deal memento, ask yourself in that moment, "What do I need in order to feel taken care of right now?" And do that right away!

Love Mantra for Self-Care

I love taking care of myself *first*.
I love taking care of myself *well*.
I love taking care of myself *every day*.
I am worth taking good care of.

CHAPTER 7

Self-Compassion & Self-Forgiveness

The choice to open your heart and be a loving witness
to yourself, without judgment, by sending yourself
waves of kindness, understanding, and forgiveness
that touch, heal, and transform your imperfections,
weaknesses, vulnerabilities, and humanness through
the presence of your unconditional love.

Self-Love Pulse Check

SELF-LOVE PULSE CHECK

Take your self-love pulse by rating each statement on a scale of one to five according to how true that statement is for you. Five indicates the statement is totally true, and one indicates that it is not at all true. Add up your first five ratings to get your LOVE # and the second set of five ratings to get your LACK #. Subtract your LACK # from your LOVE # to get the current pulse of your self-compassion and self-forgiveness.

____ I support myself to try again when I falter or fail. Instead of beating myself up, I use kind words with myself, even when I fail.

____ I forgive myself for the big and little things — past and present. I love myself even when I let myself down or things don't go perfectly.

____ I engage in more self-love talk than self-hate talk. I think compassionately and positively about myself, instead of critically and negatively.

____ I know that I am doing and have done the best I can. I remind myself when I struggle or fail that I am doing my best, and that's good enough.

____ I am not critical or judgmental of others or myself. I rarely criticize or judge others or myself, and when I do, I change my tune quickly.

LOVE # _____

____ I blame or shame myself. I make myself feel bad for things that happen, whether they were in my control or not.

____ I expect perfection — in myself and others — and become angry, controlling, or critical when things don't go perfectly. I am harsh with myself and others when things don't go the way I think they should.

____ I am hard on myself. I am more likely to see what's wrong than what's right.

____ I set unrealistic expectations and judge myself for not meeting them. When I don't clear the high bar I've set, I get angry and upset with myself.

____ I have regrets about choices I've made in the past that I can't let go of. Instead of forgiving myself, I still fault myself.

LACK # _____

Now, subtract your LACK # from your LOVE # to get your full self-love pulse for this branch.

My Self-Compassion and Self-Forgiveness Pulse _____

Let's be honest here, girl to girl, shall we? There is no one harder on you than you. It's okay, you can admit it out loud. You beat yourself up — maybe even daily — for all the things you think you should be better at, should be able to get done in a day, should be able to figure out. You blame and judge yourself often for all the ways in which your life doesn't measure up to what it "should" be. How do I know this? Because I have talked with tens of thousands of women and girls around the world, from ages six to eighty-six, from all backgrounds, races, and social statuses, and the one thing they all admitted to — when asked and when honest — was how incredibly critical they were of themselves. And how little compassion and forgiveness they were able to give to themselves.

Offer compassion to people who are sick, less fortunate, or going through difficult circumstances in life? No problem. But compassion and forgiveness for themselves? Forget about it.

Think about yourself for a moment. When you see a young child struggling to walk, a woman in dire circumstances, or a helpless animal trying to survive, what is the first feeling that wells up inside you? When you witness another being in pain or struggling, your heart instinctively opens, love flows out, and it's as if you were the Dalai Lama's or Mother Teresa's star pupil.

But what happens when *you* fail, struggle, or otherwise fall short of meeting the unrealistic expectations you set for yourself? What you likely offer to yourself is something more like a big vat of criticism, frustration, and judgment. It's as if an alter ego is waiting inside you, ready to point out all the ways in which you are failing to do, be, and have all that you think you *should*.

Some people call this voice the inner critic, but at Inner Mean Girl Reform School, a virtual school that teaches women of all ages how to transform self-criticism and self-sabotage into self-compassion and self-empowerment, we call her the "Inner Mean Girl." It's a term that Amy Ahlers and I, the school's cofounders, coined in recognition of the harsh criticism your inner critic stirs up in you and the unforgiving judgments it builds against you. These silent but powerful words, which Amy named "big fat lies," make you hurt and sting just the way you did when you were back in fifth grade or high school. When your Inner Mean Girl rants, it feels very personal, and it is. She is *you* beating *you* up. Yes, as insane as it is, you beat yourself up — emotionally, mentally, spiritually, and sometimes even physically — we all do.

Unfortunately, in today's world, this self-abuse is rampant. These days, Inner Mean Girls start stealing self-compassion from girls early — too early. We've seen this in girls as young as six and seven. Left unattended and unreformed, an Inner Mean Girl can fill a sweet heart with self-hate and self-doubt for decades. We may have learned how to be magnificent multitasking machines, professional doers, and confident achievers, but we have no idea how to give ourselves a break.

Why do we find it so much easier to choose self-criticism over self-compassion? Well, first of all, neither of the previous handbooks — the Self-Sacrifice Handbook and the Self-Esteem Handbook — included a chapter on self-compassion. Compassion for others, sure. But take that same loving energy and direct it toward yourself? Not discussed. Compassion for oneself is not an activity that our mainstream culture has embraced or placed value on, yet. Our friends at Dictionary.com reflect this sad reality by defining *compassion* as "A feeling of deep sympathy and sorrow for *another* who is *stricken by misfortune*, accompanied by a strong desire to alleviate the suffering" (the italics are mine). Do you notice something? First of all, someone very important is missing. Where are *you* in that definition? You aren't. And why does one have to be "stricken by misfortune" in order to deserve compassion? Don't we deserve compassion daily, just because we deserve gentle, kind, loving thoughts and acts, just because we are divine imprints of love? Bless our dictionaries, which are but mere reflections of the beliefs and values our bigger society holds, but we can't just stand by and let this be how we live and raise our children. It's time for us as individuals to do something to shift a culture that doesn't teach, value, or even acknowledge self-compassion, starting with reclaiming self-compassion for ourselves.

If we don't make this shift, self-criticism will continue to be second nature for girls and women around the world, including your daughters, nieces, and sisters. You know this to be true. Today, if you are honest about the self-talk running through your mind, you'd see that, almost instinctively, you criticize yourself when you struggle or fail, even though you are instinctively compassionate with others you witness in pain. But why give yourself such a hard time and give others love?

The good news is that *second nature* isn't the same as *natural*. *Second nature* denotes, of course, that something came *before* it: your *first* nature. Compassion is your first nature — you were born to instinctively be compassionate to yourself and others without condition. The question is, how far from your first nature are you operating today? And how do we get you back to being a compassion-giving love machine? First, let's check in on your current connection to unconditional compassion.

ME Moment *When Do You Deserve Compassion?*

What does it take for you to deserve compassion? A catastrophe or just a little struggle? Or can you give it without condition? Use the scale below to check in and see where your self-compassion bar — your "self-compassion set point" — is set. This is the point at which you are able to receive love in the form of self-compassion, and it is a point set by your mind and its current beliefs. Pick the rating that most accurately reflects how you feel today.

5 — I never deserve compassion.

4 — I deserve compassion when misfortune strikes.

3 — I deserve compassion when I am facing big obstacles and outside forces are stacked against me.

2 — I deserve compassion when I am having a hard time, but only when it's not my fault.

1 — I deserve compassion when I need it, regardless of fault, but there has to be some element of struggle present.

0 — I deserve compassion no matter what.

On this scale, the higher your bar is set, the more difficulty must be present for you to receive compassion — higher is not better. You were born with your bar set at 0, believing you deserved compassion unconditionally — this is your natural state. And now it's time to return to the truth: *Compassion isn't earned. You are always entitled to compassion, for one simple reason: you deserve love, no matter what and without cause.* Read the

> You deserve compassion,
> no matter what
> and without cause.

preceding statement out loud, replacing the *you* with *I*, and notice how that feels in your body. Feel the love seeping in, and feel the truth of these words in your body. Your body remembers your natural state of love, of compassion.

Daring Act of Love
Accept and Expect Compassion Unconditionally

Create a new self-love set point in your mind, becoming willing to believe that you deserve compassion no matter what. Think of a situation in your life right now about which you are currently judging yourself or being hard on yourself. Say out loud the negative self-talk you've got moving through your mind. Feel all that mean, compassionless energy you are directing at yourself. Then close your eyes, put your hand on your heart, take a breath,

"I deserve compassion."

and say out loud to yourself three times, "I deserve compassion." Say this more than three times if necessary, until you feel the energy of love permeate your heart. You'll know love is making its way in when you feel a warmth or a softening in your body, something way different from the hard, cold energy of criticism.

Remember this daring act of love the next time your Inner Mean Girl tries to tell you that you have to earn compassion. Use this Love Mantra like a piece of self-love candy you've put in your purse to calm your Inner Mean Girl down on the occasions she flares up. Let it switch your mind from criticism to compassion. Simply close your eyes, imagine flipping this magical self-love candy into your mouth, put your hand on your heart, and sweeten your thoughts by telling your Inner Mean Girl, and yourself, "I deserve compassion."

Resetting Your Crazy Superwoman, Superhuman, Perfectionist Expectations

There is another bar that needs to be reset if you are to successfully grow your ability to give yourself compassion and forgiveness: the bar that represents the *unrealistic expectations* you have for yourself. These include all the ways you unfairly judge yourself and measure yourself against unrealistic, superhuman ideals of perfection and success.

Think of all the times you've said to yourself that you *should* be doing better today or *ought* to have done better in the past. All the times you've focused on the things you think you *should* have achieved, done, or experienced by now, but haven't. All those times when, instead of finding compassion for yourself — you are human, after all — or offering forgiveness for letting yourself down, you've judged yourself harshly and held back the kindness and gentleness you so crave and need. Not because you are a sadistic monster who likes to inflict suffering on yourself, but because you've been navigating your life according to a false North Star, one pointed at unrealistic expectations that allow for compassion and forgiveness only when serious duress or misfortune strikes.

To give yourself the self-compassion and self-forgiveness you need, you must recognize and realign yourself to the true North Star: unconditional love. Then, whenever you falter, stumble, fail, or struggle, you can look up and find the warm kindness of compassion and forgiveness to guide you, instead of cold, harsh criticism and judgment.

> When you fail, falter, or feel less than perfect, turn your attention to unconditional love to lift yourself up.

It is not always easy to find the true North Star or to reset your expectations, but it is totally possible. You just need to know what you're dealing with. First, know that your Inner Mean Girl is always standing by, waiting to wag her finger at you and tell you about all the ways you've fallen short. She is armed with huge tape measures, charts, and graphs to show you all the ways in which you deserve an F — for faltering, falling behind, and failing to measure up. When you lack access to your feminine superpower — compassion — and are unable to be gentle and kind with yourself, the Inner Mean Girl overpowers you and wins almost every time, sending you into a tailspin of self-flagellation for your daily shortcomings, weaknesses, and failures.

But what if you beat her at her own game by applying some self-honesty and self-acknowledgment (which you already started growing in the previous chapters)? Let's be honest. If you were to really look at what you have accomplished in your life, what you get done in a day, and your impact on the people around you, you'd see that by any normal measure of what a human being should be able to accomplish, you are already successful. While your Inner Mean Girl may be doling out Fs based on her ridiculous expectations, it turns out that you've actually received an A or at least a solid B on your report card (and Bs are good).

Now that we've got that straight, let's outsmart and overpower that

Inner Mean Girl. Decide to make the bold move to lower your expectations (not your impact, but your expectations). Yes, I know it sounds like blasphemy to your superachieving doing machine, your overly responsible psyche. But just imagine if — instead of allowing your life and sense of self-worth to be guided by norms set by an external system whose main goal is to keep you buying, consuming, and working hard — you chose different expectations, guided by a North Star that points to unconditional love.

What if you chose to expect that over the course of your life, again and again, you would fail, falter, and be imperfect? What if you changed your mind and recognized that for the rest of your life, you will always be learning? Just like a toddler learning to walk, a little girl learning to ride her bike, a teenager learning algebra, a young woman getting her first job, a woman becoming a first-time mother, or a woman learning to start a new chapter in her life. And what if, while you learned, you were there alongside yourself — like a parent alongside his or her child learning to ride her bike, or the midwife with the new mama — reminding yourself, "You can do it. Take your time. You're doing the best you can, and that is enough." You would find it a lot easier to be compassionate with yourself for both the small ways you struggle and the big ways you fail. You would find it more natural to offer yourself forgiveness, whenever you need it, without needing to explain yourself or beg for it.

> You, more than anyone, are counting on you to be there with open arms, offering compassion and forgiveness without condition.

When you try new things, you can expect that you will stumble. Imagine having that expectation for yourself — you are most certain to meet it, if not exceed it! We'd never expect a toddler to do algebra, so why expect yourself to be perfect and masterful at everything, even if you are new at it? That's just plain dumb. Like Karen Drucker, my friend (and out-of-this-world self-love songwriter and singer), says, "Only go as fast as the slowest part of you can go." How would your experience of life, of yourself, and even of your relationships change if you were to treat yourself this way?

ME Moment *When Are You Forgetting Compassion and Forgiveness for Yourself?*

Invite your Inner Mean Girl to have a drink — could be tea, a glass of wine, or a stiff martini. Whatever you need for a good, honest, let-it-all-hang-out conversation. You and she are going to just lay all your self-criticism and underlying self-judgments on the table so that you can bring them into the light, where we can get a good look at them and go about the business of transforming them.

This date with your Inner Mean Girl will take place in two phases. Part 1 — she gets to talk. Yep, you are going to let her rip. Part 2 — you get to talk. You will take what you hear from her, and use it in a deeper conversation with your best friend, that part inside you that has been a witness to just how hard you've been on you. She is going to listen to you without judgment, hearing the harsh words you've been thinking and saying inside.

Part 1. Channel Your Inner Mean Girl

This works best if you give your Inner Mean Girl the microphone and let her rant. Act as if your Inner Mean Girl has taken over your body and is now speaking and moving through you. You can do this first step either by writing her rants out with vigor on a piece of paper, or — if you really

want to bust her hold on you and open up the channels of compassion —
by getting your whole body into it. The more you can embody her, the
more you can access the energy and feelings that are brewing inside of
you, whether you want to admit to them or not. I've written this step out
as if you are going to speak her rants out loud, but you can modify the
process and write them down instead if you wish.

Okay, brave soul, stand up and assume an "I told you so" position in
front of a mirror. Pull your finger out of your pocket and shake it at your
image in the mirror, as if you are the most judgmental person you know
and you're about to rip on you for how bad you suck. Use the following four Inner Mean Girl rant starters and speak out loud the judgments
bottled up inside you:

♥ "You should...and..."
♥ "Why don't you...and...?"
♥ "Why aren't you better at...and...?"
♥ "If you could just...everything would be fine."

Whoa. Stop and let that soak in. How does that feel? What do you
notice about the energy you just directed at yourself? Love-filled or hate-
filled or somewhere in between? This is the energy that you unleash on
yourself every time you choose criticism over compassion.

Part 2. Tell Your Best Friend the Truth

You are getting a glimmer of how your constant criticism of yourself
(for no good reason) has affected you. The way to freedom from this bad
habit starts with telling the truth and seeing it with your own two eyes.
We can't transform ourselves without truth. Get a piece of paper and use

the four truth starters below to uncover where your deep self-judgments and lack of self-forgiveness lie. Approach this writing exercise as if you were sitting down with your most trusted best friend (even if that's your dog or cat), someone you can count on to give you unconditional love, not judgment. Now write the truth. (Note that writing the truth will help you come back and soak the love in later, unlike writing the Inner Mean Girl rants, which we just wanted to release and move out of your system.)

1. "I am unhappy or upset with myself about..." Write down the areas of your life in which you are upset that things are not going the way you want. Include all the ways in which you aren't acting or doing what you really want. List at least three, but no more than five. Example: "I am unhappy or upset with myself about

   ♥ my love life: my lack of a romantic, loving relationship";
   ♥ how my body is super out of shape right now"; or
   ♥ not having enough money and spending money that I don't have."

2. "I've judged that I should..." Fill in the blank after this phrase for each of the "unhappy with me" areas you identified. For example: "I've judged that I should

   ♥ be able to find a partner who likes me enough to want to be with me";
   ♥ be thinner and be able to better control what I eat"; or
   ♥ be more financially secure and stable."

3. "What I am really thinking is..." Now here are the juicy, energetically charged judgments. Your mission is to let them rip, full force, so you

can release them from your mind and body and replace them with some good love. For each response to question 2, use the harshest, most real words to make a statement that reflects what you are really saying to yourself when you make this judgment. Don't hold back. Really let yourself give it to you — the more you can tap into the mean, critical, "what the hell is wrong with you" energy, the more you will succeed in getting to the compassionate energy in the next part of our adventure. Let yourself write freely until every judgment comes out. Here are some sample statements:

♥ "You are not pretty enough. You are too old. No one wants you. You are damaged goods."

♥ "You are fat, ugly, and an out-of-control eating machine. You are a sugar addict who can't deal with her feelings, so you stuff yourself full of food."

♥ "You are not disciplined enough. You are not smart enough. You are not worth anything."

4. "I have a hard time forgiving myself for <<insert past incident>> because I've judged that I should have..." Finally, we want you to bring into the light any instances in need of your forgiveness, by documenting them on a new sheet of paper. Take a look back through your past to find all the judgments you have stacked up against yourself: all the ways you've judged that you should have been able to do a better job, could have shown up better and stood up for yourself better, should have made better decisions, and so on. Go back in time in five-year or ten-year increments, as far back as your preteens, remembering all the times you let yourself down and recording both the past incidents and the harsh self-judgments.

Pause here and look at this list of judgments you have just recorded from all four areas. Let the energy of these statements hit you. What do your body and heart feel like when you look at and feel these words that you've been directing at you? Not so good. Which is why this requires a radical act of self-love:

♥ First, across all the pieces of paper you've used to tell the truth about the self-judgments and self-criticism you've been holding, write the words "I CHOOSE SELF-HATE" in one color.

♥ Second, draw a big, bold X on top of that statement and write "NO! I CHOOSE SELF-LOVE!"

From this day on, remember that whenever you choose to think to yourself the kind of thoughts recorded here — whether you are conscious of them or not — you are hating yourself. This is nothing to be ashamed about, because the truth is, we *all* do this. And being ashamed of it would create double self-hate. No reason for that! Now is the time to choose love. You've already taken the first step by choosing to admit the ways you haven't been compassionate and forgiving with yourself. Well done. Now there's room for the love to flow in!

Choosing Self-Compassion

Just as you would instinctively be compassionate toward a child learning to walk, a young girl trying to find herself, or a friend who is completely overwhelmed, you must be the one to put a hand on your own shoulder — weekly, daily, hourly, as often as you need it — and say to yourself,

"You are doing the best you can," not, "You'll do better next time," as if what you've just done isn't good enough. As if you have to strive for a next time in order to be okay. But instead, "You are doing the best you can right now," period. And if you're not doing this for yourself now, then you are not loving yourself enough.

From this day forward, every time you discover that your expectations are unrealistic, every time you fail, fall behind, or don't feel well, every time you are tired or are just having a bad day, you'll be there for yourself, like a best friend or the best, most loving mother. And the times when you fail to be compassionate? You'll be compassionate about your inability to be compassionate — lol!

How do you know you're giving yourself compassion rather criticism? Both are energies that you can feel physically. Self-compassion feels gentle. It's a warm energy, not a harsh blast. Compassion feels rooted in love. It lets you feel at peace, lets you know that, regardless of what you achieve or don't, and whether you act poorly or magnificently, you are enough and you deserve love. Compassion lets you feel as if you're being embraced by the sweetest, most unconditionally loving mother in the world — and you are, because you are mothering you.

> The great, all-loving mother that you have been waiting for has been living inside you all along.

Daring Act of Love
Smother and Mother Yourself with Compassion

Close your eyes, take a breath, and think of something that you're being really hard on yourself about right now. Something you're frustrated by. Something that no matter what you try just isn't working the way you want, or something you really want but haven't received yet. Allow yourself to fully feel the frustration and,

"You are doing the best that you can, and it's enough."

beneath that, the judgment and, beneath that, the sadness, despair, or exhaustion. Then, from a place of compassion, witness your struggle and then your inherent perfection. Then place your hand on your shoulder and, just as a good mother would, say these words out loud at least three times, with love: "You are doing the best that you can, and it's enough."

This is one of your new Love Mantras. Say this mantra until you can feel the compassion sink into your heart and bring you back to a state of love for yourself.

ME Art Make a Set of Compassion-Filled Love Flash Cards

Remember all those judgments you uncovered? The criticisms that have likely been carving emotional and mental grooves for years, like rivers flowing with self-hate, poisoning your psyche and eating up your self-worth? Well, it's time to dry up those polluted rivers and refill them with love using the power of compassion. While it will take time to free up your natural instinct to deliver compassion, you'll find that as you choose self-love more often, self-compassion will become easier and easier.

One of the best ways to retrain your brain is to get it to memorize different information. You can do this with flash cards like the ones you might have used to memorize the multiplication tables or vocabulary words when you were little. Once you'd memorized them, you didn't have to give them much thought; you just knew the answer or the word. Same thing here: you want to train your brain to think "compassion" right away.

Supplies:

♥   Five to ten blank index cards (no lines; I like the cards that measure 5" x 7", but choose whatever you like); alternatively, you can cut up pieces of blank paper or use the Compassion Flash Card Loveplate I created for you on www.ChooseSelfLove.com

♥   Markers, at least two colors (a different color for each card, if you can)

♥   Your list of judgments from #3 in the ME Moment (page 144), "What I am really thinking is..."

Mission:

Create a set of Love Flash Cards and reprogram your mind, replacing criticism with compassion. You're going to make one compassion-filled Love Flash Card for each critical judgment you uncovered, replacing the criticism with love. Remember, criticism comes from thoughts the mind makes up, and love comes from truth the heart knows and from the unconditional love you have for yourself.

How-to: Repeat each of the following steps for each judgment.

Step 1. Write the judgment on one side of the card and read it out loud.

Step 2. See and feel the impact of the judgment. Close your eyes, put your hand on your heart, and imagine that a woman or girl you love unconditionally is loudly saying these harsh words to herself.

Step 3. Transform the hate into love. **Keeping your hand on your heart, imagine yourself reaching out your hand to this woman or girl and placing it on her heart. What words of love would you say to** *her*?

Step 4. Write these words on the other side of your Love Flash Card. **These are your words of compassion, the words that you need to hear consistently running through your mind.**

Here's an example:

No one wants you. You are not pretty enough. You are too old. You are damaged goods.

People love you. You are so beautiful, kind, and special. And any person would be lucky to have you in her life.

Once you have your set of Love Flash Cards, you can use them in two ways:

♥   Love grooving. **Reconstruct your mental and emotional grooves by changing the running criticism to flowing love. To do this, run through the cards daily. Read the words on the Love Flash Card out loud, concentrating both on the printed word and on feeling the vibration of love pass through your lips and then your mind, heart, and cells. Over** time, and through conscious repetition, you will create new love grooves in your mind and emotional body. The best times for doing love grooving are first thing in the morning when you wake up, just after meditation or your daily divine practice, and right before you go to sleep. Pick one time that works best for you and stick to it. Repetition is key to successful love grooving.

♥ Compassion emergency. Carry your Love Flash Cards with you for the moments when your Inner Mean Girl goes mad and you need not just one piece of self-love candy but a few to sweeten her up! Pull out these Love Flash Cards and read the love side to yourself again and again, until you can feel the compassion coming back into your body, soothing your mind, and opening your heart.

Choosing Self-Forgiveness

Just as you are learning to be compassionate to yourself about the present, you also need to clean up all your self-judgments about the past. This kind of cleanup job, which can be pretty heavy duty, calls for the superpower of self-forgiveness. When you apply love in the form of forgiveness, from yourself to yourself, to all the disappointments, hurts, and times you felt let down by yourself, you clear the space for big healing to take place. What heals just so happens to be the relationship between you and you. Often when we think of forgiveness, we jump to the idea of giving or receiving it from other people, and we forget about ourselves. We become fixated on the forgiveness we want from others, and we avoid the forgiveness we need to offer others, all of which could be prevented if we just took the forgiveness fast track and forgave ourselves first.

> The person who needs
> your forgiveness most is you.
> Until you forgive yourself, no one
> can be fully forgiven.

It's time to pull out the self-judgments you've been stacking up for years in your closet. Looking back at all the judgments you found in #4 of the previous ME Moment (page 145), notice how you have criticized and blamed yourself for not doing better. The truth is, while you may wish things had been different — that you had been smarter, that there had been someone there to help you or guide you, that you had stood up for yourself and your needs — you were doing the best you could at the time. Today you are wiser, so of course you would make different decisions now, likely more self-loving ones. But holding on to what you wish could have happened does nothing but make you suffer from a lack of self-forgiveness, just as wishing you could be different from who you are does nothing but make you suffer from a lack of self-acceptance.

It's a way more self-loving choice to be compassionate and forgive the parts of you that suffered because you didn't have access to the resources, knowledge, and support you needed, when the decisions you made hurt you or kept you from going for what your heart really wanted. It's time to go back to these parts and pour love all over them!

Daring Act of Love
Write a Love Letter Full of Forgiveness to Yourself and Deliver It

Grab a pen and some paper and create a sacred space where you can feel safe while getting intimate with yourself. You are going to write yourself a love letter, starting with the words "Dear <<insert your name>>, I am so sorry that..." Look back at each of the judgments you uncovered, one by one, and feel yourself back in that moment. Challenge yourself to go beyond your thoughts about what happened, and move into the heart of what the woman or little girl was feeling while this incident was occurring for her. What did she need that she didn't receive? What didn't she know? What didn't she have access to? Write to her as a compassionate witness, telling her that you are sorry she didn't have what she needed. Use your own words. After you have sufficiently expressed

that, write, "I am so sorry that I wasn't there to help you. Please forgive me. I was doing the best I could. I am here now." Close your eyes, put your hand on your heart, and feel her forgiveness coming to you. Feel the two of you meeting as one in your heart.

For an extended visualization of self-forgiveness, one that takes you back through time to forgive all the ways in which you weren't there when you needed yourself the most, go to www.SelfLoveMeditations.com.

Love Mantra for Self-Compassion and Self-Forgiveness

I've always done the best I could do,
based on what I knew.
I love and forgive myself.

CHAPTER 8

Self-Trust

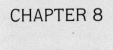

Choosing to listen to and follow the guidance of your inner voice, believing you know what is right for you, even when other people think or say otherwise.

Self-Love Pulse Check

SELF-LOVE
PULSE CHECK

Take your self-love pulse by rating each statement on a scale of one to five according to how true that statement is for you. Five indicates the statement is totally true, and one indicates that it is not at all true. Add up your first five ratings to get your LOVE # and the second set of five ratings to get your LACK #. Subtract your LACK # from your LOVE # to get your current self-trust pulse.

____ I act clearly and confidently when making choices and taking action. I make decisions about my life quickly, easily, and without much doubt.

____ I can find my way back to a calm, centered place even during times of high stress or uncertainty. I know how to find the voice of Inner Wisdom and distinguish it from fear.

____ I trust my intuition more than my purely rational mind. I trust my feelings, senses, and intuition to guide me where I need to go, even when my mind directs me elsewhere.

____ I communicate and consult with my Inner Wisdom when making all decisions. I always check in with myself before making choices, both big and small, and I listen to what I hear.

____ I listen to my opinions over those of others. I ask my Inner Wisdom before asking others for guidance. I act on my Inner Wisdom's council even when others have a different point of view.

LOVE # _____

____ I doubt myself. My mind gets stuck in self-doubt, and I start to question myself, my choices, my thoughts, my actions.

____ I have a hard time making or sticking to decisions. I become frozen, confused, or anxious often when trying to make a decision by myself. I second-guess myself.

____ I overanalyze, overthink, and obsess. Before making a decision or taking action, I run lots of scenarios through my head, talk to many people to get their opinions, and even search the Internet for hours. I then obsess over whether I made the right decision.

____ I feel anxious. I feel anxious more than calm about my decisions and life.

____ I am swayed by others' opinions or stopped by their potential judgments. I change my decisions or stop myself from commenting or acting because of what other people may say or think.

LACK # _____

Now, subtract your LACK # from your LOVE # to get your full self-love pulse for this branch.

My Self-Trust Pulse _____

Over the course of your lifetime, you will be faced with a gazillion choices, some mundane with little risk or consequence if you don't happen to make the best choice. Whether or not to meet a friend for dinner, what shoes you will wear on that first date, or what toothpaste you will buy. You make the wrong decision in one of these cases, and you waste perhaps two hours, pick the shoes that look sexy but leave blisters on your feet for a week, or have to throw away a five-dollar investment; the damage is small. Sure, you would have had a better time had you listened to that voice inside that told you, "You don't really want to go to dinner with her; you're only going because you feel like you should. Just stay home." Or, "I'd pick the red boots over the stilettos; you'll still look hot, and your feet will be happy. Nobody is worth causing yourself pain over." Or, "Spend the extra two dollars and get the natural toothpaste you love." But the damage is repairable, and the impact on your joy is small. You can stay home tomorrow, wear comfy flat shoes all week, and go back to the store.

But there are many other choices that present bigger risks, with stakes that could change the course of your entire life. Repairing the damage or altering your course should you make a bad choice in these cases takes much longer, and in some cases the damage can't be repaired, or your course can't be redirected completely. You have likely made many of these big choices already — who to date, move in with, or marry or not; what career or job you take or don't; where you live; what you invest in or don't; who to listen to when it comes to your health or the health of those you love; what choices you make about the lives of your children and other family members; and more.

When your self-trust has been strong and you've acted from that place of resolute inner knowing, what was the impact? While likely the results of trusting yourself have not been perfect, and have not been without their challenges or moments of fear or doubt, more often than not, trusting that wise inner knowing has led to more happiness, love, and peace in your life. Compare the outcomes of those decisions to choices you've made when you doubted yourself, listened to others' opinions over your own inner knowing, or let fear and your emotions confuse you. What happened? Likely drama or suffering and wasted time, energy, and money, causing you to miss the opportunities you really wanted to take.

Eventually, if you loved yourself after you made these less than optimal choices, you became more self-aware and honest with yourself, and you turned these painful experiences into lessons. But on reflection, did the lessons need to cost you so much? If your self-trust muscle had been stronger, could you have learned the lessons faster and with more love and joy than suffering and drama? While we can't avoid the lessons and some of the pain such lessons bring (this is one way in which we grow), we can get the lessons delivered faster and in ways that are more supportive. If you had listened to that inner wisdom — which may communicate as an inner voice, inner feeling, inner knowing or sense, or visual cue — when it told you something was amiss, what would have been possible? If you had been willing to take the time to dig deeper and act on what you sensed, heard, knew, or saw, rather than just on what your rational mind or fear told you, would you have made a self-loving choice rather than a self-sabotaging one?

Love Story: Smart Women Who Sabotage Themselves

For Ariane, it was an inner *voice*, rather than an inner sense, that spoke to her the day she met the man who is now her ex-husband. This voice said,

"Don't go out with this man; he will ruin your life." Not trusting this voice, and afraid she was never going to meet someone interesting, she of course dated him, married him, had children with him, and later divorced him after she learned she had married not a partner but a narcissist. She has since had to battle him in court, pay him money, and fight with him about money every month. And because of their shared custody of the children, she can't leave the state she lives in even though she hates living there and is far from her family and support system. By not listening to that wise voice inside of her, she tied herself forever to a man who doesn't support her or her dreams, and who, because of their children, has control over the decisions she makes for her life.

For Karyn, it was the inner *feeling* in the pit of her stomach, which burned every day she walked into the office. This was her body's way of trying to tell her she needed to find a different job, one where she didn't have to travel. Her body was trying to warn her that she needed to slow down and start taking care of herself. Not trusting her body talk, she rationalized the daily feeling as a symptom of her failure to eat right (she had gained thirty pounds since starting this job) and of being stressed out (she was pulling over fifty hours a week and doing the work of a team of horses).

While these logical thoughts were all true, Karyn failed to go deeper to locate the real source of the symptoms so she could find a solution. Had she stopped to feel, she would have felt her Inner Wisdom tell her, "You aren't happy. You don't want to be traveling; you want to be home, where you can create a life for yourself, instead of just working all the time." So one day, the universe delivered the message itself and slowed Karyn down. As she rushed through a crosswalk one night around 7 PM to get back to the office to work some more, she was hit by a car. A broken leg and a big scare slowed her down. But it didn't have to be that dramatic.

For Mari, it wasn't trusting her inner *knowing* that she was meant for something more than the life she was living. She had finished high school, and although the thought of going to college didn't excite her and she had a sense that it wasn't for her, everyone else was going, so she figured she had to go too. From the moment she got to her school dorm, she hated it. She didn't like her classes and didn't connect with the other students. Mari felt lost, like: Why am I here? But instead of trusting that she was in the wrong place and leaving, she stuck it out for half a year. Thirty thousand dollars in tuition later, she left.

After Mari returned home, her mother offered to pay for her to take the year to travel, to volunteer, to explore the world, to activate her artist self. (Mari has always shown artistic promise and found great joy in creating art and taking photos.) But Mari didn't want to "fall behind," so she chose not to trust what she knew inside: "I'm unhappy in school. I'm not like everyone else. I can try something else." Instead she enrolled in community college and took more classes she didn't really like, all to get an associate degree while doing something she disliked. Mari could have spent the three years finding her passion, had she trusted the knowledge that her path was different from others', and that this was okay.

I wish I could tell you that Mari found her way to self-acceptance, self-empowerment, and self-trust, but she hasn't. Someday she will, and she will look back at this time — just as you likely will look back at a time in your life when you didn't trust yourself — and she'll see that trusting herself could have led to more happiness and less suffering.

At any given moment you have two paths to choose from — the long road to your destiny and the short road to your destiny. The long road becomes your path when you make choices in response to fear, self-doubt, and shame. Responding to a lack of trust in yourself and your Inner Wisdom, you unknowingly create a reality that entails unnecessary suffering and wasted time. When we choose instead to wake up and trust the truth of what we know and feel in our hearts and souls, we end up on the short road, leading to our happiest, most fulfilled lives. And while the short road is not always easy — it too includes twists and turns and frustrations and challenges — the suffering doesn't last as long. You get to happiness faster when you choose to trust yourself. And you get to stop repeating the same life lessons over and over. And you can stop damaging your self-love tree. Self-trust affects every other branch on the tree in a big way. When you don't trust yourself, you make choices that don't honor yourself, you hold back from expressing yourself, you find it difficult to care for yourself, and it's almost impossible to have the courage to go for your dreams. Strengthen this branch, and you'll receive a return in many other areas almost instantly.

ME Moment *When Have You Failed to Trust Yourself?*

Take a moment and think about some of the decisions you've made when you didn't trust yourself. Choices that led you to outcomes that were not what you had hoped for, or that led you down a path that was hard, not happy or healthy. Think back to the beginning of your young adulthood, to times when you first started making decisions for yourself. Think about milestones, dating, and sex, about choices related to school, career, friendships, where you lived, finances, and so on. Remember the times you heard, trusted, and listened to your Inner Wisdom, and the times you did not. Remember the outcomes, the consequences, the residue that you might even still carry with you. I know, it's not always easy to go back to those places, but there is self-love gold there, I promise!

What follows is a three-step transformational process that will help you build your self-trust by transforming the self-sabotage you experience into self-love. This experience is about you telling the truth about the ways you didn't trust yourself, admitting the consequences, and forgiving yourself. It is one of the first steps in reestablishing a strong sense of trust in yourself. You see, when you made choices in the past that led you to pain or fear, you unknowingly stopped trusting yourself to make good decisions in this area. This is why in some parts of your life you find it easy to trust yourself, and in others, not so much.

Because you weren't able, for whatever reason, to act in your own best interests in the past, some part of you decided it needed to protect you — which is how your Inner Mean Girl came to be. She made it her job to protect you by using fear, shame, and criticism. The problem is that while her protection probably helped you out in the past, it now keeps you from the love, happiness, success, and peace you want. And the only way she is going to give up her post and let you listen to your Inner Wisdom is if she believes you can be trusted. What do you say? Are you ready to mend the bond of trust with yourself?

Step 1. Admit your self-sabotaging choices to yourself.

List the top three "I so didn't trust myself when I made that choice" decisions on a piece of paper. These are decisions you knew were wrong for you at some level, even if you couldn't articulate it at the time. Looking back, you can see and feel the signs that were there — you just weren't strong or wise enough to make a different choice then. But you are now, and that's what this transformation process is all about. Let's go heal the scars that those self-sabotaging choices left on your self-respect, self-honor, self-care, self-esteem, self-empowerment, and self-expression branches.

Step 2. Tell your story.

Write your story for each of the self-sabotaging choices you made, telling the truth about

♥ why you made the choice,
♥ what you really knew, and
♥ what you would have done differently had you known how to trust yourself.

Begin with "I made a choice to <<insert a choice here>>."
Continue your story using each of the following eight sentence starters in order. Each will bring you closer to truth and to trust in yourself:

1. "It was not the best choice for me because…"
2. "I made the choice because I listened to…"
3. "I made the choice because I lacked…"
4. "I made the choice because I felt…"

5. "I made it even though I really knew…"
6. "I made it even though I really felt…"
7. "I didn't trust myself enough to…"
8. "Had I trusted myself, I would have…"

Step 3. Forgive yourself.

Here's the real, honest-to-goodness truth. I want you to pause and fully take this in: You were doing the best you could with what you had to work with. You were not taught how to trust yourself, and this is why you couldn't make the best choice for yourself at the time.

Today is the day you promise to trust yourself always, and as a woman on a self-love adventure, committed to loving herself no matter what, you'll be able to keep that promise! But first, the you who wasn't strong enough to stand up for herself, guide herself, or make the best choices needs you to go back and forgive her — your little-girl self or your not-so-wise woman — for the self-sabotaging choices she made when she didn't trust herself. Send forgiveness to yourself for each of the situations, one by one, that you just brought to light. Use the following words — written, spoken, or best, both — to create a self-trust transformation for each of the stories from your past:

> You were doing the best you could with what you had to work with. You were not taught how to trust yourself, and this is why you couldn't make the best choice for yourself at the time.

"I forgive myself for not trusting myself about…
which led to…

I was doing the best I could with what I had to work with.
I didn't know that I needed to trust myself and act on that trust
no matter what, and now I do.
I love you, <<insert your name here>>.
I will always be here for you. You can trust me."

Love Story: A Self-Trust Transformation Story

This is the story of one of my self-trust transformations, made necessary by the sad fact that the first time I didn't trust myself, it cost me a lot, as happens to many girls. My story begins with the choice I made to sleep with Tim at the age of fifteen. This was not the best choice for me, because I was nowhere near ready to share my body or my sacred sexuality with another person. I didn't even know yet that I had something sacred. I made the choice because I listened to my friends who were having lots of sex with lots of boys. They said that he was cute, he liked me, and I should go for it. It was the first time I succumbed to peer pressure and let the opinions of others sway me from what I knew was right for myself.

I made the choice because I'd had no guidance about sex and my body. No one had talked to me about sex in a healthy way. The only counsel I'd received was a movie in sixth grade, the experience of watching my two best friends (who both became pregnant by sixteen), and a pamphlet my father gave me one night before he went to bed. This was no pretty picture book with heartwarming instructions on what it meant to become a woman and how I could honor my body. No, while this booklet did have flowers on the outside, on the inside it was full of pictures of aborted fetuses in garbage bags. That was my sex talk. My mother never said a word. I made the choice because I lacked adult guidance and loving support.

I made the choice because I felt like there was something wrong with me, since all my friends had boyfriends and I didn't. And I did so even though I knew deep inside that I didn't want to have sex. I knew this boy had sex with lots of girls, and that he really only wanted sex, not to be my boyfriend. And although I felt awful during the entire experience, as if I were out of my body watching it happen to me, I didn't trust myself enough to say, "Stop."

Had I trusted myself, I would have stopped him as soon as I felt like this wasn't for me. As soon I realized I had made the wrong choice for me, I would have gotten up and left with my self-honor and virginity intact.

I forgive myself for not trusting myself, which led to me not honoring myself or the sacredness of my body, my sexuality, my heart, and my spirit. I was doing the best I could with what I had to work with. I didn't know that I needed to trust myself and act on that trust no matter what, and now I do.

Daring Act of Love
Share Your Self-Trust Transformation with Someone You Love

Allowing others to witness your acts of self-sabotage is one of the most powerful ways to release the feelings of shame, fear, and guilt that are right under the surface so you can heal yourself at an even deeper level. Choose someone you trust to witness your transformation with you, someone who has your best interests at heart and who can really receive you. Explain that you would like her or him to listen to your story and witness your transformation. And then read her or him your self-trust transformation story.

Before you begin the story, tell this person specifically what you want her or him to say and do, so that she or he knows how to receive you in love. This is the part that will help you release the shame, guilt, or fear at a deeper level. Love is so powerful! For example, ask this person to say, after you have completed sharing your self-trust transformation story, something like "<<insert your name here>>, I am sorry you didn't have what you needed to trust yourself more and make a more loving decision for yourself. And I really see how you did the best you could with what you had. I love you for exactly who you are." And then ask her or him to give you a physical expression of love too, such as a hug, a hand on the shoulder, or a squeeze of your hand. Be specific about what you need. And don't be afraid to script what you want to hear. Trust yourself and ask for exactly what you need.

Growing Your Self-Trust Branch: Make It Strong

Now that we have reestablished the bond of trust between you and yourself, get ready for the best workout of your life! You are going to love it — it's way more joy-producing than any treadmill or weight machine, but it will require effort on your part. To grow a strong self-trust branch that can stand up to other people's opinions and society's judgments, that can release you from making choices based on obligations and shoulds, and that can overpower the forces of shame and fear when they arise, you need to have experiences over time that show you that when you trust yourself, good things happen. You need to be able to see that when you choose to trust your inner knowing, inner voice, inner feeling, or image or dream that your Inner Wisdom shows you, not only do good things happen, but also the best circumstances occur.

As you experience success with small things, you will start to trust yourself with big things too. The small things may include instances like making a different choice about which shoes to wear because, as you are standing in your closet, a pair of shoes seems to jump out at you. Or like choosing not to go to dinner with a friend because you feel a tightness in your stomach that, when you ask yourself about it, seems to be telling you that you won't have a good time or that you need to rest. And the big things could be very big — like changing jobs, quitting a job, moving to a new city without first finding a job there, ending a relationship, moving to a new country to deepen a relationship, having a baby, not having a baby, getting married, buying a house, and on and on. Life is full of big things, and the times when they occur are the times you really need to cut through the external and internal chatter to get to the wisdom you can trust.

Building self-trust happens in stages and over time, so make sure that you strengthen your self-trust daily. Just as you wouldn't start training for a marathon or a weight-lifting contest the day of the event (your muscles wouldn't be able to support the task), you also don't want to wait until the big stuff happens in your life before you strengthen your trust "muscles." Most of us do wait, however. When our self-trust is weak, and the hard, big, or unexpected life stuff happens, we don't follow our hearts and act in our own best interests, but instead succumb to fear, shame, societal pressure, confusion, and obligation. We fail to follow our own guidance when we need it the most.

But today marks a shift. Today you begin a lifetime commitment to strengthening your self-trust branch and, therefore, your ability to trust yourself and your Inner Wisdom no matter what. The more you practice trusting your Inner Wisdom on the small stuff, the more you will trust yourself and act in your own best interests in all matters in your life.

What follows are the four trust muscles you want to exercise consistently and often. When you go to the gym to build strong, toned arms, you don't focus only on your biceps. Similarly, strengthening your self-trust requires strong mental, spiritual, emotional, and physical "muscles." Use the following muscle-building exercises — which I invite you to begin performing without delay — along with the Daring Acts of Love and special trust-building resources to grow your self-trust branch superstrong.

Mental Muscles: Your Mind Is Just a Set of Beliefs — Retrain Your Mind to See Magic

Notice that you place more value on rational and logical thoughts, on what "makes sense," than you do on what "you sense." Notice how you trust science — what can be proven or seen — more than what is unseen and just is. Notice how you make decisions against what you are feeling just because you have some belief or thought logged into your brain that says, "This is how it is." Your mind contains a huge pile of beliefs that you've picked up along the way. When did you stop believing in magic? In miracles? In the unexplainable being just as real as something you prove with a formula? While the rational, logical, and scientific have their place, they are not more valuable or more real than magical serendipities, miracles, or other unexplainable delights. So do yourself a favor and retrain your brain to see magic and miracles too! Your little-girl self always believed in them, so why shouldn't you?

Daring Act of Love

Make Magic and Miracles with Your Magical Notebook

Writing things down makes them more real to us. Just does. Something about the tangible and visual component makes us think we can trust it. Think of all the words that have been written over the centuries that people take as undeniable truth just because these words were published in books. Now it's your turn to prove to your mind that magic and miracles do exist. Get a small notebook, title it "Magical Moments and Miracles," and keep it with you as often as you can. Whenever something serendipitous happens, record it in this magical notebook.

When a miracle shows up, write it down. When you have

an intuitive hit and you follow it, and good things happen, write it down. Keep track of all the times you experience something that may not be logical, rational, or explainable with an algorithm but which is very real. Stop saying things like "This crazy thing happened" or "I can't believe it," and start acknowledging that the magic and miracles that show up are normal. The more you do, the more will come. Retrain your mind to trust so that you can too.

Spiritual Muscles: When You Have Faith in Fear, You Cannot Trust — Choose to Have Faith in Love

Trust's number one nemesis is fear. When fear is present, it's almost impossible for you to hear yourself, let alone trust yourself enough to take action. Fear muddles your mind and generally points you in the direction of bad decisions. And as you make decisions that feel risky or stir up past unhealed feelings, fear is standing by, waiting to take over your mind, body, and spirit and start wreaking havoc. Unfortunately, the more you play big in your life and stretch beyond your comfort zone, the more opportunities fear will have to come up and keep you from trusting yourself and making the best choices. To strengthen your trust in yourself, you must become stronger than fear. The only way to do that is to strengthen your connection to the one thing more powerful than fear — love.

Daring Act of Love
Take a Self-Trust Tic Tac When You Get Scared

When fear shows up, its first ploy is to take over your mind and confuse and overwhelm you. Your job is to interrupt its transmission. Every time you do this, you will strengthen your self-trust branch. Whenever you find yourself in a situation where you feel fear — or anxiety, doubt, confusion, or a need to become overcontrolling — stop and pop in the following self-trust Tic Tac. Close your eyes, take a breath, put your hand on your heart, and repeat the Love Mantra "I choose to have faith in love. I choose to release my faith in fear." Say this mantra over and over until you feel fear release its grip. Then start up a conversation with your Inner Wisdom to see what it has to say.

If you want a great spiritual workout to strengthen your faith and trust and to lessen fear's grip on you, I have an adventure for you that will give your spiritual muscles an awesome (and joy-full) workout! Try the "40-Day Fear Cleanse," which is the source of this Love Mantra that I codeveloped with my spiritual running buddy and coleader of the cleanse, Gabrielle Bernstein. Find it at www.theFearCleanse.com.

Emotional Muscles:
Distinguish between the Voice of Fear (Your Inner Mean Girl) and the Voice of Love (Your Inner Wisdom)

The place where most people have the hardest time is knowing when to trust themselves and when not to. And it's true that when fear is coursing through you, you are *not* the best person to get counsel from. In a state of fear — whether this means worry, shame, judgment, control, doubt, anxiety, or whatever — your Inner Mean Girl is the one with the microphone. If you stop to check in with yourself about your best course of action, she is going to lead you down a path that, while it may seem to keep you safe (in her mind), will take you to the land of self-sabotage.

Emotionally you need to have the strength to take the microphone from your Inner Mean Girl and give it to your Inner Wisdom, and this will require some muscle building. In Inner Mean Girl Reform School, you go through a ten-step process that makes it crystal clear to you who is driving your actions and directing your thoughts. The process itself is an emotional workout for self-trust muscles, using superpowered tools for moving from the fear and crazy-making of the Inner Mean Girl to the peace and sanity of Inner Wisdom. The process includes this next Daring Act of Love, which you can use to become better at hearing the voice of your Inner Wisdom.

Daring Act of Love
Sleep with Your Inner Wisdom for a Week

What are you currently doing to communicate with your Inner Wisdom? Are you talking to her daily? Consulting her first whenever a big decision comes up? Using multiple ways to communicate? If the answer to any of these is no, it's time for you to commit to building an intimate relationship with your Inner Wisdom, and fast! And there's no better way to get close to someone than to share a bed with her. For the next seven nights and seven mornings, you are going to sleep with your Inner Wisdom. She is the last one you are going to talk to before you close your eyes at night, and the first one you'll talk to when you awaken.

All you need is a journal and a pen. Starting the first night, while you are in bed but before you go to sleep, take the journal and write a letter to your Inner Wisdom, telling her how much you are looking forward to building a more intimate relationship together. Write, "Dear Inner Wisdom, I am so excited that we are going to spend the next week sleeping with each other..." and then list all the things you would like to receive. Close the journal and dream loving dreams.

The next morning, when you wake up, before doing anything else, grab your journal, close your eyes, and ask your Inner Wisdom to come and speak to you. Then write the words "Dear Inner Wisdom, what would you like for me to know today?" and then jot down what comes. Or write some other question for your Inner Wisdom: "Dear Inner Wisdom, <<insert your question>>?" And then write whatever comes in response. Just let it flow, even if you can't read the writing.

Still stuck, or want more juice? Get yourself an oracle deck, which is a set of cards that can help you access your Inner Wisdom by asking a question and pulling a card (any of Doreen Virtue's decks are great starters). Or download the Inner Mean Girl Transformation Starter Kit at www.InnerMeanGirl.com, which includes seven powerful ways to connect to your Inner Wisdom so you can build your emotional self-trust muscles and make her your go-to girl and chief counselor.

Physical Muscles:
Stop and Check In with Your Inner Wisdom Daily
— and Take Small Steps before You Take Big Leaps

Remember, trust is built one small step at a time — in your relationships with others and in your relationship with yourself. Every day, you'll want to look for opportunities to check in with your Inner Wisdom first. When you find yourself needing to make a decision — such as where to go to lunch, whether to reach out to someone now or wait, or which way to drive home — check with her, and notice how she talks to you. Does she speak to you as an inner voice? Or does she show you images or patterns or appear in your dreams? Does she speak through inner sensations and feelings in your body? Or does she just know things and plant them in your consciousness? The more you talk to her, the more she will speak, the more trusting your relationship will become, and the more you will remember how to trust yourself.

Daring Act of Love
Make Your Inner Wisdom Your Magic 8 Ball

For every decision you make today, stop and check in first with your Inner Wisdom to see what she says. Just like one of those Magic 8 Balls that you shake in order to receive its answer, your Inner Wisdom will magically supply an answer for you. Make it a game. To check in with your Inner Wisdom, all you have to do is stop, close your eyes, take a breath, ask your question, and then wait for an answer.

The answer may come in the form of a message you hear. It may come as a visual image that flashes through your mind or an image that catches your eye. It may come in the form of a feeling in your body, a sensation. Or it may be a knowing, something you can just tell. Sometimes it may even feel as if someone is pushing you in a certain direction, or as if someone is trying to stop you from moving in a certain direction. Pay attention to all signs, and make your decisions accordingly. At the end of the day, sit down with your Magic 8 Ball — your Inner Wisdom — and tell yourself what you learned about self-trust and how your Inner Wisdom communicates to you.

Love Mantra for Self-Trust
I hear my inner wisdom.
I feel my inner wisdom.
I know what is best for me.
It is safe to trust myself.

CHAPTER 9

Self-Esteem

A strong belief in and regard for yourself. A strong confidence in your ability to do and be anything.

Self-Love Pulse Check

SELF-LOVE PULSE CHECK

Take your self-love pulse by rating each statement on a scale of one to five according to how true that statement is for you. Five indicates the statement is totally true, and one indicates that it is not at all true. Add up your first five ratings to get your LOVE # and the second set of five ratings to get your LACK #. Subtract your LACK # from your LOVE # to get your current self-esteem pulse.

___ I believe that I can do, be, and have anything, and I go for it. I know that if I put my mind to something, or I work hard, I will get what I want.

___ I have a high-level of self-confidence and self-regard. My confidence in my abilities is strong, and it takes a lot to shake that inner belief.

___ I stand up for my beliefs and ideas unapologetically, even if others don't agree with me. I am certain of my beliefs and ideas and will stand up for them regardless of others' opinions.

___ I am proud of what I accomplish and accept attention and acknowledgment easily. I know that I am good at what I do. I accept praise without excessive concern that others will feel reduced because of my success.

___ I strive to be the best me that I can be. It's important to me that I always give my best effort. I value my effort and talents.

LOVE # _____

___ I experience self-doubt and feel inferior. I get waylaid by inner feelings of anxiety, doubt, or fear. I often feel mediocre or inferior.

___ I put myself down. When others praise me, I deflect the praise. I am more likely to say something negative about myself than something positive.

___ I give up easily or stop short of going for what I want. I settle for less than I really desire, because deep down I don't believe I can do it.

___ I don't believe I am good enough. While I may say I really want something, deep down I don't believe I deserve it.

___ I keep my thoughts to myself even though I really want to speak up. I keep my opinions and beliefs to myself, to a fault.

LACK # _____

Now, subtract your LACK # from your LOVE # to get your full self-love pulse for this branch.

My Self-Esteem Pulse _____

While we all experience moments of doubt about and wavering confidence in ourselves at one time or another, there is a clear difference between a blooming self-esteem branch and a failing one. Which type you have comes down to two things: your belief in yourself and your valuation of yourself. Most women seem to have one or the other — a blooming branch or a failing branch — without a lot of middle ground. Self-esteem is pretty black and white. If you have high self-esteem, you know you do. You believe you can do and be anything you set your mind to. You hold yourself in high regard, and, even though as a child you may have received negative attention for being smart or special, you've believed in yourself, at least usually. You've been willing to shine brightly, and you have shone. You may have dimmed the brightness slightly to keep from standing out too much, but inside you have remained confident in your abilities.

You may have even overdeveloped your self-esteem branch, over-compensating with self-confidence and self-regard for a lack of self-love in other areas — a lack of self-compassion, self-acceptance, self-pleasure, self-honor, and so on. See if any of this sounds familiar: You present as an outwardly confident overachiever, but inside you have a hard time giving yourself a break; you are overresponsible and so you overwork, overdo, and overcommit; and honestly, you value your ability to do and achieve more than the ability to be and receive. You are driven, you believe in yourself and your abilities, and whether you openly admit it or not, you know there is a cost to how hard you drive yourself.

If this sounds like you, your path to healthy self-esteem is about recalibrating your belief in yourself and your abilities by reassessing where your high sense of value stems from. Keep shining your light, keep believing in yourself, and begin to become more aware of how your overdeveloped self-esteem could be stopping you from experiencing the pleasure, joy, peace, and love that come from giving energy and attention to the other branches. And, as we go through this chapter, challenge yourself to go deeper into the source of your self-esteem, what you have tied your value to, and from where your motivation to achieve hails. Make it your mission to, by the end of this chapter, become clear on the answer to these questions: Is your value tied to outward achievement more than to inner fulfillment? You've proven you can do anything, and that you are a strong woman, but are you hiding something behind your brilliant confidence, something more vulnerable?

Or perhaps your relationship with self-esteem is different. Maybe you don't currently have a strong self-confidence or conviction in your ability to achieve anything you set out to conquer or amass. If you wouldn't say that you possess an almost unshakable belief in and regard for yourself — your abilities, ideas, contributions, and value — then you have a self-esteem branch in need of strengthening, even if you don't like admitting this. Of course, no one wants to be labeled with "low self-esteem." That's like being branded with a scarlet letter or being called a leper in a society that prizes high self-esteem over just about any other human quality. Our society values winners, competition, achievement, and confidence, and it preys on and shames anything that looks like weakness, inferiority, or vulnerability.

You can breathe easy, knowing that in our magical storybook of self-love there are no scarlet letters, lepers, or shaming finger-pointers. No categories, no "better than" or "worse than." The truth is, a woman with an overgrown self-esteem branch accompanied by a dinky branch of self-compassion is no better off than a woman who lacks self-confidence, but can be kind and gentle with herself when she fails. We don't compare in self-love land, remember. So if you feel any shame about not having a big self-esteem branch, or you feel superior because your branch is rather big, drop the shame or superiority right here. There will be no contest in which we compare branch sizes — lol! As it turns out, because of our hyper-focus on self-esteem and external achievement as a culture, the self-esteem branch of almost every woman and girl needs some loving.

The goal for all of us is to have balanced, healthy branches of self-esteem — not too big or too small, but just right. If we can do this — be self-confident and self-compassionate women; value self-compassion, self-pleasure, and self-care as much as we do self-esteem; and teach our children to do the same — then together we will gain the power to shift the very basis of our individual and collective systems that determine women's and girls' self-worth. Shifting our relationship with self-esteem, and its relationship to all the other branches, will be good for everyone, today and for generations to come.

And while certainly much more can be said about healthy, balanced self-esteem, it can, in my experience, be pared down to the following essential belief and habit. Discovering these for yourself is the adventure that I invite you to take throughout the rest of this chapter.

Self-Esteem Belief and Habit

NEW BELIEF: "I am gifted, and my gifts are valuable."

NEW DAILY LOVE HABIT: Value and give your gifts fully. Cherish your specific gifts, and give them every day. Believe that your gifts have great value, and live accordingly, regardless of the value others give them.

You Are Gifted:
Dare to Be Special and Embrace Your Gifts

Let's start with you believing and owning just how ridiculously fabulous you are, which means that you become willing to own every proclamation that follows. Say these statements out loud and notice what bubbles up, or doesn't, as you make these proclamations about yourself:

> "I am fabulous."
> "I am talented."
> "I am special."
> "I am wise."
> *"I am gifted."*

It's all true; you are, you know, fabulous, talented, special, wise, gifted. How does it feel to say these things out loud about yourself? Supereasy? Joy-full? Like: of course I am! Or uncomfortable? Phony and forced? Like: I don't really believe this. Either reaction is okay. Just notice what's true for you. And then answer this question: Are you willing to believe that these things *are* true of you? You don't need to know yet what your gifts even are; you just have to be *willing* to believe that it's possible you are talented, special, wise, and, yes, gifted.

You see, every single person, including you, came to this planet with gifts. We are all born with them. Your gifts are the things that come naturally to you in a way that they don't come naturally to every other person. When you focus on and apply energy to them, your gifts and you grow exponentially. If others were to put the same focus in the same place, they would not receive the same results — their gifts are different. But we are all *gifted*.

Think of gifts this way. Imagine one of the best concert pianists in the world. This person has practiced for hours, years even, to be able to play the kind of music that stirs your senses. There is no doubt that this person has a magical gift, and that because someone noticed that gift at some point and helped the pianist focus her or his energy on growing that gift, this master pianist now fills the hearts of the world's people with love. You and I could practice for a gazillion hours on the piano, but if we didn't come in with the divine gift to stir people's souls that way, we will never play at the level of that gifted pianist no matter how much we practice.

We could develop a talent, learn a skill — like playing the piano well — but a gift is different. A gift is given to you at birth by the divine. Gifts are always given by someone; these gifts just happen to be given to you as part of the unique imprint of divine love you were born as. The challenge of saying yes to your gifts is that they often feel like too much, as you might imagine receiving a gift from the divine would be! They are brilliant, and they showcase how special you are. And while the divine intended for you to come to this planet and share your gifts openly and fully, you've been getting other messages to the contrary.

Bragging, standing out, or otherwise being different or special has been generally frowned upon by mainstream culture for a long time. As a result, you've learned to dim your light or to shine it brightly but only in ways valued by your culture. But here's the good news: Everyone on this planet received a gift, or multiple gifts, from the divine, which means your specialness has nothing to do with anyone else's. Everyone gets to be special and bring his or her gifts out to play in big ways in the land of happy, healthy self-esteem. So what do you say? Ready to play and display your divine gifts?

Daring Act of Love
Get Bragged On, and Add On!

Let someone you love tell you in person, face-to-face, what gifts she or he sees in you. Pick a person you trust, but one who will happily and fully play this game. Standing or sitting across from this person, ask him or her, "What do you love about me?" The person then replies by saying, "<<insert your name here>>, what I love about you is…" As that person talks, your only job is to listen and receive what is said. Look your friend in the eyes, open your heart, and receive this love. Afterward, just say, "Thank you," and mean it. Stay in your heart; don't move into your head or start to giggle to dissipate the energy. Do this for at least one minute. Set a timer to keep you going. Then, you get to add on to what your friend said! Set the timer for another minute and express to the person who has just loved on *you* what you love about you, by saying something like: "That was so helpful. It's helped me open up to express what I love about me. Can I share with you?" And then go ahead and say out loud to this wonderful witness, "What I love about me is…"

Double Dare: Ask if you can do the same for your friend — if you can brag on her and then witness as she brags on herself. Seeing others' gifts helps us embrace ours even more.

ME Moment *What Are Your Gifts?*

If you think you already know the answer to this question, I encourage you to slow down and take this adventure anyway. This exercise is not about finding your strengths, identifying your skill sets, or praising your talents. This adventure can give you answers that no self-assessment you've done at work or in school ever gave you. This is about you seeing and embracing your *divine gifts*, the ones that came from the universe as a direct expression of divine love.

If you are shy about owning your own brilliance, use this adventure as a way to boldly step out, let yourself be seen, and take up space. Have the courage to reveal, embrace, and own your divine gifts.

Step 1. Make a gift list.

Write the words "My Gifts" at the top of a piece of paper, preferably in color, in BIG, BOLD letters, to reflect the brilliance of the package called "you." Write down the following seven statements, leaving plenty of room for adding your own words to them. Finish each statement with as many things as you can think of. Let your heart and soul — not your head — tell it like you are. No holding back! There is no one reading this but you. Practice believing in and valuing yourself.

- ♥ "I am really good at — not just ordinarily good at — but really good at..."
- ♥ "When I was little, I just loved..."
- ♥ "I feel happiest and most alive when I..."
- ♥ "People always tell me that..."

♥ "I affect people. When I am really in my zone of brilliance, I notice that people..."

♥ "You can always count on me to..."

♥ "I know that I am gifted at..."

Be sure to include *everything* that you can remember people saying about you, all the things you often brush off as if they were no big deal. Include compliments that are hard to take. Include the things you do naturally, or that you notice people come to you for again and again. There are always gifts under the things we take for granted. They come so naturally that we assume everyone has the same experience or ability. But they don't.

Step 2. Ask for your gifts.

This next step may make you feel vulnerable. Good. It's supposed to. Your mission is to ask at least five people who know you to answer the following four questions. Send the questions via email so that they can write the answers to you. Choose people from different parts of your life, not just the safe people. Don't skip this step even if you are tempted to do so. Your heart wants to be seen, even if it's scared. Be daring!

1. What do you think I am really good at? Give an example or tell a story about a time you experienced me this way.

2. Why do you think I am gifted at these things? Be specific. For example, if you say I am a good cook or writer, what is it that makes me a good cook or writer?

3. What makes me special, unique?

4. When you spend time with me, what can you count on? **How do you feel or what do you experience during and after our encounters?**

Step 3. Gather up and sort out your gifts.

You've got all kinds of gifts coming your way — from all the people you've asked and from your own gift-finding expedition. Now it's time to get a sense of what you've collected.

1. Gather up. Take all your responses from the first two steps. Imagine that you just had a wild and fabulous birthday party where you received tons of presents reflecting how loved and appreciated you are.
2. Sort out. On a fresh piece of paper, create three or four lists of your gifts by grouping together similar gifts. Perhaps after birthday parties, you like to put your gifts into piles to help you sort through what you've received? Do the same thing here. As you sort through your gifts, notice the words, phrases, and strings of words in the different descriptions that feel similar and group those together in separate lists. These similarities will point to the common thread of what the gifts reveal about you.

Step 4. Reveal your gifts.

Now that you have your three or four lists of gifts, it's time to reveal what's really here, time to decipher the real gift. Often the true gift gets hidden underneath a talent, strength, or quality, because that's how we've been trained to think. As you look at each list, challenge yourself to look beyond the obvious, seeing not with your mind but with your heart to find what truly makes you *you*. Ask yourself, "What truly is my gift? What is special about how *I give* this gift?"

The table below, "True Gifts," offers some examples. These statements are more than just laundry lists of strengths, qualities, or talents. Remember: this is all about you owning your magical, amazing gifts, not about spouting your three biggest strengths or top qualities. You want to be able to really feel these words inside you so that you can receive the powerful energy that comes from seeing who you are and owning how special that is. The gifts listed in the table are gifts of real women I've coached or who have participated in one of my transformational programs.

True Gifts

Strength: Tenacity. ➡ Gift: My gift is never giving up, and inspiring people to believe that they don't have to give up either.

Talent: Singing. ➡ Gift: My gift is feeling the common experiences we have as humans and then singing those emotions using words and song.

Quality: I make people laugh. ➡ Gift: My gift is finding a sweet humor in everything, which makes people breathe and not take themselves so seriously.

Strength: Honesty. Gift: My gift is saying what everyone else is thinking but is too afraid to say.

Quality: Others feel at ease around me. ➡ Gift: My gift is making people feel welcome and comfortable and at ease.

Talent: Decorating with style. ➡ Gift: My gift is creating beauty and grace wherever I go.

Now it's your turn. Go back to step 3, where you compiled your gifts, and find the truth of what your gifts are — beyond simply the quality, impact, strength, or talent. Go deep into the heart of the gift. Dig into what the words are telling you about you. Then, in your own words, from your heart, write out a phrase that reflects your gift. Practice saying the words out loud to help you find the ones that best express your special gifts. Do this for each of the three or four lists you made, so that you identify at least three of your gifts. Keep writing and playing with the words until you have phrases that feel like you when you say them out loud.

Step 5. Receive and own your gifts.

Create a gift proclamation page by taking a clean sheet of paper, writing the words "My Gifts" at the top, and listing each of your gifts. Record each one on a separate line, starting with the words "My gift is..." Then, put yourself into a powerful physical stance, proclamation page in hand, and proclaim your gifts by reading them out loud. Let them sink into your body. From this day forward, promise yourself to embrace these gifts by taking them out in the world boldly, believing in them, their value, and yourself, doing everything you can to share them, regardless of what anyone else has to say.

Your Gifts Are Valuable: Value Yourself

Just as we don't compare the size of our self-esteem branches, we don't compare the size of our gifts. Bigger packages don't mean better gifts. Your gift may involve playing to thousands of people on a stage, being a public figure, or running a big company. Or your gift may be to immensely affect the life of one person, to provide a small service that people need, or to simply show up as an example of a loving human imprint every day. What is essential is that you value your gifts and that you choose to actively give them fully to the world.

When you don't give your gifts fully, the world, and you, suffer. You were given your unique gifts because the divine knew this world would need them, which makes them inherently valuable, like pure human gold. Your gifts are direct expressions of divine love. Gifts carry such power. No matter what the shape and size of the gifts that are expressed through you — whether they're fierce and fiery, passionate and powerful, serene and sensual, or compassionate and courageous — gifts, when you give them, always influence people in a way that creates more love, happiness, and peace. And if you haven't noticed, these are greatly needed by the world, by everyone you know, including yourself. You give your gifts, people receive more love, happiness, and peace, and you receive more love, happiness, and peace. What a great deal! Yet more often than not, you have resisted fully giving your gifts. Why? There are many excuses, but really only one reason: you are afraid.

Your brand of fear may differ from that of another person, but almost always the misuse or underuse of one's gifts stems from fear. People with overdeveloped self-esteem branches, who are often outwardly successful, may find that fear shows up in their belief that their gifts can't support them financially, or that their gifts don't apply to their work in the world. Fear keeps them overly focused on trying to appear strong and confident. They rely too much on their socially acceptable strengths, instead of showing the world their true gifts, which would make them way more vulnerable. If this sounds like you, fear may be causing you to place more value on the money, status, approval, and security that external systems provide than on your divinely given gifts.

If you are a person with an underdeveloped branch of self-esteem, you too may be hiding your gifts away. You may be afraid to be seen, and so you may prevent attention from coming at you in a big way. Fear may cause you to keep yourself small and hidden in many ways, including by settling for only dabbling in your gifts or not living them at all. When you don't believe you have gifts, are unsure of yourself, or value others' gifts over your own, you become afraid to step out and do much of anything. None of these are winning scenarios. You lose, and the world loses.

Love Story: The Courage to Both Believe in and Live Your Gifts

My client Rhonda, a big thinker, a woman with a talent and love for writing, knew she had a gift but didn't believe enough in herself and her gifts to use them to do and be what in her heart she knew she was born for. Rhonda had a gift for seeing beyond the obvious and into the possible, coupled with a gift for using words and big ideas to express the common, but often hidden, experiences of humanity. She had the ability to be a thought leader, writer, and agent of social change. But instead, she toiled away in a job she didn't love, working with people she didn't fit in with, doing work that wasn't meaningful. Instead of spending her days coming up with big ideas that created positive change, she came up with ways to sell consumer commodities that weren't even healthy for people. She was like Amelia Earhart grounded, selling plane tickets rather than flying her plane around the world.

Rhonda's self-esteem branch, which had been strong at birth, had been battered by a big weed whacker: a schooling system that labeled her a daydreamer because she wasn't a hyperachiever (except for her writing teachers, who saw her genius). So she began to value achieving over seeing. She was influenced by narcissistic men — husbands, lovers, and business partners — who poisoned her belief in herself by injecting doubt into her heart. And she was influenced by relatives who loved her but who were proud only when she succeeded in getting a big salary and title in a corporate setting, causing her too to value such things and, in the process, devalue her very core.

Rhonda's regard for and valuation of herself became tied to external sources. She lost her internal belief in herself and her abilities.

If you had asked Rhonda, "Do you believe you are smart?" she would have said yes. If you asked her whether she had gifts, she probably would have said yes again. And if you had asked her if she valued her gifts, she'd have said yes, but her actions would have said otherwise. If her self-esteem branch had been stronger, and she'd valued more of who she was, she would have found a career among people who valued her, stopped looking outside herself to feel valued, and become the person who in her heart she knew she was — a gifted being, one of a kind. Rhonda.

This is the journey of self-esteem that Rhonda and many other women whose gifts were devalued when they were young are on today. They must reclaim their conviction that their unique gifts are as valuable as other gifts that are currently valued by our culture.

ME Moment *Do You Really Value Yourself?*

Time to stop for an honest conversation with yourself. There is only one question to ask yourself, but it's a critical one: "Do my life and the actions I take and the choices I make reflect that I really value my gifts and what's important to me?"

This question is a deep one, and you may or may not be able to answer it right off the bat, and that's okay. As you work on deeper and deeper levels of self-esteem, which has a direct correlation to your sense of self-worth, it would serve you well to ask yourself this question periodically. Hold a superpowered honesty hearing (see chapter 4) to check in with yourself and see how your actions and choices are aligning with your gifts and the truth of who you are. Another way to look at this question is "If I really believed in myself, if I really had a high regard for myself, would I be living the life I am living today? And if not, what would I change?"

If all that is a bit much for you to take in, start by asking yourself one of the following questions, and commit to taking one step toward assigning greater value to the gifts you've been given.

♥ What value do I currently attach to my gifts, to what makes me special? Look at your gifts one at a time and rate them on a scale from one to five. Five indicates that you absolutely value the gift, and your actions and choices reflect that. Three indicates that you value the gift but your actions don't show this. One indicates that you don't value the gift. For anything less than a five, you need a revaluation!

♥ How am I not currently fully valuing and giving my gifts? **For every gift on which you scored less than five, consider how you devalue that gift in these different parts of your life — career, relationships, finances, and health. How do your choices not align with your valuing and giving your gifts?**

♥ What is one small but mighty, and maybe even daring, action I can take in the next thirty days to bring my life into alignment with my gifts, and to show that I value the divine gifts I possess? **Ask this question about each of your gifts, and then boldly take that one action.**

ME Art Make an "I Love Me" List

One surefire way to amp up your self-esteem is to reflect back to yourself just how awesome and special you are. Today you are going to reveal 108 things you love about yourself!

Supplies:

♥ A piece of blank paper (if you want to make a ME poster) or a small, purse-size notebook with a cover that feels like you

♥ Fun, colored markers and pens (get ready for some serious fun!)

♥ Optional: Printout of the "I Love ME List" Loveplate I made for you at www.ChooseSelfLove.com

Mission:

Take an inventory of all the things you love about yourself, and list 108 things. Not 10, not 100, but 108. Why? Because 108 is one of the most powerful numbers in the universe. There are 108 beads in a *mala* (the prayer beads you often see Buddhist monks wearing), the distance between the earth and sun is 108 times the diameter of the sun, there are 108 pressure points on the human body according to many traditions, and the list goes on. I am a big believer in using extra cosmic energy from the divine whenever possible, because why not?

How-to:
Step 1. Make a list of 108 things you love about you.

At the top of the page write, "I love me!" Then start listing what you love about yourself, and don't stop until you have 108 quirks, realities, and essences written down. Use the following love starters to get your self-love flowing:

"I love that I am . . ."
"I love that I always . . ."
"I love that I remember . . ."
"I love that I have . . ."

Thinking up 108 ways that you are superduper special may seem daunting, but it is totally possible. And the act of stretching yourself to acknowledge the 108 will force you to go past the surface into a more intimate relationship with yourself, where you really value *you*. If you can't get to all 108 in the first go-round, that's okay, but at least get to 70. Then, every day, add at least one thing to the list until you get to 108.

Step 2. Put your list where you can use it.

Make your list into a mobile reflection of what you love about yourself, and carry the list with you always. Fold it up and put it in your wallet, or write it in a small notebook you can carry in your purse. Or choose to create a poster out of it, frame it, and hang it where you can see it every day. That way, when you need a love boost, you can read the list.

To try out two Daring Acts of Love, The Self-Love Serenade and the Add On/Brag On, or watch a daring video demonstration, take yourself to www.SelfLoveTV.com.

Love Mantra for Self-Esteem

I am gifted.
I am valuable.
I am special.
I am me.

CHAPTER 10

Self-Empowerment

Choosing to take charge of and responsibility for your life by acting to create the life you really desire, without apology or requiring approval from others.

Self-Love Pulse Check

SELF-LOVE
PULSE CHECK

Take your self-love pulse by rating each statement on a scale of one to five according to how true that statement is for you. Five indicates the statement is totally true, and one indicates that it is not at all true. Add up your first five ratings to get your LOVE # and the second set of five ratings to get your LACK #. Subtract your LACK # from your LOVE # to get your current self-empowerment pulse.

____ I take responsibility for my life circumstances. I am not a victim or martyr. I believe that I am responsible for the state of my life.

____ I change what I don't like about my life. I am the captain of my life, and I make shifts whenever needed.

____ I go for my dreams. I know what I want, and I am actively making my dreams a reality.

____ I feel strong and act courageously. I take risks in order to go for what I want, even when I feel afraid.

____ I am unafraid to live my life differently, even if that means upsetting others. I don't need permission from others to do what I want or live the way I want.

LOVE # _____

____ I wait for things to happen. I am reactive rather than proactive about my life.

____ I feel powerless and stuck. I feel like I don't have control over, or the power to change, my circumstances. I blame others or external forces for the things I don't like about my life.

____ I allow others' opinions to influence my choices. I allow what other people say or think to stop me from doing what I want.

____ I feel afraid. I stop myself from making changes or going for what I really want.

____ I look to others for approval or acknowledgment. If I am not receiving external validation or assurance, I get nervous or I think I'm doing something wrong.

LACK # _____

Now, subtract your LACK # from your LOVE # to get your full self-love pulse for this branch.

My Self-Empowerment Pulse _____

Are you in charge of your own life? Are you sure? Or have you unknowingly been giving your power away? And how do you know? Many people get *self-esteem* and *self-empowerment* confused, and while these branches reside right next to each other and are indeed very close, there is a marked difference. Self-esteem is the belief that you can do and be anything you set your mind to; self-empowerment is the ability to actually take action and go for what you want, no matter what, without asking permission or acknowledgment from anyone else. You can have a boatload of self-esteem, and believe yourself gifted and special, but without a strong sense of self-empowerment you will find yourself waiting around for life to happen to you or listening to others' opinions about how you should live your life. Self-empowered people take the reins of their lives into their own hands; they choose to *reign over* themselves, not to be reigned over.

The word *reign* is the perfect word to express the energy and essence of a truly empowered woman. Like a queen, she is a *sovereign* being, presiding over her own kingdom — or queendom, to be exact — which is herself. The word *sovereign*, although not often used in our society, is one of the most powerful words a woman can apply to herself. A sovereign being is by definition a person with supreme rank, and for once I can agree with the peeps at Dictionary.com. The problem with sovereignty lies not in its definition but in who we choose to give supreme rank to when it comes to our lives — be that a person, a group, an organization, or a system. When our self-empowerment is strong, we know without a doubt that this supreme rank is ours; we need no person or establishment to tell us so, and we would never think of handing the power of our lives over to another.

A sovereign woman has supreme authority over her choices and life

— present and future. She gives no one power over her; she chooses how to live her life. She gives no one power over her body, mind, or spirit. Sovereignty is akin to independence. A woman with sovereignty needs no other person to complete her. She knows she can take care of herself, and she does it. She knows that if she needs something, she can find the resources and provide for herself and her family. She is not needy, co-dependent, or in need of others' acknowledgment or approval. If she needs something, she gets it. She never makes the choice to feel like a victim.

Imagine if you lived your life as the queen of your own domain. The queen of your destiny. The queen of your decisions. The monarch of your dreams. As a woman who takes charge of her life and charts her own course. A queen who may take counsel from others but always makes decisions according to her own heart. A self-empowered woman who doesn't look to any person or establishment to give her power, status, or recognition, but who instead draws power and permission to act from inside herself. Imagine courageously leading your own life, being willing to step over, and step past, the fear and limiting beliefs of others and into the glory of the life you know you were meant to live.

How would your life be different? How would you be different? How would you more completely be your powerful self?

Choosing to own your power and wield it with love and courage is a branch of self-love that you, like every woman, must face at some point in your life, or you will never live the life you were meant to live. I don't mean live according to your parents' ideas and hopes, your partner's ideals or demands, or even the proclamations and edicts of society. You must be willing to stand on your own, as the queen of your life, sovereign, independent, and empowered, doing as you see fit, even when it doesn't align with the vision others have for you. True queens

- ♥ lead from their hearts,
- ♥ have visions of what they want to accomplish,
- ♥ act courageously, and
- ♥ trust their own consciences above all else…and they act accordingly.

ME Moment *How Are You Giving Away Your Own Power?*

Of course, no one wants to admit that they see themselves as powerless, that they give away their power to
others or are afraid to be powerful, but that is what all of
us with weak self-empowerment branches do. And whether you want to
admit it or not, if you are unconsciously or consciously making choices
that give away your power, the only way to stop is to admit the truth to
yourself first. Hold an honesty hearing with yourself, looking truthfully
into each of the following three areas to find the places where you are
undermining your own sovereignty and empowerment:

1. In what ways or areas in your life do you feel powerless? Look at the major
    areas of your life, such as finances, career, home, health, and relation-
    ships. Where do you feel like you have no ability to change your real-
    ity? That no matter how much you try or how much you do, nothing
    will change? Or do you feel that because of the circumstances you find
    yourself, in you can do nothing to alter the state of your life?

Act of Empowerment: List all the ways in which you feel powerless today or have felt powerless in the past, using the following structure:

"I feel powerless to...even though I know..."

For example, you may have felt powerless to leave an unhealthy relationship, or felt trapped in a dead-end job, felt unable to become healthy, or believed you were without the resources to rise up and out of poverty. So you might write, "I feel powerless to leave my relationship even though I know it's not good for me" or "I feel powerless to leave my job even though I know I am really meant to do something else."

2. Who or what have you given your power to? Perhaps you have convinced yourself that you could not survive or thrive without this person, this group of people, or the establishment you have connected yourself to. You believe — consciously or unconsciously — that they have things you need, things you cannot provide for yourself. This might be unconditional love, financial security, acceptance, recognition, stature, safety, stability, intimacy, affection, health care, and so on. You allow the opinions and support of these people, and your connection to and reliance on them, to prevent you from doing what is truly right for you.

Act of Empowerment: Make a list of all the people, groups, and establishments you have given your power away to — past and present. Then for each, answer these two questions:

♥   What do you believe they can give you that you cannot give your-self?

♥   What are you afraid you will lose or be unable to gain if you dis-connect or distance yourself from them or make a decision that goes against their wishes, expectations, or standards?

For example: You may have let your parents' approval keep you from dating someone you loved because you were afraid to lose their love and support. You may have allowed your family's financial support to prevent you from going for a dream that, although it wasn't rational, was true to your heart, and you may have done so because you believed your family gave you financial security. Or you may have let a corporate job with health benefits stop you from becoming an entre-preneur or taking a year off because you believed that without those benefits, you couldn't take care of yourself or get the care you needed.

Your statement might look like this one: "I am giving power to the company I work for. I believe they give me health care and ben-efits that I can't get otherwise. I am afraid that I will not be able to take care of my health needs if the company isn't paying for my health care insurance."

3.   In what ways have you not stepped into your power? Perhaps you are not actively creating your life but are passively letting life happen to you, waiting for your big break. Or you may have simply become resigned to the idea that this is how life is. You coast along, dabbling in your dreams but never fanning the fire inside and going for your dreams. You go through life unheard and unseen, except on the rare occasions when you get so tired of holding back that you burst with emotion,

and usually not in a graceful or healthy way. You are afraid of your power, and — whether you like to admit it or not — are a mere courtier instead of a queen.

Act of Empowerment: List all the actions you have wanted to take, but haven't, in the past ten years. And for each one, list the truth of why you didn't take it. What stopped you? Complete the following sentences:

♥ "I was afraid I couldn't..." Articulate what you were afraid you could not do for yourself.
♥ "I was afraid I wouldn't..." Say what you would have gone without or lost if you had done it.
♥ "I was afraid others would think..." List what you believe others would have thought or said if you had done it.

For example: "I wanted to quit my job and travel the world for a year. I was afraid I couldn't make enough money to survive. I was afraid that I wouldn't be able to find a job after I came back. I was afraid that others would think I was irresponsible."

As a last step, take a step back and look at all you have discovered about yourself while having this ME Moment. Ask yourself the following questions:

♥ How does all this make me feel? Use a feeling word, not a judgment: "I feel..." (sad, mad, excited, scared, and so on).

♥ What circumstances would I like to be different from what I see now?

♥ What needs to shift for me to recognize that I complete myself, and that there is nothing anyone can give me that I cannot receive from myself?

♥ Am I willing to make my life different, to empower myself to change it? Remember, all you have to be is willing.

Take Your Power Back: Reclaim Your Sovereignty

No one can give you anything or empower you with anything that you have not already given yourself. This is the bottom line of self-empowerment. With sovereignty you demonstrate that the power is within you. You've just reexperienced some of the ways in which you have been looking outside yourself to receive the power only you can bestow. Think of this as placing a crown of self-empowerment on your own head as a token of your sovereignty and your status as chief decision maker in your life.

ME Art Prepare Your Proclamation of Sovereignty

Your next order of business as the queen of your domain is to properly empower yourself to be empowered. And this piece of ME Art, which incorporates much of the previous ME Moment, is set up to do just that. So put on your crown (even if it's just a pretend crown for now) and become the queen of your own domain.

Supplies:

- ♥ Two pieces of paper, preferably ones that would suit a queen — no shabby, stained, or crumpled-up messes; only nice, crisp, powerful pieces of paper will do
- ♥ Two different colored pens or markers or crayons
- ♥ Optional: Printout of the "Proclamation of Sovereignty" Loveplate at www.ChooseSelfLove.com

Mission:

To make and state a powerful proclamation of your personal power. This proclamation process — from the creation of the words that reflect your sovereignty and self-empowerment to your act of verbalizing the words and proclaiming them to be law in your domain — is a sacred self-love ritual. It has the juju to empower you to create mighty, marvelous shifts in your life.

How-to:

Step 1. Create your power statements.

Go back and study what you uncovered in the ME Moment — what you are willing to do differently to assert your inherent power in your life. Also, take a look back at all the ways to think of yourself as an empowered individual — as a sovereign, a queen, a courageous navigator charting your own course, as someone who is committed to making your dreams real no matter what, and so on. Come up with four to seven statements that reflect the stand you are taking in order to do the following:

1. feel powerful,
2. take back your power, and
3. step into your power.

For example:

♥ "I am the queen of my own life."
♥ "I may take counsel from others, but I make my own decisions according to my own conscience, my own heart."
♥ "I ask permission from no one to live my life the way I see fit."
♥ "I embrace my destiny and live my dreams into reality, no matter what."
♥ "I lead myself into the life I actively choose to create for myself."

On one of the pieces of paper, rewrite the statements again and again until the words reach what you feel is a power level of at least eight, on a scale of ten, when you say them out loud. Ten means "Wow! I so feel that in my cells." Eight signifies "I can feel the power in there, ready to be released even if I am unsure exactly how this will manifest in my life." You will know the words are at the power level you need when you can feel them vibrate in your body, your heart, and your mind. You'll feel courageous, bold, strong, and grounded when you say them, even if they feel a little scary. At a core level, deep inside, you'll know that this is how you desire to be and live — and that you are ready to do whatever it takes to make it so.

Step 2. Make your proclamation of sovereignty.

Now it's time to draft the official paperwork that must accompany all proclamations of power. Take the other fresh piece of spiffy blank paper and, at the top, draw a crown with the words "I AM POWERFUL" inside it. Then, under the crown, in a different color, write the following:

Proclamation of Sovereignty

I, << add your name here>>, by the authority invested in me by me as the queen of my own domain, do powerfully swear to uphold the following proclamation to the best of my ability from this day forward.

Then write your proclamation of power on this document, including your charged-up power statements. Use the two different colors to add some extra life and energy. Feel the intention and energy behind the words that you are about to proclaim as law. Feel yourself stepping forward to claim your birthright as a self-empowered woman responsible for charting the course to her dreams and destiny, without looking for permission from anyone else to do so.

Daring Act of Love
Conduct a Coronation Ceremony

Wait! You aren't done yet. Oh, no. All proclamations require one very important component to really lock in the power — the pomp and circumstance of a ceremony. You, my dear, are hereby dared to create a Coronation Ceremony in which you anoint yourself with the power to uphold this proclamation. Think of this ceremony as a ritual that marks a transition between how you showed up in your life previously — whether as a jester, a maiden, a victim, a sergeant, or a courtier — and how you will show up now as a newly empowered individual. Rituals — although mostly ignored or downplayed in our society, or done only by those we've given our power to — are extremely powerful. When a woman takes back her power to create and to lead her own rituals, she reclaims her inherent power to initiate herself into new realms. You have the power to create a ritual and wield its power whenever you want. Try it now.

1. Claim your mission. To create a ceremony that holds the energy of the power you desire to cultivate.
2. Choose your wardrobe and environment. Anything that makes you feel powerful. The colors of sovereignty are emerald green and gold. The flower is the sunflower.
3. Prepare. Set a date for your ceremony, and do it up right — really, when was the last time you got to play dress-up and create a sacred ritual for yourself? Let loose and engage in some theatrics. Evoke the energy of sovereignty with music that makes you feel powerful and bold, and don the colors and clothing that make you feel more powerful when you step into them. Engage in an empowered act to find a space for yourself to have this ceremony, whether that means asking your roommates or family to take off for a night, going to a one-day retreat, or going out into nature.
4. Conduct your ceremony. Get your royal garb on, have your proclamation papers handy, and find a self-love stage for yourself where you can deliver this proclamation, a place of power — in front of a fireplace, on a balcony, on top of your bed, in front of the mirror, or just in the middle of a room. Close your eyes, take a big breath,

and put your hand on your belly. Your belly is the place in your body that gives you access to your deep feminine power, and if you can speak your proclamation from there, as opposed to just speaking from your voice box or through your nasal passages, you will run the power through your body and up through your heart. Your heart is, of course, where your courage lives — and let's be real, your proclamation is courageous. Proclaim yours with the love that beats in your heart for yourself — and have the courage to love yourself so much that you will do whatever it takes to give yourself what makes you happy.

Double Dare: Take yourself to a sovereignty double feature before your coronation. Get the energy of sovereignty racing through your veins by watching two of the best movies about a self-empowered woman, *Elizabeth* and *Elizabeth: The Golden Years*, both starring Cate Blanchett. You will witness this maiden turn into a queen and, afterward, turn into a woman who loses her sense of self-empowerment, who gains it back, and who finds the courage to defend her domain and walk into her destiny. After watching these, reflect on your own journey to being your empowered self, the queen of your heart and destiny.

Love Story: From Esteemed Maiden to Empowered Queen

Meet Jennifer, a maiden struggling to become a queen. At the age of thirty-five, she was still looking outside of herself — to her parents and boyfriend — to provide her with the approval she hadn't yet given to herself, and to her job for financial security. (Money and love — what we won't trade away for those!) She didn't like her job as a lawyer and, in retrospect, was starting to see that she had chosen this path mostly to make her parents happy — a hard truth to swallow, and one she discovered only after a heated argument with her parents regarding her boyfriend, James, a man they disapproved of but tolerated.

On one particular Sunday afternoon, all came to a head at the family kitchen table when Jennifer mentioned to her mother and father that she was considering moving in with James. While she didn't expect a ticker-tape parade, she also didn't expect what ensued. Without missing a beat, her mother spoke first and, with a pronounced frown and stern voice, informed Jennifer that if she moved in with this man, they would promptly disown her. The problem was, Jennifer already had moved in with James — six months earlier — without telling her parents. Too afraid of what they would think, still dependent on their approval and support, and unconsciously terrified she would lose the emotional and financial safety net her parents still represented for her, Jennifer had not possessed the courage to even run the idea by them until now.

What happened next would become a major defining step on Jennifer's self-empowerment path. In response to her mother's statement — Jennifer later told me — she felt like she was having an out-of-body experience, watching what was happening from a distance, like a scene from a movie. While she didn't have the language to describe it at the time, what Jennifer was having was an "empowerment epiphany." When this kind of epiphany hits, like a cold bucket of water in the face that instantly washes away the film or fog, you see clear as day — often for the first time — that you have been giving your power away in all kinds of ways.

In that moment, Jennifer saw that she had let her parents choose her career and let their unspoken disapproval prompt her to lie about someone she loved. She also saw that the same dynamic was playing out in her law firm and that she believed she was stuck in a career she didn't like. Now, at the age of thirty-five, she stood at a crossroads. She could submit and give away her power again, and let her parents dictate the course of her life, or she could stand up and be the queen of her own domain and choose her own destiny, at the risk of losing the support and approval of her parents.

Jennifer took a deep breath, looked at her parents, and said, "I appreciate you for all you have done for me in the thirty-five years I've been your daughter. You put me through college, helped me buy my first car, my first condo, and you've always supported my ambition to be the best I can be. I am grateful for that love and support. I am not a child anymore, I am a grown woman, and I know what is best for me. Regardless of how this relationship works out with James, I know this is the best next step for me. I hope you will support us with your love; and if you can't, I will be sad, but that will be your choice, not mine." Jennifer's parents just stared at her as she delivered this proclamation of sovereignty. When she finished, there was a long pause, and — Jennifer told me later — while she was literally shaking in her designer boots, she'd never felt so empowered.

Now you might expect that what occurred next was the fairy-tale ending, in which her parents rose up, hugged their daughter, and had a truly tear-jerking Hallmark moment. But the truth of a queen's life is that sometimes our biggest fear comes true and we have to remain standing, connected to the inner knowing that we can survive, that we have everything we need inside ourselves. Jennifer's mother spoke first: "Well,

I guess you'd better leave then, and take your things. You have another home now, so you aren't welcome in mine." Jennifer looked to her father, whose head was down, staring at the newspaper left from that morning. She wasn't going to get support there either, at least not right now. Saddened and, truthfully, a little scared, she turned, empowered in her sovereignty, and walked out.

Three years would pass before Jennifer would speak to or see her mother again. Her father, while he didn't see his daughter in his home during that time, was more compassionate and kept in touch. What finally broke the ice was a family tragedy — the illness of Jennifer's younger brother — which created an opening for a new type of relationship to develop between Jennifer and her mother, one based on respect, woman to woman. Jennifer eventually broke up with her boyfriend and left her job as a lawyer to work with young women, empowering them to go for their dreams. If asked today whether she regrets her choice to move in with her boyfriend instead of acting as her parents wished, she would say no. While it was painful and difficult to be separated from her mother that way, she was proud of herself for choosing what was right for her. It was this choice, Jennifer said, that gave her the courage to step over the threshold to becoming a woman, to take charge of her life and make the changes she knew in her heart she must.

Be the Monarch of Your Dreams

What dream or desire are you sitting on? Are you waiting for something "out there" to shift before you do what your heart and soul are craving now? What dreams have you put on hold because they feel too big or otherwise not possible? Or not even dared dream for fear they would not come true? An empowered woman waits for no one to tell her it's time to act in accordance with her heart — she just does it. She doesn't put dreams on a shelf; she lives them into reality, one small but mighty step at a time. Even when she doesn't know what the outcome will be, and she doesn't know all the steps to take, she revs up her power and goes for it.

Many people misunderstand self-empowerment, believing that people who act courageously and who wield their full power are not afraid. This isn't true. You don't think Joan of Arc was afraid when she rushed onto the battlefield? Or Amelia Earhart when she made her first solo flight? Or the suffragettes when they stood up for their dreams and were jailed because they believed so much in their vision of creating a world where women could vote? Of course these women felt fear, just as you have when you've faced something you really desired but didn't know how to get. Just like when you were called to greatness and the calling felt too big. And like you, they too probably had moments when they felt disempowered or looked for something out there to tell them it was okay to go for it, moments when they stood waiting rather than going for their dreams. The difference is, they didn't stay there.

The distinguishing factor between a self-empowered woman who acts as the monarch of her dreams, moving them from vision to actuality, and the one who just thinks about living her dreams is not the absence of fear. It is the presence of courage.

*ME Moment   If You Stepped into Your Power,
What Dreams Would You Go For?*

Give yourself permission to dream with absolute courage. Close your eyes and imagine yourself standing in a
room with shelves on the walls full of picture frames of all
shapes and sizes. Each of these picture frames represents a dream of yours
that you have put on hold or stuffed way down deep. This is something
your heart knows it wants to experience, create, birth, have in this lifetime,
but which you have let fear or others' judgments stop you from pursuing.
Look at each one of the picture frames representing your shelved dreams
and, on a piece of paper, draw the frame and the dream. Then pick four
of these dreams that you are willing to make a reality now, and put a big
heart on the frame of each to activate it with love. You don't have to know
how these dreams will come to fruition; you just need to be willing to take
them off the shelf and engage in a Daring Act of Love as your next step.

Daring Act of Love
Go Public with Your Dreams

Share the four dreams you've chosen with at least four people,
preferably in person or by phone. Email works too, but don't
chicken out — use this as an opportunity to be seen. Yes, putting your dreams out in public is scary, because you are opening

your heart to be seen. But that's why we call these Daring Acts of Love! And when you share your dreams with people you love, they can hold those dreams for you too — which means the dreams are a gazillion times more likely to come true.

Love Boost

To add more power to these dreams, I've created two love boosts to take you deeper and start empowering you to take action. Take yourself to www.ChooseSelfLove.com to get both.

The Dream Wheel. Think of this as a cosmic dream-catcher with the power to move dreams forward. This Loveplate will help you create a piece of ME Art that will empower you to make your dreams a reality.

Meditation. Not sure what dreams are sitting on your shelves, or which ones you want to take down? Check out the Dream Wheel Meditation on www.SelfLoveMeditations.com to help you decide.

Love Mantra for Self-Empowerment

I am the queen of my own domain.
I chart the course of my life.
I make my dreams reality.
I am powerful.

CHAPTER 11

Self-Respect & Self-Honor

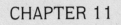

The unwavering commitment to making only choices
that respect and honor the sacred soul that you are.

Self-Love Pulse Check

SELF-LOVE
PULSE CHECK

Take your self-love pulse by rating each statement on a scale of one to five according to how true that statement is for you. Five indicates the statement is totally true, and one indicates that it is not at all true. Add up your first five ratings to get your LOVE # and the second set of five ratings to get your LACK #. Subtract your LACK # from your LOVE # to get your current self-respect and self-honor pulse.

____ I respect all parts of me — my spirit, mind, body, and feelings. I don't discount, disregard, or degrade my body, my intelligence, my feelings, or my experience.

____ I expect people to be good to me, and they are, or I don't have relationships with them. I have relationships only with people who are kind, loving, and respectful to me — no matter who they are.

____ I respect others, but not in lieu of respecting myself. I give the respect I desire to others, while still respecting myself.

____ I share my body and spirit only with those who honor her sacredness. Romantic partners always honor and respect me and my body, or they do not remain my partners.

____ I stand up for myself. If I find myself in a situation in which I am not being honored or respected, I speak up and take action to change it.

LOVE # _____

____ I disrespect myself through my words and thoughts. I say or think mean things about myself.

____ I discount my feelings and importance. I feel diminished or embarrassed when I show my feelings. I feel that I matter less than other people.

____ I have unhealthy relationships and make self-destructive choices in them. I have codependent, toxic, or physically, emotionally, mentally, or verbally abusive relationships.

____ I let people use me or treat me poorly. I still talk to people who are mean, lie, backstab, gossip, or do other bad things to me. They hurt me, yet I can't end the relationship.

____ I make excuses for people who treat me disrespectfully or badly. When others tell me someone is treating me poorly, I defend the person, especially if it's a relative, longtime friend, or romantic partner.

LACK # _____

Now, subtract your LACK # from your LOVE # to get your full self-love pulse for this branch.

My Self-Respect & Self-Honor Pulse _____

Have you ever walked into a temple or a church and felt that something was different about the way the space felt? As if you should quiet your voice, pull your energy inward, and show reverence? You instinctively knew that you were to show respect for the space and honor the people in it — that you were standing in a sacred space. What you may not know is that every day you stand in sacred space, because every day you stand in your body temple. It's your duty to treat her as such and make sure everyone else does too.

> Your body, just like a temple or church, is sacred space. It's your duty to treat her as such and make sure everyone else does too.

Perhaps you've been blessed with the opportunity to hold a newborn child in your hands. And had the experience of feeling the preciousness of this new soul, the innocence emanating from this beautiful clean spirit wrapped up in a tiny, wrinkly human body. As if you could feel the pure love, fresh from heaven, you held this little being and knew to instinctively honor the child by showering it with adoration and love. And while your body may not be fresh from the mint any longer, your soul is still a sacred expression of the divine that deserves to be honored at all times.

> Your soul, just like a newborn child, is a sacred expression of love. It's your duty to ensure that it is honored as such in all relationships, including the one with yourself.

There is a tradition in many spiritual centers in which the children are brought up to the front of the church or temple for all the adult congregation to see. The children march in a long and happy procession up the middle aisle, and in that moment, if you were to look around, you'd notice every adult face in the house softening and smiling. As the children turn to face the congregation, the adults raise their hands with their palms facing these children and together, with the most heartfelt emotion, say to these little sacred beings, "You are a divine being of God. You are love. You are perfect just the way you are. Thank you for being you." It is like witnessing a sea of love wash over every person there — adults and children alike.

What goes unsaid but not unnoticed is that while it may appear that the adults are the ones helping the children to remember who they are so they don't ever have to forget, it's really the opposite. The adults, as they express their heartfelt emotions to, and recognition of, the divine in these children, are also talking to themselves.

> *You* are a sacred being who deserves to be honored and respected by all people, in all situations.

How many weeks have you been on this planet? Multiply your age by 50 for a quick calculation. If you are 20, that's about 1,000 weeks; if you're 30, about 1,500 weeks; if you're 40, about 2,000 weeks; and so on. Imagine if for every one of those weeks you had received the gift of an entire sea of people reflecting back to you the notion "You are a sacred being, a reflection of divine love. We see you. We love you." Whoa! Imagine that kind of honor and reverence seeping into your cells hundreds or thousands of times. Might you have then remembered you deserve respect? Might you have remembered your body is sacred? Might you have felt better supported and guided to make choices and have relationships that honored that sacredness? And empowered to end ones that didn't? You bet!

While we can't go back in time and change the past, and can't shrink our bodies so we can get in on the kid action happening in the fronts of these spiritual centers, you can in this moment make the choice to reclaim yourself as a sacred being who deserves to be both honored — body, mind, emotions, and spirit — and respected, showered in love. A being who, if she finds herself in circumstances where her sacredness is not reflected or respected, has no qualms about removing herself and finding circumstances where it is, period.

Reclaim Yourself as a Sacred Being

You want to be honored and respected, right? Of course! Who doesn't? Yet in how many situations or relationships throughout the course of your lifetime has someone disrespected or dishonored you? Trashed you? Verbally, emotionally, or physically assaulted you? Used you? Spewed their garbage all over you? Offended or discounted you? Treated your body, feelings, mind, or spirit as neither important nor worthy of honor?

Take a moment and count them out on your fingers right now. Did you use up all ten fingers yet? Unfortunately, most of us — having grown up in a world that as a general rule doesn't treat a lot of things as sacred, including beautiful divine imprints of love such as you — have long lists of ways in which we were not treated as sacred. Some likely happened way before you had the choice to remove yourself from the situation or relationship, and plenty came after you were of an age when you could have made a different choice. Many of these could have been avoided had you been taught to remember that you are sacred, had you been guided to keep your temple sacred in all ways and supported when you did so. And here's the piece I really want you to get: All those ways in which you didn't uphold your sacredness, those times that you didn't respect and honor yourself by the choices you made — you can forgive yourself for them right now. You were doing the best you could with what you knew. If you didn't have someone telling you just how sacred you were, how the heck were you supposed to know? So go ahead and forgive yourself; grab on to the self-compassion and self-forgiveness branch for some love. It's not your fault that you didn't know you are sacred. What's important from this moment forward is that now you do.

> You cannot receive from others what you are not willing to give to yourself. You must respect and honor yourself if you want others to honor and respect you too.

ME Moment How Are You Not Honoring or Respecting Yourself?

Take the self-love flashlight out and get up close with yourself to see what parts you may not be honoring and don't even know it. Following are common areas where we fail to honor ourselves and, as a result, enter into dishonoring situations and relationships. Answer all the questions with a yes or no to find where you most need to be reminded just how absolutely sacred *you* are. Then jump into the ME Art and Daring Act of Love that follow, and watch your self-love pulse rise, rise, rise!

Feelings

Do you do any of the following?

♥ Apologize for your feelings? Apologize for tearing up, crying, or otherwise being emotional?
♥ Ignore your feelings and stuff them down?
♥ Make fun of your feelings or brush them off, especially after you realize you've shared them in public or with someone else?

To how many of these questions did you answer yes? If one or more, your feelings need some R-E-S-P-E-C-T!

Spirit

Do you do any of the following?

♥ Have a daily and weekly practice that feeds your spirit? Do you talk to your spirit every day and know that you wouldn't leave home without connecting to your spirit?
♥ Value your spirit as much as you do your mind and body? Do you spend as much time, money, and energy on making sure your spirit is happy as you do on making sure your body is fit and your knowledge level is keen?
♥ Have meaning and purpose in your day-to-day life? Do you feel that what you spend your time, energy, and money on matters to both you and to the world, that you and your work are connected to something bigger?

To how many questions did you answer no? If one or more, your spirit needs some R-E-S-P-E-C-T!

Body

Do you do any of the following?

♥ Have sex with people who don't treat your body as sacred? Do you have sex when intoxicated, with people you don't have a sacred relationship with? Sex with people who are in relationships with other people who don't know about you? Sex with people you'd like to have a sacred, intimate relationship with but who are, you know deep down, really there only for the sex?

♥ Put trash into your body temple by filling your body with unhealthy foods, sugar, and sodas?

♥ Hate your body? Do you tell your body she's fat, ugly, unattractive, and worse?

To how many questions did you answer yes? If one or more, your body needs some R-E-S-P-E-C-T!

Mind

Do you do any of the following?

♥ Frequently think negative thoughts? That is, of the sixty thousand thoughts you have in a day, are a large percentage of them negative?

♥ Go to sleep with the computer and wake up with your phone or other digital device? Is your to-do list always turned on, and is your mind always turned on too?

♥   Call yourself stupid, get on yourself for not being smarter, or judge your performance harshly?

To how many questions did you answer yes? If one or more, your mind needs some R-E-S-P-E-C-T!

Which of these four parts do you need more R-E-S-P-E-C-T for — feelings, spirit, body, or mind? These are the parts of yourself that you are not currently honoring as much as is needed, as indicated by the yes and no answers you gave. Wherever one or more of your answers indicates that, yes, you do need more respect, the self-love medicine is sacred healing, and you are just the person to give it to yourself... with the help of some ME Art.

ME Art Create a Sacred Self-Love Altar for a Part of Yourself That Needs to Be Honored

Honoring the parts of you that need to remember their inherent sacredness is crucial. Your body, mind, spirit, and feelings are your temple, and it's time to pay homage and feel that honor in your veins. You can't think your way to honor; you have to feel it in your heart. An altar is the perfect way to focus on the part of you that needs your love, and you can supply it in whatever form that part of you needs most — reverence, reflection, recognition, respect, remembrance.

An altar is simply a space where you create something for yourself.

Its purpose is, first, to visually cue you to think about what you desire to create in your life. Second, it creates a physical space you can come to and sit in or near, a space apart from the crazy-making external world. And third, an altar is a place you come to in order to connect with yourself and with the divine. A place to pour love into yourself as well as plug into your communication channel. That's it. Simple, but powerful. It can be as elaborate or low-key as you want.

Mission:

To create an altar that you come to and receive love from yourself and from the divine.

How-to:

Step 1. Choose your intention.

What is this altar going to honor? Your mind, feelings, body, or spirit? Pick one or two. Focusing on one intention, or two at most, is recommended for maximum benefit. If you'd like to grow your honor and respect for yourself in all four areas, choose one for each month and change your altar on the new moon each month. New moons are the best time to clear the slate and start something new.

Step 2. Pick your place.

No place is too small to fit an altar, so don't worry if you're thinking you don't have the space for one. Nightstands, the tops of dressers, windowsills, folding tables, shoeboxes, and hatboxes will work just fine. It doesn't have to be private — as in, only you can see it — but if that's important to you, get a pretty cloth to put over it when you're not using it, or slide it under your bed or a bigger table.

Step 3. Make your self-love altar.

Do a short meditation in front of the space you have chosen. Close your eyes, put your hand on your heart, take a deep breath, and say to yourself what part of yourself this altar is for: "My body . . . my feelings . . ." And then ask that part of yourself, "What do you need in order to feel sacred?" Ask for images, colors, sounds, and pictures, and just notice what comes up. Write down all the information you receive from your Divine Downline, and then use it to build your altar. Great altar items include candles, rocks, photos, art, poems, crystals, special mementos, pretty cloths, aromatherapy scents, inspirational sayings, books, even stuffed animals. And, of course, continue to add to your altar as you go.

Step 4. Visit your personal altar daily.

Sit in front of this altar every day — make it the place you go before you look at your computer or phone, and the last thing you see every night, even if only for three minutes (set a timer if you need to). As you sit there, either close your eyes or keep them open, and repeat to yourself the Love Mantra:

"My *body* and *spirit* are sacred."

Keep saying the mantra over and over again, feeling the honor and sacredness seep into the parts of you that need to be respected and honored.

Add any other words as inspired to do so. And yes, at first this may feel awkward — just fake it 'til you feel it. If you keep coming to this sacred space, there will be a day that something inside you shifts. It always does.

For a video on creating your personal self-love altar, go to the Self-Love TV section on www.ChooseSelfLove.com.

Daring Act of Love
Say You're Sorry and Make a Sacred Vow to This Part of You

Chances are, you've done some damage to the parts of you that aren't feeling so sacred, even though you did the best you could at the time. In circumstances such as these, whether we are in a relationship with someone else or ourselves, the best policy is just to apologize. Take a trip to your altar and have a heart-to-heart with the part of you that you currently disrespect and dishonor, or have disrespected and dishonored in the past. Tell it from your heart — yes, just like you're talking to a person — how sorry you are and specifically why you are sorry. Just let the love rip. Then ask this part of you to forgive you. To receive the forgiveness, put your hand on your heart and feel yourself reconnect with yourself — just like when you make up with a friend or a romantic partner. End

by making a sacred vow to this sacred piece of you: "I promise to honor and respect you from this day forward, no matter what."

Stand Up for Your Sacredness — Require Respect in All Your Relationships

How would you like to be honored as the sacred being you are? Have the capacity to say "bugger off" to any relationship or situation that didn't honor or respect you? Have only loving, respectful relationships? And have these things because you hold yourself in such high regard? Everything starts with you, with your willingness to take a stand for yourself. Say those words out loud: "I take a stand for myself. I take a stand for myself. I take a stand for myself." Stand up and say them out loud again: "I take a stand for myself." And notice how taking a stand for yourself feels in your body. Notice your posture shifting as you move into respect for yourself.

It's like when certain people walk into a room and, all of a sudden, you notice that you and everyone else in the room is now sitting three inches taller. You've moved your body and energy into a position of attention. This person, whoever she or he is, commands respect — you can feel it. Sure, he or she may have a position that gives him or her a title, but without this person's ability to command respect, people wouldn't sit up like that. There is something inside him or her that knows he or she deserves respect, and so everyone

> You must take a stand for yourself and require respect in every relationship you have.

in the vicinity offers it. While you may not be walking into a room of hundreds or thousands of people who are going to sit three inches taller out of respect, you are in many relationships, and those relationships will either lift you up and help you soar, or push you down and keep you small.

Love Story: Trading Self-Respect to Get Love from a Boy

It wasn't until the age of thirty that I realized men were *supposed* to be nice to me. Three weeks into dating Noah, the man I am married to today, he said to me, "Christine, you can't like a guy just because he's nice to you. He's supposed to be nice to you." I can still remember cocking my head to the side and looking at him as if he had just told me he was the child of mutant ninja turtles. I, a smart, successful, educated woman, had never considered the notion that I should expect a man to be kind, gentle, and compassionate, let alone that I should make it a requirement for having a relationship of any kind with me, including romantic ones. Instead, I had come to expect men to be controlling, short-tempered, hypercritical, immature, and unpredictable, and so I allowed the men in my life to treat me that way.

In my professional life, my expectations for myself and others were very high. But when it came to what I'd accept in my personal relationships — especially the primary one (with my former fiancé) that I relied on for love — I set the bar very low. And I had a high tolerance for pain. I learned to turn the other cheek when my former fiancé hurled expletives at me that would make a sailor blush, or grabbed my wrist hard enough to hurt. I told myself it wasn't abuse because I didn't have black-and-blue marks on my skin, but in truth, he frequently battered my spirit and my feelings. We loved each other — dramatically and passionately — but there wasn't much sacred about the way either of us treated the other, except when we went too far or found ourselves in a short-lived truce.

When I looked around at my girlfriends, I saw the same low expectations and high tolerance of pain. What we all needed, but didn't have, was a very important permission slip with this piece of wisdom on it: "Respect and unconditional love are not upgrades; they are mandatory. If a person doesn't offer these to you, he or she doesn't deserve to be part of your life. No exceptions."·

I learned that the reason so many of us set the bar so low in our personal relationships, and have such a high threshold for pain, is this: unhealthy relationships indeed cause us massive pain, but the pain of feeling and dealing with our emotional wounds and fears — emotional holes, which I call "love cracks" — is way worse. So we cope by stuffing our emotional holes, which we often receive very early in life, with these unhealthy relationships. And then we just keep making them bigger by continuing on in the unhappy, disrespectful relationships and situations that dishonor us.

We settle for relationships that provide us with some kind of love — any kind of love will do. It doesn't matter if the love is tainted and has strings attached. We're happy to take a conditional or codependent relationship if we can squeeze any amount of love out, no matter how tainted. After years of living with gaping emotional holes and the dreadful feeling of loneliness, and of being unloved, unseen, and unsupported, we find that anything feels better than nothing. Like love-starved lunatics, we take whatever pain we must tolerate in order to get our fix of love, even if that means disrespecting and dishonoring ourselves in ways we'd never allow our children to accept. Remembering that we are sacred beings who deserve to be honored and respected sure would make for a much better experience!

Daring Act of Love
Demand Respect without Apology

Next time you have an interaction with a person who does not meet your requirement for respect and honor, take out your permission slip and recite these words from it: "Respect and unconditional love are not upgrades; they are mandatory!" Then add a personal piece: "So if you want to be in a relationship with me, I need you to respect and honor me." You may be shaking in your boots as you get these words out of your mouth, and likely the person you are saying them to will be shocked. But damn, you will be proud of yourself when you're finished. Nothing like standing up for yourself to get the heart racing, full of love for yourself.

Once, during a heated fight between my sister and me, I put the "Demand Respect without Apology" Daring Act of Love into action. My sister had decided to turn her mouth into a verbal gun to assault me with every expletive she could think of. Fresh back from some time spent at my self-love altar, and with my self-love vow, I looked her square in the eye and said, "I refuse to engage with you until you can be respectful." This was not my usual tactic — in the past I would have hurled expletives back at her, a talent I had developed to survive in my unhealthy relationships — but this time I put out a big dose of R-E-S-P-E-C-T. She was stunned speechless, and her jaw dropped to the floor. I stood my ground and then left the room. I was proud that I'd demanded respect, but even prouder of the choice I made at that moment: instead of attacking her back, I'd taken a stand as a person who also operated only with respect. Loving and respectful relationships had become the only acceptable kind of relationship in my life, and I knew the change had to start within me.

Reflect Your Sacredness: Respect and Honor Others

It's as simple as this: do unto others as you wish them to do unto you. Just as you can't expect to receive that which you don't give yourself, you can't expect to receive what you aren't willing or able to give to others. And just as you are a sacred being, so is every other soul on this planet. If others are willing to honor and respect you, you must be willing to honor and respect them in return. And sometimes you will need to be the one who takes the initiative and gives respect first.

This, of course, does not mean you become a doormat — queens do not become doormats. If you are in a relationship with a person who disrespects and dishonors you, then you must love yourself enough to end that relationship or distance yourself from it — no matter who this person is.

And this does mean you must give careful consideration to the words that come out of your mouth and the actions you take with other people. You might be surprised at how often you disrespect others in even small ways that matter. Today, engage in a Daring Act of Love and amp up your self-respect and self-honor by cleaning up your words and actions — temples don't allow trash and neither shall you.

Daring Act of Love
Give Up Gossip and Name-Calling...for Good!

Become impeccably respectful by speaking your words with love, honor, and respect. And engage in these two Daring Acts of Love: give up name-calling and swearing at others, and give up gossip — of all kinds. The first dare is self-explanatory. You are going to have to find new words to express yourself that don't include profanity or calling people names. Let's be explicit about the second, though, because you might be surprised at how much you do gossip. Gossiping is saying anything about someone else that you wouldn't say if she or he were in the room. And this includes people you know personally and those you don't. In the

"40-Day Inner Mean Girl Cleanse" we offer through the Inner Mean Girl Reform School, giving up gossip has proven to be one of the biggest challenges women face. But here's the truth: you dishonor yourself by gossiping about others, because it's a reflection of your disrespect for yourself. So go ahead, I dare you: give up gossip for a day or week to start; then you can make it a lifetime, and watch what happens!

Daring Act of Love
Proclaim Your Sacredness

As a last act to establish your sacredness, perform a powerful ritual with yourself in which you claim yourself as a sacred being. In the same way that you proclaimed your self-empowered self, claim your sacred self. Dress in your most sacred attire. Create sacred space. And engage in these two daring acts:

Feel your sacredness. **Find sacred music.** Write the words *I am sacred* on your body with lip liner. And dance for at least thirty minutes, feeling your body become a temple that is sacred, honored, respected, and revered.

See your sacredness. **Find a mirror.** Write on the mirror with lip liner: *I am sacred.* Look into the mirror for at least thirty minutes, seeing into your sacred soul — recognize her, remember her, reflect back to her the beauty and sacredness you see.

Love Mantra for Self-Respect and Self-Honor

I am sacred.
My body is sacred.
My feelings are sacred.
My mind is sacred.
My spirit is sacred.
I honor the sacred temple that is me.

CHAPTER 12

Self-Pleasure

Choosing to consistently create, receive, and experience joy, ensuring that your soul is fully fed and nourished.

Self-Love Pulse Check

SELF-LOVE
PULSE CHECK

Take your self-love pulse by rating each statement on a scale of one to five according to how true that statement is for you. Five indicates the statement is totally true, and one indicates that it is not at all true. Add up your first five ratings to get your LOVE # and the second set of five ratings to get your LACK #. Subtract your LACK # from your LOVE # to get your current self-pleasure pulse.

____ I feel happy more than unhappy. Even in moments of high stress or unhappiness, I can return to joy quickly.

____ I have a healthy balance of work and play. Even when I work hard, I don't go a day without doing something fun or pleasurable.

____ I feel joy-full and fulfilled. I am fulfilled on all levels, emotionally, mentally, spiritually, and physically.

____ I savor life. I stop often to smell the roses and enjoy life, no matter how busy I am.

____ I know when I need more play and pleasure, and I don't feel guilty about doing what I need to get it. Just like I get medicine to tend a cold, I get my pleasure medicine to tend my soul.

LOVE # _____

____ I feel unhappy and don't know why. I wake up unhappy or find myself going for days without smiling or laughing.

____ I play or give myself pleasure only after I have worked hard or finished my to-do list. I give myself permission to play and have pleasure only if I feel like I've earned it.

____ I try to get pleasure in quick spurts or by bingeing on it. I wait until I am starving for fun and joy, and then I overindulge — eat, drink, spend, or sleep too much.

____ I don't remember what I actually like to do for fun and pleasure, because it's been so long. I can't name more than a few things that I like to do for the sake of pure joy.

____ I am too busy to enjoy the small pleasures. I am so consumed by my to-do list or work-load that I don't take time to slow down, and do things like notice beauty, connect with nature, spend a day in bed reading a nonwork book, or savor my food.

LACK # _____

Now, subtract your LACK # from your LOVE # to get your full self-love pulse for this branch.

My Self-Pleasure Pulse ____

Play, pleasure, and fun — when was the last time those made the top three of your to-do list on any given day? Superwoman doesn't have time for such things! You've got work to do, people to take care of, and fires to put out. When was the last time you saw Superwoman out on the golf course, curled up reading for an entire day, or hanging out at the farmers' market squeezing tomatoes? Or saw her hang up her cape for the day to eat a delectable meal, soak in a lavender bath, or have a private dance party in her living room? Not recently, if ever. And for Superwoman, that's just fine; she didn't come to this planet to soak in the sun, delight in the tastes and sounds, or appreciate the massive beauty. She came here to work and to save people. You, on the other hand, came to this planet to enjoy yourself. Notice that word — *en-joy*. You came here to live in joy! Sure, you have work to do, people to assist, an impact to make, and all that, but one of the core reasons your soul came to this planet was to have a good time and to soak in this wonder-filled world. Didn't you get the memo? It reads:

> Make sure you remember to fill up on joy daily, or your soul will shrivel up and starve. Pleasure shall be one of your top priorities while you live on planet Earth.

Oh, right, that didn't make it into the Self-Esteem or Self-Sacrifice Handbooks. *Pleasure* is like a foreign word to many of us, one whose meaning and actuality continually elude us. When thinking about self-pleasure, most of us don't get beyond the ideas of sex and masturbation. Let's translate. Yes, masturbation is one aspect of self-pleasure, but defining self-pleasure as masturbation is like saying Disneyland is only the tea-cup ride. Sure, it's a great ride, but there are way more attractions and magical experiences to be had. Self-pleasure includes any act or experience you engage in that creates joy for you. This could be as simple as smelling a flower, as fabulous as taking yourself to your favorite restaurant and savoring every bite of your meal, and as silly as skipping down the street with your friend just because it makes you smile.

It's happy medicine, a prescription for pleasure — and there isn't anything wrong with that, right? Yet saying out loud, "I am going to pleasure myself," or, "I am going to get pleasure for myself!" feels almost shameful, as if you should definitely feel guilty or keep it to yourself. Try saying the words out loud. Weird, right? You can thank the Self-Sacrifice Handbook, which taught us to feel guilty for putting our happiness first or doing nice things for ourselves, and the Self-Esteem Handbook for teaching us to pursue happiness rather than create joy. Really, I don't know about you, but I'd much rather *experience* joy than *pursue* happiness — nothing pleasurable about the pursuit, and frankly, it's exhausting.

Let's write a new chapter, shall we, and correct this translation once and for all? Say these words out loud:

> "I take a stand for making my happiness and my quality of life a top priority."
> "I choose to create pleasure every day for myself. I make sure I experience joy every day regardless of what there is to do or to take care of."

You'd never hear a seven-year-old say, "Nope, sorry, I can't go to Disneyland. I have to clean my room." The seven-year-old has no problem with choosing fun and play, or making her happiness a priority, even when there is work to do. And you won't either, once your self-pleasure branch starts to grow again. Today you give yourself a giant lifetime permission slip to get the love you need through the pleasure that comes from creating and experiencing joy, beauty, and all that makes you feel alive.

> Your soul needs pleasure to survive. Just as your body needs breath, your soul needs to experience joy each day.

Your soul is counting on you to love it so much that you will do whatever it takes to make sure your "pleasure center" stays full. No guilt, no excuses, and no exceptions. Just as you feed yourself food to keep your body full of energy, you must find pleasure even on your busiest days. When your pleasure center is full, it has food to feed your self-love tree. When it's depleted or bankrupt, you suffer and you feel less loved and cared for. When your immune system gets run down, you go to the store to get yourself nutrients to amp it back up. When your pleasure center is running low, stop, take a pleasure-power pause, and get yourself some joy, beauty, or play, pronto! In the same way that you must make exercise a priority every day to keep your body healthy, you must also make pleasure an everyday priority to keep your soul happy.

I'm going to show you how, but first a love story.

Love Story: I'm Taking My Happy Back!

I remember the day that I realized my soul was starving. Even though I was living my passion, doing great work in the world, meeting a lot of my goals, and making enough money to get by, I found myself at the tail end of a three-week busy binge with little room for pleasure and play, leaving me, in one word, crabby. It had gotten to the point where my assistant would come in and ask me first thing, "Christine, how are you feeling today?" just to gauge how best to navigate the day (and me) and how close she was going to stick by (or not). And I couldn't blame her. I felt that way about me too. Problem was, I couldn't get away from myself! So I held an honesty hearing with myself. My first question was simply "Christine, what is going on with you?" And instantly I realized that I was unhappy, really unhappy, and had been for weeks. My reply was "What? I am one of the happiest people I know. How could this be?" My Inner Wisdom shot back: "Because your soul is starving. You have been so busy giving, so busy working, so consumed with being a joy for others that you've forgotten to experience joy for yourself."

Whoa! In that moment it was as if I could feel a hole inside me. I was empty, starving for nourishment — my pleasure center was empty of joy. So empty, in fact, that in that moment I couldn't even remember what actually brought me joy. And that is when I knew I needed a radical intervention — a Daring Act of Love.

I invited my seven-year-old self to join me on this adventure, and with a handful of markers and a piece of blank paper we began to create my Joy Portrait, a picture of everything — no matter how silly, simple, or seemingly insignificant — that brought me joy. About forty-five minutes later, we had a full portrait. I remember sitting there staring at the words and pictures for some time. For the first time in a long while, I was able to see that I had pushed a lot of pleasure out of my life because my life was so full of the things I was doing, giving, and trying to achieve. They were good things but things that had shoved my work-and-play equation out of balance. I had almost completely stopped spending my time and energy on the "optional" activities — the ones that delivered only plea-sure, not profit or productivity — including things like dancing, taking a day to read an entire book, spontaneous evenings with friends, monthly craniosacral massages, Thursday-night dates with myself, reading *Sunset* magazine, and eating blueberry pancakes on Sunday mornings with Noah (really, he makes the best pancakes!).

The realization of how little pleasure I had afforded myself, and of how starved my soul was for joy, was definitely a "self-pleasure epiphany."

I took immediate action by applying love to this branch that was in such dire need. I made a self-love promise that, no matter how much I worked or how busy I was, I would create space for pleasure every day. I would make nourishing my soul as important as fulfilling my destiny, because the truth was, if my soul wasn't full, wasn't well taken care of, then no matter how hard I worked I would never have the impact I desired on the world and those closest to me. I'd be too burnt out. Without the cooling and peaceful energy of joy, my passion for helping others was like an out-of-control forest fire. My soul needed both; my body and mind needed both.

I made this promise on February 13, the international day of self-love, and promised to make the self-pleasure branch my #1 self-love focus to nourish and grow for the entire year. As soon as I set that intention, mira-cles started to occur. Over the previous three years, I'd had a goal to start tap dancing lessons and dance with Noah on a regular basis. I had put it on a vision board and written it down as a goal, but had never been able to materialize it. Not until I made this promise. Within a month, I took my first tap dance class in twenty years — and did my pleasure center ever ignite! I began tripping the light fantastic with Noah at least twice a month, igniting more pleasure in our relationship and in my own. And that inspired an impromptu family dance-off involving an Xbox, Donna Summer, and dance moves to rival Michael Jackson's (well, maybe)!

How Do You Keep Your Pleasure Center Full?

What gives *you* the most pleasure is unique to you and your soul, and there are two major sources you can turn to in order to find what fills you up — one, that which brings you joy, and two, that which brings beauty and love to you through your senses. Get familiar with these two sources by engaging in the following three self-love adventures: the ME Art exercise, ME Moment, and Daring Act of Love. All of these are designed to open you up to receiving more and more pleasure — joy, creativity, beauty, fun, play — than you ever imagined! Your mission is to use them to discover more about yourself and, through those discoveries, find new answers and insights that liberate you to let the pleasure in. Oh, yeah!

Pleasure Source #1. Make Joy for Yourself!

Joy can be created out of thin air without having to run up your credit card bill, get on a plane, or make an appointment, if you know where to look. What makes you happy? Such a simple question, but when was the last time you stopped to ask yourself that? Sure, you might ask yourself questions each year like "What do I want to accomplish?" or "What are my goals?" or even "What are my dreams?" But are you certain that your choices, the pursuit of your goals and dreams, and the way you spend your time are all making your life more pleasurable? More joy-full?

✏ ME Art Create Your Joy Portrait

Supplies:

- ♥ A piece of paper
- ♥ Color-infused, joy-generating writing utensils
- ♥ Optional: Get and print out the "My Joy Portrait" Loveplate at www.ChooseSelfLove.com

Mission:

Claim your bliss by creating a physical portrait of what really brings you joy, so that you can see it, remember it, and feel it. Then make the commitment to go out and create joy for yourself — every day.

How-to:

Step 1. Put joy back on your map.

In the middle of the paper, write the word *Joy* in a big, bold, happy way. Underneath the word *Joy*, write, "What brings me joy?"

Step 2. Tap into your joy.

To get your joy motor moving (it may have been sitting quiet for a while), close your eyes, put your hand on your heart, and take a few deep breaths. As you take each breath, feel yourself going back in time to different points in your life when you can remember experiencing great joy, bliss, and happiness. Almost as if you're watching a movie playing in your head, see yourself in these moments, feel yourself in these moments, and remember what joy felt like for you. If you need additional help accessing your joy center, go to www.SelfLoveMeditations.com and get the self-pleasure meditation.

Step 3. Fill up with joy.

Take what you've seen about your joy moments, and what your soul already knows about following your bliss, and fill your entire page — your personal Joy Portrait — with everything that brings you joy. Use words, phrases, and symbols. Make this page joy-*full*. Use the following joy starters to find your bliss. You don't have to write the entire sentences on your portrait, just the words that reflect the actual action, activity, experience, energy, circumstance, or feeling that brings you joy.

♥ "I am happiest when..."
♥ "I feel most alive when..."
♥ "I feel most free when..."
♥ "I can't help but smile and laugh when I..."
♥ "When I was a little girl, I loved to..."
♥ "My soul gets nourished when..."
♥ "I feel most cared for when..."
♥ "I just love..."
♥ "I find great joy in..."

> When you en-joy your life, you live in joy. When you live in joy, you enjoy your life.

Step 4. Ask your soul what it needs...and make sure it receives it.

Once the page is full, completely full, stop for a heart-to-heart with yourself. Take a good heartfelt look at this reflection of your joy that you have created. And tell yourself the truth in response to these four questions:

♥   What do I see and notice?

♥   How is my life in alignment with my joy?

♥   How is my life out of alignment with my joy?

♥   What's one way I can redirect my life now to attune it to joy and get what my soul needs to thrive?

As a completion ritual, write the words *I attune to joy* on your Joy Portrait, and make a self-love promise to attune your life to what brings you joy.

ME Moment What's Blocking You from Giving Yourself Joy?

What beliefs or habits do you have that keep you from giving yourself joy and experiencing pleasure?

1. What beliefs and opinions about play, fun, work, and duty did you learn from your family of origin, religious or educational institutions, or community while growing up? Examples:

    You have to finish your work before you can play.
    You don't have time for play; there is too much to do.
    Just buckle down and get the job done (there's no time for fun).

2. What beliefs and opinions about spending money or time on things that bring you joy or pleasure did you learn from your family of origin, religious or educational institutions, or community? Examples:

You don't have enough money to waste it on <<insert thing>>.
Don't spend your money on frivolous things. Be practical.
Don't waste your time on <<insert thing>>.

Look at your inventory of beliefs and opinions and decide which of these aren't actually yours or no longer serve you. Get your mind to recognize that pleasure is good, and pleasure is a priority, by removing the mental blocks that keep you from letting pleasure in. Take one or both of the following actions to remove these blocks and open up the way for more joy:

Belief release. Write the blocking beliefs and opinions down on a piece of paper and then rip the paper up, saying out loud, "I release these blocks that prevent me from receiving joy. I deserve to have joy and experience pleasure just because I am alive. My soul needs joy and pleasure to survive."

Belief rewiring. For each block, create a joy flash card by writing a joy-creating or pleasure-inducing statement on an index card, one that reflects the opposite of the joy-blocking belief. Then every morning for forty days, as soon as you wake up, run through the flash cards. Each night before you go to sleep, do the same. In no time, you will rewire yourself to be a joy-creating powerhouse!

Daring Act of Love
Check on Your Joy Center and Keep It Joy-Full

For seven days, take a pulse check of your soul every morning when you wake up. Ask it, "How joy-full am I feeling?" and rate your joy level on a scale of one to five, with five meaning you feel full. If your level is anything less than a four, look at your Joy Portrait and find one way you can create joy for yourself that day. Do it, without fail. Check in with yourself that evening to see if your joy meter jumped. Keep creating joy for yourself until you're filled.

Pleasure Source #2. Experience Each Day through Your Senses

As a culture, we have been indoctrinated to live through our minds. Like human thinking machines, we tend to process most of our experiences as thoughts, which then inform our experiences, rather than through the powerful pleasure-seeking devices — our five senses — that we've been gifted with. No wonder we are so pleasure starved! Thinking your way to pleasure is a weak substitute for experiencing pleasure through your senses. It's the difference between sitting at your desk and thinking about a rose, and walking in a garden and stopping to smell the rose.

You could close your eyes and imagine the flower as best you can, but without *sensual* stimuli, the best you are going to get is a pretty picture and a small blip in your pleasure center. But look at a picture of a flower, and your visual sense center awakens, and so does your pleasure. Find a real flower that you can get up close to, smell, and touch, and this beautiful being will activate at least three of your senses and jolt your pleasure meter big time. Add romantic music and a partner gently caressing and kissing your arm with the flower, and hang on for a geyser of pleasure — four sensual centers activated!

Your senses love receiving the energy of beauty and love. Food made with love. Beautiful fabric. Beautiful scents. Loving touch. Breathtaking scenery. Beauty and love are like miracle fertilizer for your branch of self-pleasure. When your senses find and take in the energy of beauty or love, you have a *sensual* experience — one that awakens your senses and, as a result, creates pleasure for you. This is the nature of *sensuality* — a must-have for any woman with a blooming self-pleasure branch and, unfortunately, another misunderstood word in our culture. For many years sensuality has been associated mainly with sex. But you can have a sensual experience right in the middle of your office cubicle, standing in line at the grocery store, or walking down the street, which is exactly how this planet and you were meant to interact. You were built to be a pleasure-making, pleasure-receiving being, having sensual experiences — to evoke pleasure — simply by opening up your senses and experiencing the simplest objects and acts through them.

Think of it this way: The great creator in the sky could have designed your divine human imprint to plug into an outlet to refuel, not to have the experience of tasting yummy food that delights your senses and produces pleasure. Your vision could

> Fill your soul with joy, beauty, and love every day, and your soul will smile.

have been designed simply to keep you from bumping into things, not to enable you to see and experience beauty and love. Your ability to smell could have been created just to alert you to danger (as a smoke alarm does), not to allow you to inhale aromas that titillate you and open you up to receive beauty and love. Thank goodness that wasn't the model! Instead, you came equipped with five vibrant, pleasure-seeking devices ready to fill your pleasure center to the max. The question is, are they turned on and working?

ME Moment *Are Your Senses Working for Your Self-Pleasure?*

Are you living a sensual life? Are you touching, tasting, hearing, seeing, and smelling your way through life? Are you experiencing the pleasure of the sounds, tastes, touch, sights, and aromas that you came to this planet for? Or have you dulled your senses and ceded control to your mind, missing all the pleasure that surrounds you, just waiting for you to grab it, because you've become a thinking machine instead of a feeling and sensing being?

The only way to know for sure is to go out into the world with your senses and see what happens. You can't talk to your senses from inside your head — you have to be with them in an experience.

Daring Act of Love
Live through Your Senses for Five Full Days

For the next five days, give your thought-producing mind machine a rest by making it the copilot and handing over to your senses the keys to how you orient and experience your life. Focus on one sense each day. Each morning before you get out of bed, activate one sense and invite it to take charge for the day. Your mission is to experience your entire day primarily through that sense, following its lead and giving it your attention and affection all day long. Imagine you and this sense are having a superintimate all-day date and you want to be as close and attentive as you can. Before you go to sleep the night before, decide which sense you will hang with the following day, so you'll know who you are waking up with. Use this three-part self-love daily practice to guide you:

AM wake-up: Start your day with one sense. First thing when you awaken, open your eyes, close your eyes, and connect with that sense. If it's hearing, then listen. If it's taste, move your tongue around; lick your lips. If it's sight, look around your room and notice in a new way what you see. Be in this sensual experience for at least three minutes.

All day: Savor and acknowledge that sense and the pleasure it provides. As if you were seeing, tasting, hearing, touching, or smelling for the first time — like an alien who has just arrived on this planet, and who is going to leave the next day and so wants to experience as much as she can — amp up your awareness and appreciation of everything this sense can bring you. Savor moments by slowing down, paying attention, and noticing things you probably took for granted before. For example:

♥   For taste, engage in no other activities while eating — no talking, watching TV, or reading. Chew each bite slowly. Notice the texture and flavor of the food. Sip your drinks. Let everything sit in your mouth longer than usual. As you eat or drink, love the food that you are bringing into your body, and thank your taste buds for allowing you to have such a beautiful experience.

♥ For sight, see everything as if for the first time — notice the colors, forms, and interactions in your surroundings that you might have taken for granted or missed altogether. Watch people, notice intricacies, take in color, see beauty. Acknowledge what you are seeing, and appreciate your eyes for allowing you to see it.

♥ For sound, hear everything as if your life depended on it, as if it were your go-to sense (like that of a blind person). As you hear the sound, notice the thoughts it creates or the feelings it stirs up. Listen more carefully as people talk, as if you were hanging on their every word. Appreciate the sounds you like, and notice the sounds you don't. Appreciate that you don't have to lip-read. Try different volumes of music and different kinds of music, and again, notice your feelings. Thank your ears for doing such a great job of hearing for you.

♥ For touch, notice everything that your body comes in contact with — from the sheets you wake up on, to the toothbrush against your teeth, to the clothes on your body, to the chair you sit in, to the human touch you receive. Stop to touch things, rub things, caress things, and notice your reaction. Appreciate the beautiful things you can touch, and thank your hands for touching for you.

♥ For smell, breathe a lot, from the moment you arise and all day long, and take in at a cellular level the aromas you smell. Set the timer on your phone to go off once an hour to remind you to breathe deeply, and then smell what is in the air. Activate your sniffer all day long when you can remember to. Take the opportunity to smell all kinds of things — food, flowers, clothes, heck, even another person. Savor aromas that make you feel good. Appreciate your sniffer for bringing in beautiful-smelling things and for warning you about ones that aren't.

PM bedtime: Go to bed with your sense. Take one last excursion with your sense as you get ready for bed. How would this sense want to experience going to sleep? Make your choices for your nighttime ritual and sleep accordingly — from the pj's to the room to your bed to what you do in the hour before bedtime to what goes into bed with you. Then, once you are all cuddled up together, and your sense is feeling superappreciated and the level of your pleasure meter is sky-high, have a nice, intimate dialogue. Ask yourself:

♥ What did we experience today?
♥ What did we notice today that normally I don't?
♥ What can I remember about today and then take into my everyday experiences?

Love Mantra for Self-Pleasure

I fill up with joy.
I fill up my senses.
I feel full of pleasure.
I love savoring life.

CHAPTER 13

Self-Expression

The choice to let the world see you, fully, truthfully, and without apology or holding back. Full, free expression of your heart and soul.

Self-Love Pulse Check

SELF-LOVE
PULSE CHECK

Take your self-love pulse by rating each statement on a scale of one to five according to how true that statement is for you. Five indicates the statement is totally true, and one indicates that it is not at all true. Add up your first five ratings to get your LOVE # and the second set of five ratings to get your LACK #. Subtract your LACK # from your LOVE # to get your current self-expression pulse.

____ I openly express myself in all parts of my life. I am myself whether I'm at work or with my friends or family.

____ I express my thoughts, feelings, and gifts fully and freely, even when this makes others uncomfortable. I shine brightly without shrinking back.

____ I feel seen for who I really am. Many people know and see the real me.

____ I bring my unique flair to everything I do. I am myself, even if that means I do things differently from everyone else. I don't need to blend in.

____ I feel like I am living full out, in full color. I am truly living a life that reflects who I am. I feel alive and my life feels vibrant.

LOVE # _____

____ I shrink back, hold back, and suppress my thoughts, feelings, and gifts. I want to express myself or offer my gifts, but at times I don't.

____ I feel like I am living someone else's life or like my life is only half-lived. I go through the motions of life rather than living my life fully.

____ I admire creative people, but I don't consider myself creative. I admire other people who can fully and freely express themselves, but that's not possible for me.

____ I hide or change parts of myself to fit into the situation or relationship. I am afraid of what others will think, so I let external influences dictate how I express myself.

____ I keep myself protected and don't let others see the real me. Some people see some parts of me, but I do not make myself vulnerable and let people see who I really am.

LACK # _____

Now, subtract your LACK # from your LOVE # to get your full self-love pulse for this branch.

My Self-Expression Pulse ____

We all want to be seen for who we truly are. Every single person on this planet wants more than anything else to be seen and loved, but most of us do the exact opposite of what is required to be seen. Instead of stepping forward boldly, saying to the world, "This is me, hear me roar, see me shine, watch me dance, feel my passion," we shrink back, hold back, and hide behind masks. Because it feels safer, we keep our magnificence and true beauty hidden or tamped down. But safer is not better in this situation, as self-expression isn't about feeling comfortable with how others see you; it's about your willingness to step forward and stand naked on the stage of life and let others see your heart and soul, regardless of what they perceive. For in your truest and fullest expression, you are safe because you are protected by the pure and powerful love that comes from expressing your spirit.

> Are you willing to let others see your heart and soul?

Consider this. You have been invited to perform on the most magnificent stage, where there are red curtains, wood floors, and a big audience. As you walk out from behind the curtain, the room goes silent, all eyes on you. Every person is there to see you express yourself so fully that each one leaves that room tremendously affected by your presence. The crowd is dark, the spotlight is on you, and you know this is your moment to step forward and shine. What do you do? Do you step out and give it all you've got, sing the song in your soul, and be as bright as you can? Or do you freeze and shrink back into the darkness? Or do you grab a mask from behind the podium and give a good performance but never let us see the real you?

Your self-expression branch thrives on your ability to be vulnerable (that is, your ability to let others see the truth of who you are) and on your willingness to express yourself fully, freely, and for real — regardless of whether that fits with the program, and regardless of what any critic has to say. The degree to which you can be vulnerable, express yourself fully and freely, and be your most real self will determine how fulfilled and free you feel inside and how vibrant you are.

You see, *you* have a unique way about you that must be expressed. You have opinions and beliefs that must be spoken. Your body moves in a special manner and must be free to dance her unique patterns and expressions. Your spirit, which when fully expressed can make the room come alive like no other, must be free to express itself authentically in all areas of your life. Your heart has gifts that will make this world a better place, gifts that must be offered and received. Your unique human imprint and your special divine soul came here to express something, and unless you're expressing yourself freely, fully, and for real, you won't be seen or feel seen. And when you don't feel seen, you feel sad, depressed, frustrated, angry, hopeless, and more. You feel sick — mentally, emotionally, and physically. Withholding the truth of who you are is like bottling up your essence and holding it captive. Your soul will feel as if it's dying to get out.

Set Your Soul Free...Express and Embody Your Essence

We spend a lot of time in our culture talking about knowing our qualities, strengths, and traits. While these are important to know because they give us insight into who we are, we can't fully know or be who we are if we see ourselves only through mental and emotional constructs; we must also deeply know and express ourselves spiritually. Self-love is not a mental exercise; it is a spiritual journey. In order to experience the levels of love, joy, and peace that you came here to experience, you must go deeper — into the spiritual realm — to find them. To ensure that your self-expression branch really thrives and feels alive, this means discovering and embodying the *essence* of who you truly are, and then expressing that essence freely and fully, without holding back, without apology, without trying to be or emulate someone else. That is where the magic happens, the love happens — where *you* happen!

Henry Kimsey-House, cofounder of Coaches Training Institute and a genius at self-expression, summed it up for me with this story about the power of expressing yourself from your essence, and the struggle that happens when you don't. Henry coached actors for many years, and during that time he uncovered a fascinating difference between the actors who got booked often and the actors who didn't. Those who auditioned by playing the part as the person they thought they needed to be, instead of basing their characters on the essence of who they naturally were, were significantly less successful. They were trying to be something other than who they were in order to get the part. But the actors who embraced their natural energy and used their essence to energize the role won parts again and again. They didn't try to fit into roles but instead expressed their true selves fully; and in doing so they affected their audiences so much that the actors got the parts they sought.

You can tell when you are expressing your essence by how you feel inside — you feel alive and unencumbered, even if what you are expressing isn't happiness and sunshine. Because you are aligned with your truth, you feel free. When you feel compelled to jump to your feet and give a standing ovation at a performance, or when you watch a performance and begin to feel your heart swell inside you or tears well up, or when your brain goes quiet and you become absorbed in the experience, it's because you have been touched by the essence of the person or people you are witnessing. You are seeing and feeling their essence, and this stirs you. You too have the ability to do this just by choosing to express your essence.

Finding and claiming your unique essence is a powerful process of finding phrases or combinations of words that reflect, emanate from, or hold the energy of your natural self-expression. When you say these words out loud, you can literally feel their truth ring throughout your body. And as you share them with others, their heads nod *yes*! Essence differs from gifts, in that gifts can be used or not, but essence, while it may be tamped down, still seeps out no matter what, and people notice because they can feel it.

> Your essence is who you are in the core of your soul.

You can find your essence in many ways — some are simple, and some are daring. To start, you can look back at your gifts that you found in the chapter on self-esteem and locate words that *describe* you at an energetic level or a feeling level, as in: "This is how I naturally *express* myself." My own title, inspirational catalyst, was born from this process. I have the gift of inspiring people — even if we are just out for a cheeseburger. I'd go to lunch with people, and often they would say to me, "Christine, I go out to have a meal with you, and I leave inspired to make changes and be the best and happiest me that I can be." Amy Ahlers, my partner at Inner Mean Girl Reform School, took a bold approach to discovering her essences. She went to an airport with a friend and put on different outfits — first a professional suit, then a jogging suit, then a clown nose and a brightly colored outfit, and then several others. As Amy donned each of these different outfits, her friend was standing nearby handing out clipboards with pages covered with lots of different words. Her friend asked people to circle the words that best described Amy. No matter what she wore — sweats or a business suit or something else — she received the same responses: things like *Sunshine. Bright. Morning. Dawn.* This led her to the title "wake-up-call coach."

Your essence is part of you. You can't change it. You can dim it and try to hide it, you may bury it underneath layers of repression, but it's much better to just accept it and go with it. When you freely express your essence, you feel happier because you are freely being you. There is happiness and fulfillment in liberation. People more often reach out to meet you, and because they can feel your authenticity, they have the experience of seeing you.

ME Moment *Who Do You See Yourself As?*

Samantha Bennett, poet, creativity and productivity expert, and founder of the Organized Artist Company, has a gift for seeing and uncovering people's essences. She says that one of the best popcorn trails to follow if we want to uncover our essence and our desire for self-expression is to take a close look at the people we admire. The people we are infatuated with, find intriguing, and wish we could be like, and who resonate with us are actually activating something inside us — our essence — that isn't yet being expressed, at least not at the level we would like or that we need in order to feel seen. For example, if you love Madonna, one or more of your essences may, like hers, be sensual, eccentric, power-diva-tastic. If you have always felt inspired by someone like Amelia Earhart, your essence may include adventurousness, independence, and rule- and barrier-breaking. We each have an essence that is composed of multiple "essences" that reflect different parts of our spirit. As a self-loving woman, your mission is to uncover your unique blend of essences that make up the complete essence of you!

What follows is a self-discovery exercise that Samantha developed, and which I've used with many of my clients and students — as well as with myself — called "Sheroes and Heroes." Follow these four steps and complete your "My Sheroes and Heroes" Loveplate on the next page:

1. In each row of the "name" column, write in the name of a person, living or dead. Choose the names of people you resonate with, admire, or are intrigued by, and who fit into the categories listed in the far left column. You can choose more than one person for each category. Fill out only the "name" column in this step.

2. After you have filled in the entire "name" column, fill in the spaces in the "quality" column. For each name, list all the words you can think of that describe this person. Let your ideas flow, and write whatever comes up. Write as many words as you can. Fill in the entire "quality" column with these words.

3. Once you complete the "quality" column, go back through the words listed and circle the ones that best describe you too. It doesn't matter if you express these qualities in your life yet or not. As you read through the list, you will recognize the ones that resonate with you the most. Follow your Inner Wisdom on this one. If some of the words feel a little daring or bold, great! Circle them. Chances are this is a piece of you dying to be expressed.

My Sheroes and Heroes

SHERO OR HERO FROM:	NAME	QUALITY
Your own field of work		
Literature (list an author of fiction or nonfiction)		
Business		
Fashion		
Television		
Films		
Cartoons		
Books (list a fictional character)		
Music		
Politics		
Cooking or another food-related field		
Ancient history		
Sports		
Myths or children's stories		
Other		

4.   For your last step, grab a clean piece of paper and write down all the words you circled. If other words or phrases come to you, include them too. The goal is to have a sheet of paper listing a bunch of essences that resonate for you, as you. These words and phrases are the expressions of your essences, which, in the next Daring Act of Love, you are going to turn on and try on.

Daring Act of Love
Come Out of the Closet...Express Yourself!

From your essence list, choose four words or phrases that reflect your essence. You can group the similar words and phrases together to create really juicy essence buckets. Just make sure there is variety among the four sets of words. Then, each day for four days, perhaps from Monday to Thursday, dress to express one essence of yourself. Find the appropriate clothes in your closet — or a girlfriend's, if needed — that really express this part of you. Or head to a vintage store to pick up a few clothing options that really hold the energy of this essence. Dare to be bold in your choices; even go a little over the edge. Think color, fabric, style, accessories. If the essence is sunshine, you might pick a bright yellow or orange dress. If you were to get even bolder, you'd find a matching hat and perhaps a handbag with flowers on it.

When your exterior is aligned with your chosen essence, it's easier to express that essence. Your job is to be that essence in your most authentic way. Play with amping it up and turning it down. The next day, switch to the next essence, and after that another, until you have completed four days of trying on different parts of yourself and showing them off to the world. Each day, notice how you feel, and notice how the world around you reacts. Think about what keeps you from taking this piece of yourself out of the closet more often, and imagine what would be possible if you did.

ME Moment *See Your Heart and Soul*

Your heart and soul came into this life programmed with all of the information that expresses who you truly are — kind of like heart-and-soul-essence DNA. This essence DNA doesn't change as you get older, but it often gets corroded by all the influences that make you feel afraid to express yourself or let yourself be seen. The good news is that you can always find your way back to your essence, that place of pure love that you started this life with, when you had no doubt about who you were and no qualms about expressing her, regardless of what others had to say.

When you go back to that source of pure love today, you can reconnect to parts of yourself that you have forgotten or have put away for safekeeping. You will remember what you love, not because of who you are supposed to be or what you should be doing, but because this is who you are at the core of your soul. You will remember what makes you come alive, regardless of what others may think, and begin to find your way back to being unafraid and unapologetic about letting this aliveness course through your veins and express itself in whatever way fits you. Reconnected, you can stop living as a fraction of yourself and start expressing the whole, beautiful, fabulous you! With your heart and soul free, you'll find your way to levels of happiness and love you probably knew were possible, but could never get access to, because the access point was inside you.

Take a best-friend moment and ask yourself the following essence-revealing questions. Close your eyes and see yourself on a stage, sharing the truth of who you are with the audience. As if you were opening up a window to your soul to allow us to see into who you really are, say these essence-statement starters out loud to express yourself:

♥ "Ever since I was a little girl, I've just loved to..."
♥ "You can always count on me to..."
♥ "I am happiest when I am just..."

Write the answers in your journal, and take several minutes just to soak them in. Say these things into a recorder, and then play them back for yourself to hear. Let this ME Moment be a time for you to soak in your heart and soul — the essence of the divine imprint of love that you have always been. For a full guided meditation, visit www.SelfLoveMeditation.com.

ME Art Make a ME Print: See Yourself and Let Yourself Be Seen

It's time to play! I have used this self-love adventure with women of all ages and types (and men too), and the results are profound. Put away your brain, open up your heart, and dive into a creative love bubble that is all about you seeing you!

Supplies:
♥ Full-body-size sheet of butcher paper (from any art store or office supply store). Choose one thick enough to glue magazine clippings to and long and wide enough to fit your entire body on.
♥ Magazines. Collect ten or so magazines with pictures and words. Choose a variety — a few healthy-living, self-empowerment, or travel magazines, or others like that. Stay away from trashy tabloid magazines; you don't want that essence in your ME Print.

♥   Scissors
♥   Glue stick
♥   Marker, for tracing your body outline
♥   Two hours. This is a powerful and fun experience, and to do it really
      well, give yourself at least 120 minutes.
♥   Helper to trace your body on the paper. Or better yet, a friend who
      wants to make a ME Print too! You could do this exercise on your
      own, but it's more powerful if you make a date with a friend to do it
      with you. If you can't find someone, no worries. Just trace yourself
      and be your own b.f.f. for the day.

Mission:

Create a personal collage of yourself — a.k.a. a ME Print — using,
of course, your own body. This collage will reflect the essence of who you
are — all of you! And then, after you're done, you'll put this silhouette up
in your home and notice what you see. If you're really daring, you will let
yourself be seen by others; you'll invite them to come over and tell you
what they see in your ME Print.

How-to:

Step 1. Create your space.

Gather all the materials, put some music on, and lay your piece of
butcher paper out on the ground.

Step 2. Lie down on the paper, strike a pose, and trace your body.

Find the pose that most feels like your truest expression. Ask your helper
to take a marker and trace your body on the paper, or do it on your own.

Step 3. Find the pictures and words that express your essence.

Spend about forty-five minutes to an hour ripping out pictures and words from magazines that fit who you really are (and are growing into). Setting a time limit works well, because otherwise you can be here for hours. The challenge is not to think, not to do it perfectly, but to follow your intuition about what images to pull and where to put them. As you cut the pictures out, use the glue stick to paste the images inside the silhouette, wherever you feel they should be placed. Again, no linear thinking allowed. Just go with the flow. For the most effective flow, do the parts of this step in this order:

♥ Go through the magazines and tear out the photos and words that resonate with you.
♥ Cut the photos or words into the shapes you want.
♥ Paste them into your silhouette.
♥ Add your name or any other words or images you want on your ME Print.

Step 4. Cut out your silhouette and put it up where you can see it.

Tape it to the wall, attach it to a hanger and hang it from a nail on the wall, or use whatever creative solution you have. Point is, display it. After you clean up your materials, come back and move on to step 5.

Step 5. Soak yourself in.

Stand in front of your ME Print and notice what and who you see. Soak in what you feel, and notice what comes up. Get a piece of paper and write these words down: "I see in me..." Then write down all the things you see in your silhouette self. Don't use your mind to explain the ME Print. Instead, open your heart and tap into your Inner Wisdom, and notice what you feel about what you see, what you intuitively know about it, and what patterns you see. Write about these things.

Step 6. Play "I See in You" (a daring adventure to do with friends).

One by one, each person takes a turn standing in the middle with her ME Print. The person in the center says, "What I see in me is...," and tells the others what she sees about herself in her ME Print. Once she is finished, the looking glass turns, and for three to five minutes she *receives* as her friends tell her what they see in her, beginning with the words "<<insert the subject's name here>>, what I see in you is..." That is, they tell her what they see when they look at her silhouette. It's important to begin the comments with "<<insert the subject's name here>>, what I see in you is...," because, when we hear our names and the words "I see in you," our hearts open, we feel seen, and we receive the love we need. This loves gives us the power to go out into the world and express ourselves fully. Filled up on love, we have less fear about being who we are, full out, freely, and for real, without apology.

Love Story: A Call to Liberation

Every year in February, in honor of the international day of self-love, I set my intention to create experiences where people can fully liberate themselves to express themselves. I call this part of the day the "My Body Is My Temple" experience. At the events I host around the world, I invite a woman with a vibrant self-expression branch to lead the others through an experience that transforms the idea of full expression into a visceral, cellular experience. Among those who've joined us for these events are real-life temple dancers, divine circle dancers, yoginis, Nia practitioners, and more — and these are always among my favorite parts of the day. My one goal is to get people out of their seats and into their bodies — moving, grooving, and expressing the magnificence and beauty of who they are.

Here's what always happens. The music starts, the leader begins, and the women sit there staring at her. She invites them to join her, calling them forth with her hands, and still most of the women sit. You can see that, inside, these women are dying to get up and move their body temples, but something keeps them glued to their seats. They want to be her, the temple dancer, the yogini, the divine feminine circle dancer, free, open, moving their bellies and hips, expressing themselves the way she so confidently does, but they can't. They're trapped inside their austere, hard-pewed body temples, where their Puritan or sexually repressed ancestors have locked the doors from the outside.

Anticipating this, the masterful dancer spots a few women in the crowd who are — as she can tell by the swaying of their bodies — ready to bust their temple doors open. She comes down off the stage and invites those women to join her onstage. With that one invitation, those women are up on their feet, temples swaying full force and free.

And then a miracle happens. The room fills with the energy of joy and liberation. Women grab the hands of other women and pull them out of their seats and onto the stage, giving them permission to move their bodies, uninhibited by any thoughts or fears of what others might think, including themselves. And within minutes, the entire room of women is moving and grooving — yes, self-expression (and self-pleasure), without alcohol necessary to make it happen.

Where do you fall on the liberation scale? On a scale of one to ten, how easy is it for you to dance in public? Ten is your number if you are totally free. One, at the other end of the scale, indicates you remain glued to your seat, not even moving. Five means you want to get up, and if someone came over to invite you to dance, you might do it. Pick a number — the number that describes how readily you'd join in without a social lubricant to inspire you. With what level of ease can you let go, while sober, and express yourself in public through movement in the moment? Anything less than a ten is too low, so guess what? You get to practice moving and grooving your body temple in tune with the spirit of your beautiful, powerful, and magnificent essence.

Daring Act of Love
Dance Your Freaky Self Full Out!

Now that you have seen yourself, it's time to feel yourself in your body. With all that you have learned about your essence, choose three songs that resonate with and express who you are. You are about to have a private dance party where you move according to your essence, no matter how silly, outrageous, or different it may look. Your goal is to find the movements that express your essence. Sing out loud, dance freely, move your body as if the two of you were having a private *Soul Train* session. Don't bother worrying about who can see you. That's the whole point: you don't care. This is about you liberating a part of yourself that has been stuffed away, afraid to express herself. Dance, be bold, and fly free!

As you listen to the music, bring in the different essences you have discovered through our adventure together in this chapter, and try out body movements that relate to the words of the songs. Use your body to express the words and bring your essence more fully to life. To enhance the staying power of your newly embodied and enlivened expression, make this daring act of love a daily or weekly practice. Use the same three songs, have the same private dance party, continuing to move your body as she needs to in order to express your essence.

Double Dare: Do this dance in your driveway or backyard — where the sun or the stars and moon can see you. There is something superliberating about dancing outside. Sure, someone may see you, but who cares? This is a private dance just for you and you.

Love Mantra for Self-Expression

I love expressing myself.
Fully.
Freely.
Out loud.
ME.

AMPLIFY the LOVE!

Secrets to Cultivating
a Long-Lasting, Loving
Relationship with Yourself

CHAPTER 14

Make a Self-Love Promise

STAY COMMITTED TO CHOOSING LOVE FOR YOURSELF

ongratulations on lavishing loving on your ten self-love branches! Can you feel the branches and roots of your self-love tree getting stronger? Your relationship with yourself deepening? Your commitment to you solidifying? The really good news is, the love doesn't stop here. It just keeps on growing, every day, for the rest of your life, if you choose. Your self-love tree needs constant care, however, and, just like the trees in your yard, sometimes it will need a good pruning to get it and you growing in the healthiest direction. The more attention you pay to this beautiful tree of yours, the more your love for yourself will grow; and as a result, more love will flow to you. Gardeners use tools to take care of their trees, and you too need tools to care for and grow your self-love tree.

This chapter and the next will give you two of the most powerful tools I know: the self-love promise and the self-love practice. One has the power to cement a deep level of commitment to yourself to help you make the decisions you must make every day from a place of self-love. The other will help you develop powerful emotional and spiritual strength and stamina, both of which will determine your ability to choose to empower, trust, accept, know, forgive, express, pleasure, and value yourself — or not.

The best way to learn to use any tool is to use it, with intention. Our first step, then, is to get you focused on the branch of self-love most ready and willing to grow, right now. While all ten branches of self-love are critical to the health of your relationship with yourself, if you try to concentrate on all ten at the same time, you will get overwhelmed, your resources will be spread too thin, and your tree will suffer. The best way to ensure you have the most beautiful, blooming tree of self-love, and the best relationship with yourself, is to focus on one branch at a time, putting all your resources — time, energy, money, and love — there. As this branch receives oodles of attention and adoration from you, it will become stronger, you will become stronger, and it will grow and blossom. As a result, the branches surrounding it will also benefit, because they are all connected via the trunk. And as all that love wells up in the center of your tree, the roots of your self-love tree will feel the love and deepen. The entire system will be stronger because you chose to focus on one branch at a time.

ME Moment *Which Branch of Self-Love Will You Grow?*

Now, you may be thinking, "How can I pick just one branch? There are so many that need love." Or maybe you're drawing a big blank — no clear choice has emerged. Have no fear, love is here, right inside your heart. Just tune in by using one or all of the following techniques:

1. Think your way to choosing your branch. Go back and flip through each of the ten chapters on the self-love branches. Pick the branch with the lowest score on the Self-Love Pulse Checks. If there is a tie, pick whichever one makes you most excited and joy-full, or the one that scares you the most. Either one will give you a thrilling adventure!

2. Feel your way to choosing your branch. Flip back to the illustration of the tree of self-love in part 1. Take a moment to take in the entire tree. Look at each of the branches — acceptance, compassion, honesty, esteem, and so on. And instead of thinking your way through the tree, allow yourself to feel your way through. Put your hand on your heart, close your eyes, and take a deep breath. Go through your own inner tree of self-love, branch by branch, and allow yourself to feel the health of each branch today. Does it feel healthy and strong? Or does it feel weak and in need of love? Ask the branch most needing your love to show itself. To be guided on a visualization that will help you choose the branch of your self-love tree that needs love most now, go to www.SelfLoveMeditations.com, where you can receive both an audio and a video version.

3. Divine your way to choosing your branch. Download a copy of the self-love tree at www.ChooseSelfLove.com and print it out, or open up your book to the self-love tree illustration. Grab a penny, hold it in your hand, and ask this question: "What most needs my love right now?" And then throw the penny up and let it land on the self-love

tree. Whichever branch it lands on or near is the branch to choose. If it lands between two, pick the branch that most excites you, remembering that when one branch is loved, all neighboring branches benefit.

Once you have your self-love branch identified, you are ready to move to the next stage, making a promise that helps you stay committed to that branch all year.

The Self-Love Promise

Now that you have the branch you want to grow, you are ready to make a self-love promise that will help you define and keep a commitment to this part of your relationship with yourself. The promise will make your commitment actionable, tangible, and achievable, and if you stick to it, it will give you a sense of real growth in your ability to love yourself.

What Is a Self-Love Promise?

A self-love promise is a sacred contract between you and you, made from love. It acts as a binding agreement that compels you to choose loving actions toward or thoughts about yourself, and to take bold stands for yourself, no matter what. When life gets hard, and loving yourself seems a million miles away, the vows you've made to yourself will pull you through to the other side, to love. They empower you to choose the path of love even when fear, shame, or obligation demands that you choose it instead. How can a simple promise be so powerful?

Remember a time when you promised to do something for a person you loved, and how that connection to him or her and the promise of your word energized you and allowed you to follow through? The same thing happens with the self-love promise: it gives you the strength to choose love for yourself. The promise acts as an anchor to keep you connected to the intention behind it. And it gives you the power to find your way back to love for yourself in any situation.

So in moments when you let yourself down, engage in self-destructive habits, or just totally fail, instead of beating yourself up, feeling afraid, alone, or ashamed, or continuing to sabotage yourself, you have another choice — self-love in its many forms, including compassion, honesty, and acceptance. Your loving promises to yourself give you the power and path to choose self-love instead of self-hate, self-criticism, or self-abuse. Over time, as you choose self-love more and more often in your actions, beliefs, and thoughts, your self-love branches will strengthen and your relationship with yourself will soar. One day, the promise you made becomes a vow you keep no matter what. And then you return to your first nature, loving yourself unconditionally.

The Art of the Self-Love Promise

How you *make* a promise is the number one determinant of how well you will actually *keep* the promise. We've been trained to make them to others — from the everyday "Yes, I will do that for you" to the big "Yes, I will marry you" — but most of us are novices when it comes to making and keeping promises to ourselves. And while promises made to others are important, making promises to yourself is essential. But not just any kind of promise. The promises you make to yourself should always create more love.

If you're like most women, on the rare occasions you have made commitments to yourself, they have entailed self-punishing, self-depriving sacrifices, such as not eating sugar, drinking coffee, or engaging in some other activity that you derive pleasure from. We women love to tell ourselves, "This is good for me, no matter if it makes me miserable." And, of course, the sacrificial promise gets broken and we end up beating ourselves up for failing.

How many stress-inducing plans have you made whose results never materialized (think diets)? Or "God-I-promise-I-will-never-again" pleas that never stuck? Or bargains that cost you happiness and pleasure in the present in return for some hoped-for future result? You know the old "I promise that if...happens, then I will..."? Did making bargains like that let you feel better, or worse, about yourself? Rarely do such bargains lead to more love and happiness. Instead we usually gain more fear, guilt, and extra pounds. Why do such promises always go sour? Because their origin is sour. The source of these self-depriving, self-judgmental, *should*-ridden promises is *fear*, *shame*, and *guilt* instead of *love*.

> Love is the most critical part of any vow, whether addressed to yourself or anyone else.

If, for example, your goal is to achieve a fit body, there's a big difference between making that promise from a place of self-love and making it from a place of shame and fear. Examples of the two types of promises might look like this:

SHAME-AND-FEAR PROMISES:

"I will lose this extra weight if it kills me."

"I won't eat dessert ever."

"I will eat salad every day for a month."

"I'll do whatever it takes not to be fat."

SELF-LOVE PROMISE:

"I consume healthy foods because my body deserves to be healthy and fit."

Notice the difference? The first promise is full of self-judgment (I'm fat), is devoid of self-acceptance (I'll try to morph my body shape into someone else's body type rather than accept my own), and lacks communication with your body (I'll eat salad every day even if my body needs something different). The self-love promise, in contrast, comes from self-care, a loving desire to have a fit body so you can be healthy and vibrant. Which one do you think you'd be more likely to stick to; which one is more likely to get you the results you want? The self-love promise, of course! We've all tried the shame-and-fear promise, and you know that motivating yourself by "fat fear" never works. Usually you end up feeling worse about yourself, not to mention a few pounds heavier. This is true for all promises to yourself — skip the fear and shame and go for the l-o-v-e! Let's mark this moment with a commitment to not make fear-riddled, shame-based, or guilt-induced promises ever again.

Daring Act of Self-Love
Clean Up Your Self-Talk

Imagine that you have a broadcasting station inside you that controls your thoughts and talk. This station broadcasts over two channels — 88.9 FM FEAR and 108.00 FM LOVE. For the next week, notice when your words — whether you are thinking, feeling, or saying them — are coming from the 88.9 channel and filling your mind, body, or environment with vibes of fear, shame, self-degradation, or anything else that hurts you (or someone else). Be like your own Federal Communications Commission and clean up your station — no fear, shame, or self-degradation allowed!

As soon as you notice that these vibes are trying to make their way onto your airwaves, change your words or thoughts into love. Stop, close your eyes, take a big breath, and think or say the words "I choose love!" and then rephrase the negative statement you made a moment before. Just as if you were changing the dial in your mind or mouth, stop yourself mid-thought or midsentence, if possible, and change your words so that they send waves of love through you. Change your words and thoughts, change your life!

Six Tips for Making Self-Love Promises That Stick

1. Make the promise for yourself and yourself alone. **Your motivation cannot be to keep a guy or girl, make someone else happy, fit in, or follow along.**

2. Words matter. Choose the words that feel right for you. **Choose words that resonate specifically with your heart and soul. Just as you can hear if a piano is out of tune when you strike a key, so too you can hear and sense if a word is discordant when you say it out loud or write it down. The art is in listening to what feels right, what resonates**

for you. You may need to keep writing and rewriting, choosing new words and moving words around. But when you tune in to what you really want to promise, you will feel it as soon as you hear it.

3. Omit the words *want, try,* and *can.* Include the words *I promise* or *I vow.* *Want, try,* and *can* create weak commitments that are, as a result, unsecured anchors, and we want you strongly committed and supported in your self-love promise. Saying "I will try to..." when making a promise is like quitting before starting. Lead your promises with the words *I promise* or *I vow,* and these words will reflect and hold the resonance of your resolve and commitment.

4. Make the promise visual and verbal. Promises cannot be thought into existence; they must be stated out loud so the sound vibration can pass through your lips, and your cells can vibe on the self-love waves. Your brain also needs to see the words through your eyes, allowing you to register this commitment in all the crevices of your mind, so write them down first, and then read them out loud. Pronounce and proclaim! That's the name of the game.

5. Promises can be aspirational as long as they are believable. Some promises will feel like a stretch — and that's good! Promises have the power to pull you forward into ways of being that you haven't yet experienced or mastered. So yes, stretch! But don't lie to yourself. Make sure you can commit to what you're saying, or your promise won't pack the power needed to inspire you to keep it. How can you tell the difference? It's all in the way the words feel coming out of your mouth and landing in your body as you say them out loud. Notice whether, when you say the words, you feel the following:

♥ Do you feel grounded and empowered? Are the words resonating in your body, mind, and spirit? Thumbs up!

♥ Do you feel queasy or nervous, but as if you can at least sense the possibility of this promise being true? Thumbs up! This is a stretch, but a good one.

♥ Do you feel as if you'd really like to make this promise, but that it seems airy and ungrounded? Stop, reword, and restate your promise until you find words that feel as if they land in your body.

♥ Or do you feel nothing, or as if hot air is spewing out of your mouth? Stop and check in with yourself. Ask yourself, "What's blocking me? What am I afraid will happen if I take this promise?" Then ask, "What promise am I willing to make right now?"

6. Be willing, not perfect. Most of the time when you make a promise, you won't know what that promise will actually require you to do or become. Of course, you will have a feeling about what you are stepping into, but your mind cannot begin to even imagine how life will test you and gift you because of this deeper level of commitment to yourself. It is not important to have a plan or pretend that you are perfectly ready to meet every challenge you'll face. What is important is that you are willing. If you are *willing*, you are ready.

ME Moment *What Self-Love Promise Are You Willing to Make?*

You know which branch is ready to grow, and you understand the art of making a self-love promise. Now the only question is, what do you want to promise yourself? Use the following four questions to get clear on what vow you are ready and willing to take today to carry you forward and bring you more love and a better relationship with your most important partner, yourself! With this greater clarity, proceed into your magical, fantastical ritual of the self-love promise.

1. What do I need to say no to in order to grow this self-love branch?
2. What do I need to say yes to in order to grow this self-love branch?
3. What would make me super-happy to experience as a result of this self-love branch's new growth?
4. What promise comes immediately to mind, given all of the above?"

Don't censor or edit yourself; just say or write the first thing that bubbles up: "I promise..." This is the self-love promise that you will craft into a super-love-powered promise that can keep you coming back to love for yourself again and again!

Complete a Self-Love Promise Ceremony

Every year on February 13, the international day of self-love, people from all over the world pause to choose a self-love branch and make a self-love promise to themselves that they will keep all year long. This one promise, which they may make in the privacy of their own homes or in a roomful of others at a Madly in Love with ME Celebration or self-love event, becomes an anchor for the entire year, empowering them to choose love again and again, no matter what. To join us for these self-love celebrations each year, be sure to go to www.ChooseSelfLove.com and sign up to be a Love Ambassador.

While you are invited to join us every February 13 for the rest of your life, you don't have to wait until the next one to make a promise. You can make self-love promises anytime you like. The great thing about self-love promises is that they are cumulative — new ones build on the ones you've already made. Use the following six action steps to make your specific self-love promise to grow your chosen self-love branch:

Act 1. Get Present

Ideally, when making a promise, put yourself in a space where you can soak in the words and feel this commitment in your heart. A quiet and beautiful space is always nice: candles and low lights, or outside in nature. Being with yourself, being present, is required — as is, of course, being completely unplugged. Doing without electronic devices and other gadgets (except those needed to create music) during this event is essential. Clearing space for yourself physically, emotionally, and energetically and creating beauty in your surroundings sets a sacred tone, fitting for an event such as making a promise to yourself. You wouldn't make a promise to your best friend while checking emails or helping your kids with homework. No, you'd be present. Give yourself the same respect. And of course, if you need to make a self-love promise pronto while in an airplane, at a restaurant, or in the car, go for it. Choosing a time when you're by yourself is better, but if you're in a public space or with other people, simply create your own private Idaho, close your eyes, take a breath, and imagine everyone else disappearing. Then imagine sitting by yourself in your favorite place in the world. This will let you feel present, and then you can continue.

Act 2. Pronounce the Promise

Say the words out loud. Be as present as you can, and allow yourself to hear and feel the words as they come out of your mouth and vibrate through your body. As you say the words, ask yourself, "Do I mean them, really?" Can you say to yourself, "Yes, I want to make this promise. I can make this promise. But most important, I am willing, even though I may not know just yet what this vow entails"? Empty word calories won't do, but willingness will.

This first promise you make is a mark in the sand that says, "I am committed to loving myself and growing that love." If you've already been actively loving yourself for some time, great! You are ready to deepen your relationship with, and love for, yourself, and taking this new vow will only strengthen your self-love commitment. Married couples renew old vows and take new ones all the time, so why shouldn't you?

Act 3. Pick Your Words

Because this is your promise, the words have to feel right for you. Always test the words out for yourself. First, write the promise down that you uncovered in the previous ME Moment. Then say the promise out loud a few times, changing the words as needed so that it feels right for you. Cross out words, put in new ones — whatever you need to do to get these words jiving on your love vibration. Once you have the right love words for you, proceed. (Note for the perfectionist: Do not obsess over finding precisely the right word. *Right* in this case means one that is "in alignment with love" or one that "resonates with love." You'll know the right words when they feel good and strong in your heart. This is not a mental exercise, nor is it anything that you can do wrong. Trust yourself, tune into love, and have fun!

Here are some sample promises that people have made on Madly in Love with ME Day:

Self-trust: "I promise to *always* trust *me* (on the deepest level in my heart) totally and completely."

Self-expression: "I promise to value myself and my self-expression no matter what!"

Self-pleasure: "I promise to make sure I am having *fun* in my life, no matter how busy I am."

To see more self-love promises from people around the world, you can stop by www.ChooseSelfLove.com and get inspired.

Act 4. Make Your Promise Pretty

Beauty is a sign of self-love, so unless you are in an airport and in need of an emergency self-love promise, and all that's handy is a cocktail napkin, treat yourself well and write this promise prettily — put it in your journal, on a note card, or even a Post-it Note (pink, green, or yellow, three of the colors of self-love). Make it pretty enough that you'd like to visit it again. Seeing a promise over and over allows it to seep deeper into your cells.

Act 5. Seal the Deal — Proclaim Your Promise

How you make a promise has a lot to do with how successfully you will keep it, so do not skip this step. Do treat this step as a sacred promise to your heart and soul. Put yourself into a "promise state of mind" by creating a quiet space where you can be with yourself. Great places include in front of a mirror so you can see your face, or lying down, or sitting somewhere that feels supercomfy and intimate.

If you are in front of a mirror, keep your eyes open and look into them while you repeat your unique promise three times. Otherwise, close your eyes, put your hand on your heart, and repeat it three times. As I mentioned earlier, vows with yourself are always repeated three times — it's a rule I learned from one of my spiritual teachers, one of those rules without explanation. And it works. You'll just have to trust me on this.

Act 6. Soak in the Promise

Congratulations! You just made one of the most important promises to one of the most important people in your life — you! Now it's time to let this vow soak in. Take a bath, a nap, or a walk, or have an evening out with yourself and wear this self-love promise like a locket around your neck with your beautiful promise inside. Too often we move on from one thing to another without letting what we've just done settle or soak in. It is a great act of self-love to give yourself the space to bask in the love you have just promised to yourself.

And then tomorrow...

Daring Act of Love
Make a Morning Love Mantra

Keep the self-love flowing and growing by turning your promise into a Love Mantra, a promise repeated again and again in order to amplify its power and therefore its presence in your life. As you repeat these words of truth about love, you program the love into your mind, heart, body, and spirit. You can keep the words exactly as they stand in your promise, or you can shorten them so that they feel more like a jingle run- ning through your mind, body, and spirit. The secret of using a mantra is the repetition of the same phrase over and over again. Just as doing fifty squats a day would give you strong quadriceps, doing fifty morning Love Mantras will strengthen your rela- tionship with you.

Your Love Mantra Here

It's best to commit to a specific time of day to repeat the man- tra — mornings rock for starting the day supercharged with love. Every day, some time before starting work or after dropping the kids at school, say your mantra out loud fifty times. At first this may feel weird and forced. Keep going anyway. Keep up the mantra until the day you feel the words sink in deep or until a new mantra shows up. You'll be surprised at how Love Mantras just start pop- ping up as if they're excited to help move the love through you.

CHAPTER 15

Engage in a Radical Act of Self-Love

PRACTICE SELF-LOVE FOR FORTY DAYS STRAIGHT

The self-love practice is a phenomenon I stumbled on during my own self-love adventure. It empowers anyone who uses it to make big shifts in a short amount of time. This miracle-creator, the "40-Day Self-Love Practice," has something in common with a cleanse, training for a marathon, or taking on a project in order to reach a desired result. Each one of these practices takes you through a process that leads to a personal shift on the inside and outside, leaving you in better shape than before you started. Each practice offers structure, and it prompts you to supply the focus and diligence you need in order to stick to whatever self-love promise that particular practice supports. As a result, it delivers revelation upon revelation about the underlying motivations, beliefs, and patterns that keep you from the self-love you so desire but haven't able to generate no matter how hard you've tried.

You want to make decisions and choices aligned with your highest good, right? You want to take good care of yourself, express yourself, and have only loving relationships, including a loving one with yourself, yet sometimes it just seems impossible. Why? Because there are about a gazillion beliefs running through your mind that prevent you from acting in your own best interest, the way a best friend would. These beliefs formed habits and patterns that have kept your mind running in the same rut over and over again, making choices you know aren't feeding your self-love tree. As a result, it has been impossible for you to engage in the acts of self-love you deserve. Not because of a lack of will or desire, but because you just don't know another way.

It's like your drive to work, or your drive to anywhere that you've been going for years. You've created a pattern, and almost unconsciously you follow that same route over and over again. Even if it's not the prettiest or the most serene, you've stopped even considering that there might be a different route. And then one day, you decide to make a right turn where you normally go straight, and you find yourself on this entirely new, much more scenic road, and you're much happier. You discover that by following this new path, you end up where you need to be — but faster and happier. And eventually, after following this new route for several weeks, you forget about the old blah route and this new route becomes your everyday pattern. The same can happen with beliefs and habits; hence the power of the 40-Day Self-Love Practice!

Yogis, metaphysicians, and brain scientists all agree that if you can do anything for forty days continuously, you can change habits, break patterns, and rewire your brain. By focusing on one thing — in this case a self-love promise and self-love branch — for forty days, you experience emotional, mental, physical, and spiritual shifts that change you from the inside out, on levels you couldn't attain if you were to simply read information or experience a short burst of shift. This is why you can attend a fabulous weekend workshop and then return to your usual life within days — you revert to old habits. And it's why you know in your head how to stop the self-sabotage and self-criticism but can't stop these negative habits. It's why you know all the things you should do to take care of yourself but don't do them.

You want to take care of yourself — but no matter what you do, you can't keep up a daily practice, keep your sabbath sacred, or stop exhausting yourself every three months. Yes, you want unwavering self-respect and self-honor, but you can't seem to end that relationship with the person who isn't always nice to you. Yes, you want to stop being so dang hard on yourself; you want to have more self-compassion, self-acceptance, and self-forgiveness; and you want to stop the chatter of that Inner Mean Girl. Wherever you are on this self-love path, if you find yourself wanting to make things different, and if you try to make changes but they just don't stick, it's time to call in the big lightsaber of love to cut through all the crap and get to the l-o-v-e — the 40-Day Self-Love Practice.

Creating and Engaging in Your 40-Day Self-Love Practice

The first 40-Day Self-Love Practice I ever did was a 40-Day Comparison Cleanse. I was determined to grow my self-compassion branch by giving up my very toxic habit of comparing myself to other people, women especially. Comparison is one of the six most toxic habits of the Inner Mean Girl, and if you have an Inner Mean Girl Comparison Queen, you know what I'm talking about.

At the time I decided to give up comparison for forty days, my Inner Mean Girl Comparison Queen, Mean Patty, was stealing my joy and my ability to celebrate the success of publishing my first book, *Choosing ME before WE*. She was consumed with comparing me to the likes of Oprah, Marianne Williamson, and Barbara Walters, women twenty years my senior, women who had spent many more years than I building a career. But these were facts Mean Patty couldn't care less about. She was busy comparing me, and I was spending a lot more time, energy, and money than I needed to because of the confusion, anxiety, and self-doubt Mean Patty was generating. At my wits' end with her negative self-talk, I took a radical act of self-love and put us on a 40-Day Comparison Cleanse.

I based this cleanse on my self-love promise to give up comparing myself to other people, including the person I *thought* I should be. What I didn't know at the time was that practice meant *practice* — meaning I had to actually follow the practice and keep my promise. Just thinking about not comparing myself, or just saying some affirmation without engaging in any action, wasn't going to work. Trying to think my way through the problem hadn't worked so far — I needed a structure that held me throughout the day, helping me to make decisions and choices in the moment, from a place of self-compassion and self-acceptance instead of self-criticism. And so I created a three-part practice, which has been the basis of every 40-Day Self-Love Practice I've engaged in since. Here are the steps of the proven super-love-powered formula that works:

Act 1. Morning Wake-Up Practice

Before leaving the house, and often even before leaving your bed, you start your morning in self-love, connected to yourself and your divine wisdom with the use of two powerful self-love tools — the Love Mantra and the Divine Downline.

Upon waking, open your eyes, then close your eyes, and then repeat the mantra to yourself again and again until you feel something shift in your body. You may have to fake it 'til you make it, which may take several days or even a few weeks. Often people don't feel anything at first. And that's where the power of the forty-day practice comes in. Because you have committed to a forty-day practice, you will keep taking this action every morning. And then, one day, you will feel the shift.

> Love Mantra: a phrase that reflects and captures the love-generating belief or habit you are practicing.

For the 40-Day Comparison Cleanse, my Love Mantra was "I am exactly where I am meant to be." I'd lie in bed with my hand on my heart, sometimes curled up in a gentle ball, other times flat on my back, but always conscious of how I placed my body, so that the words could easily find their way into me. Over and over I'd repeat the words "I am exactly where I am meant to be," and as the days passed I began to notice a calm come over me, and a difference in how I reacted throughout my day.

Remember, how you start your day is how you live your day. Starting with a Love Mantra anchors you to that mantra and its fundamental love-based statement for the entire day, so that you can come back to it again and again. Then, throughout the day, whenever something comes up that tries to pull you into fear, self-sabotage, self-criticism — whatever non-self-loving habit or pattern you're trying to shift — you connect back to self-love by saying the Love Mantra to yourself.

After your Love Mantra has made you all nice and toasty inside, and has opened your heart to receive, this is the perfect moment to connect to the divine, ask a question, and gain insight for your day ahead so that you can keep moving and grooving toward experiencing more love. It's best to keep the question simple, and it will be most powerful if you ask the question as if you were asking your wisest and best friend for her advice. The point of the question is to give you permission to act in ways that previously you have not. Remember, you are shifting patterns and habits here, which means your mind is going to come up with all kinds of reasons to keep you from doing, thinking, and acting in ways that align with this new way of being. Your mind, especially in the early days of the practice, will be stuck in its rut. Divine wisdom will keep you on track to creating a new road to self-love.

> Divine Downline inquiry: the question you ask the divine to give you the wisdom and support you need to make self-loving decisions that day.

For my Comparison Cleanse, I knew that I needed an answer that would prompt me to take action, even if that action were to be passive. The Love Mantra worked well on the *being* level, but as an achiever, I also needed something to *do*. Not as in the pursuit of an accomplishment, however, and not busywork. I needed new ways of being and thinking and acting that I could explore and experience, ones that would facilitate the kind of quantum shift I desired.

My Divine Downline inquiry every morning became "What do I need in order to feel good about where I am in my life right now?" I'd close my eyes, still lying in bed with my hand on my heart, and dial in this question to my Divine Downline. And then I would wait for an answer. Sometimes I would receive a word that popped into my mind; other times I'd hear a phrase, perspective, or set of directions in my mind; and other times an image would appear in my mind, giving me the guidance I needed, even if I didn't always like what I heard.

Dialing in your question to your Divine Downline may be easy or hard for you, depending on how you and the divine communicate and how often. Not to worry. The more you dial in, the better the connection will be, and the more you will learn about the style of communication of your Divine Downline. Yours may be audio-based, so you'll hear words or phrases. Or it may be visual, so you'll see images or movies or colors. Or yours may be based on feelings, which means you'll feel something in your body — and if this is the case, you can ask that body part what it wants to tell you. Or yours may be based on a sense of simply *knowing* the answer — as soon as you ask the question and it sinks in, you'll just know what you are to do.

As you begin these practices, you may ask your question and get nothing. In that case, have no fear! There are lots of ways you can plug into your Divine Downline, including listening to guided meditations, journaling, using an oracle deck, or drawing pictures. Almost always the direction you'll receive from one of these methods will include an action to take or a perspective to adopt. Which brings us to the second part of all self-love practices.

Act 2. All-Day Practice

You're anchored to your Love Mantra, and you've gotten your divine directions; now it's time to go out into the world and practice choosing self-love in all the moments and situations that show up to get you to do anything but. This is where the real shift happens, where you build your emotional and spiritual muscles, increase your self-love, and ultimately rewire patterns, habits, and beliefs to serve you. All 40-Day Self-Love Practices work directly in your life — you don't have to take off work, leave your family, or spend thousands of dollars to travel to exotic destinations (although sometimes that is nice!). You get to go on an adventure and still take care of all the things that need your attention. Remember, self-love is all about both/and. Your mission throughout the day is twofold:

Mission #1. Deliver on the divine direction you received.

Whatever your Divine Downline told you to do, you must now do, be, try, practice, check out, or follow through on. No matter how unreasonable or unimpressive it sounds. This is where miracles occur. It is in your willingness to let go of control, to *trust* that the divine is on your side and is wiser than you could ever be, that you open up to new possibilities. As you experience these new possibilities and receive more love and happiness in return, you begin to trust new ways of being, doing, and thinking, and in that trust you step beyond the love block. Things you once thought impossible become normal. And all those ruts in your mind about how things are? They disappear and, with them, the block goes away. Love begins to flow freely through the new routes you've created.

Mission #2. Be aware of the beliefs, habits, and patterns that show up, and make a conscious choice to shift them.

Something powerful and magical happens when you commit to a 40-Day Self-Love Practice. It's like you send a letter to the universe saying, "Hey, I am so ready to shift this old habit or belief. Can you help me out? I am totally ready to remove this block to love!" And then the universe shows up and delivers all kinds of opportunities for you. All of a sudden you begin to see habits and beliefs you didn't even know were there. You come face-to-face with truths about how these habits and beliefs affect your life (and they're not always pretty). You get challenged to make tough choices, not because there isn't a clear answer to which decision is the best for you, but because your mind has you tricked into not trusting your divine inner guidance. And because you are supported by the 40-Day Self-Love Practice, by your Love Mantra, by your divine connection, and by your commitment to practice and make a shift, you are able to meet these challenges in an entirely new way. Each 40-Day Self-Love Practice can be approached like an experiment — try it out, try new things, and see what happens. Test new theories, challenge old ones, and watch the insights, miracles, and love come rolling in!

One day, while I was on a 40-Day "Receiving" Self-Love Practice, in which I was committed to transforming my habit of overdoing and overworking, and to growing my self-care branch, I received the direction from my Divine Downline to not start work until 11 AM that day. The thought of this terrified me. I was programmed to start always at 9 AM, even though I had been working for myself for over three years. I had a presentation that evening. And a lot to do in order to get ready for it. But I had made the commitment. So I stayed in my pajamas, made a nice breakfast, and got in the car (pj's still on) to pick up my intern. On the way, I stopped and pulled the car over (by divine direction), turned the engine off, and sat in the car for twenty minutes in the sun, letting the sun fill up my body with energy. In the process of my sitting there and "doing nothing," I *received* the entire two-hour workshop I was going to give that night. Then I picked up my intern, and she did all the work of getting the copies made, pulling the materials together, and so on. By the time I arrived at the 6 PM workshop, I was full of energy and able to give fully to the women assembled because I had filled myself up first. What I learned in this process at a deeper, cellular level was that I could trust that I would receive what I needed, and that I could do this by taking care of myself first, by valuing *being* as much as I did *doing*.

Had I been doubtful or afraid, and not followed through on my commitment, I would not have experienced the shift early in my forty-day process that led me to uncover a huge and incorrect belief: that *I had to drive and strive in order to survive*. Through my 40-Day Self-Love Practice, I was able to transform a belief that had once served me, and which had begun exhausting me.

As you begin to open up your awareness and keep it open throughout your entire day, your self-love assignment is to notice what happens to you and for you on all levels — mental, physical, emotional, and spiritual. Notice what emotions, what type of resistance, and what beliefs surface throughout your day in relation to the self-love practice you have taken on. By the end of the forty days, it is possible to make a major shift on all levels — emotional, mental, physical, and spiritual, if you stick to the forty days. You can begin to experience shifts in seven days, have big insights in twenty-one to twenty-eight days, and by day thirty, may even feel that all is good. But it's not enough without the final ten days. Forty is when the emotional, mental, physical, and spiritual come together to make lasting change.

You've already experienced shifts within seven days during some of the Daring Acts of Love, which were designed to give you quick openings and insights into new possibilities. Now you are ready to take on the big shifts; the magic number now is forty days.

As you embark on your first 40-Day Self-Love Practice, use the practice as a lens through which to better see your interactions and better understand your behaviors, motives, and thoughts. Challenge yourself to let go of old ways of thinking and doing, and stand tall as a champion for yourself — a woman committed to being her own best friend no matter what.

Act 3. Evening Reflection

Alice Walker, a Nobel Prize–winning author, says in her book *We Are the Ones We've Been Waiting For*, "Wisdom requests a pause. It is the pause that gives us clarity, certainty. It is our time of reminding ourselves of what we want for ourselves." Every forty-day practice you embark on is guaranteed to leave you wiser, and wisdom can come only when you stop to hear it. Just as you began your morning connected to yourself and your Divine Downline, you will end your day with yourself and the divine.

This need not be an elaborate sixty-minute exercise. You can reflect in as little as three minutes each night — and of course, if you have more time, then give it to yourself. Each evening before you go to sleep, check in with yourself and the divine by asking the following three simple questions:

1. What did I learn today about <<insert the focus of your self-love practice>>?
2. What do I want to remember tomorrow about <<insert the focus of your self-love practice>>?
3. What am I proud of myself for today?

You can simply lie in bed and close your eyes and say the answers to yourself, or journal them, creating a cozy way to fall asleep loving yourself!

Ten Steps to a Successful 40-Day Self-Love Practice

What follows are several tips for ensuring that your self-love practice yields powerful results for you. After creating and teaching these practices to thousands of people, myself included, I've found that if you stick to these steps, you'll have an experience that leaves you better able to love yourself well for the rest of your life — the shift sticks!

1. Choose the branch of self-love you want to grow. Which of the ten branches needs your love and attention now? Choose one.

2. Pick a start date and end date, and put the dates on your calendar. Mark a big "40" with a red heart around it on your calendar.

3. Tell someone you trust about your 40-Day Self-Love Practice. You can ask that person to join you or just support you. Simply sharing the news of your undertaking will amp up your success ratio a ton.

4. Pick a Love Mantra and Divine Downline inquiry to start with. Do this knowing that you may very likely change them along the way.

5. Start your 40-Day Self-Love Practice as an experiment and adventure. Go into this thinking of it as work, or with the attitude that you must change yourself, and you'll fail right off the bat. You'll never make the forty days. Go in with the attitude "I can't wait to see what I discover," as well as with the energy of unattachment, openness, curiosity, anticipation, excitement, and commitment to yourself, and you'll do great.

6. Share your insights. Share the love with friends in whatever way makes you happy — just go public. Any positive acknowledgment will be fuel to help you keep going!

7. Use the Daring Acts of Love and adventures for support. Go back to the chapter on the branch you are giving big love to, and engage in its Daring Acts of Love during the 40-Day Self-Love Practice. Even if you have already engaged in the act, doing it again will take you deeper and you will discover more.

8. Keep a journal of some kind. Record your insights and Aha! moments somewhere, even if only as notes on your phone or other digital device.

9. Day 40! Celebrate! **Plan and do something special for yourself that reflects the shift you've just made. Reward yourself in a loving way for loving yourself enough to focus on your relationship with you for forty days!**

10. Name and claim your self-love practice. **Naming your practice gives it power, making it easier for you to talk about it, stick to it, and stay focused. Use any of the follow four options to name yours:**

   a. The promise itself. **For example, a 40-Day I Am ME without Apology Self-Expression Practice, in which you are committed to being yourself regardless of what anyone else thinks.**

   b. One of the branches. **For example, a 40-Day Bring on the Self-Pleasure! Practice, in which you commit to growing your self-pleasure, or a 40-Day Radical-Self-Care Practice, in which you push away the boundaries around and patterns of the beliefs that keep you from taking good care of yourself.**

   c. A self-sabotaging habit you want to change. **For example, undertake a 40-Day Toxic-Relationship Cleanse Self-Love Practice and commit yourself to giving up relationships that aren't good for you.**

   d. A self-loving habit you want to create. **Try a 40-Day Receiving Love Self-Love Practice, in which you commit to receiving more love from many places.**

Claim and name your self-love practice. Write the practice right here in the book, or write it down on a piece of paper:

I, _____,
hereby commit to a 40-Day "_____"
Self-Love Practice, in which I am committed to

_____,
commencing on _____ and ending with
a celebration on Day 40 on _____.

Two Ways to Superpower
Your 40-Day Self-Love Practice

Removing the blocks to love and rewiring old patterns and beliefs can bring up old stuff that needs to be cleared on levels that can be hard to clear on your own. And even with the best intentions, it can be hard to stick to the forty days without someone else creating a structure for you, or without the camaraderie of other people who are engaged in 40-Day Self-Love Practices at the same time. I've been in all of these situations, which is why I am going to make sure you don't have to be! Whether you need a 40-Day Self-Love Practice that leads you along, or you want to be part of a group participating in a 40-Day Self-Love Practice together, I've got you covered.

40-Day Self-Love Practices That Lead You

I've created a handful of 40-Day Self-Love Practices focused on some of the biggest blocks that most people have, and on the areas in which people most want to grow their self-love. Anyone, including you, can engage in one of these practices anytime. They are fun, daring, and shifting, and they give you everything you need in order to successfully move out the blocks and move in the love — weekly teachings from me, daily love-filled emails, weekly dares and adventures, guidebooks, videos, special interviews, and more. Plus, there is an entire community of people who have engaged in, and are engaging in, these 40-Day Self-Love Practices, and who gather on our special virtual playgrounds to inspire, support, and share the love with one another. When you sign up for a 40-Day Self-Love Practice, you get invited.

Here are a few that are ready for you to roll right into:

Self-Expression, Self-Esteem, Self-Awareness:
The 40-Day Fear Cleanse

This self-love practice busts through blocks caused by fear and leads you to actively pursue whatever it is that your heart and soul really desire. Forty days to choosing faith in love over faith in fear. For more information, go to www.theFearCleanse.com.

Self-Empowerment, Self-Respect, Self-Honor:
The 40-Day "Choosing ME before WE" Self-Love Practice

A self-love practice that empowers you to take back your love power and create the happy, full love life you deserve, making the promise to never settle for less than your heart and soul desire in relationships again. Forty days to creating the best relationships of your life, starting with your relationship with yourself. I invite you to read more about it at www.ChoosingMEbeforeWE.com.

Self-Compassion, Self-Forgiveness, Self-Acceptance, Self-Trust:

The 40-Day Inner Mean Girl Cleanse

A self-love practice that transforms the six most self-sabotaging, toxic habits of your inner critic — gossip, comparison, judgment, unrealistic expectations, perfection, and obligation. Forty days of turning self-sabotage and negative self-talk into self-love. Read more about this 40-day cleanse at www.InnerMeanGirlCleanse.com.

Self-Pleasure, Self-Care:

The 40-Day "My Body Is My Temple" Self-Love Practice

A self-love practice that transforms your relationship with your body and turns your body into a temple you adore, adorn, nurture, and move in. Forty days of shifting your relationship with your body to pure love. Read more at www.ILoveMyBodyTemple.com.

To discover all the 40-Day Self-Love Practices out there for you, go to www.40DaysofSelfLove.com.

Invite a Friend

Whether you are creating and leading yourself through your 40-Day Self-Love Practice, or doing the same thing but in the company of other people who are choosing love, invite a woman or girl (or even a man) to take the 40-day plunge with you. I've seen people deepen their friendships, their marriages, and their relationships with their sisters and daughters because they've taken this "trip" together. Plus, when you have someone with you, you are more likely to stick to it and be successful, and you have a helping hand if you fall off the train.

CHAPTER 16

Be a Love Ambassador

USE YOUR LOVE POWER TO GENERATE LOVE FOR YOURSELF AND OTHERS

One of the best parts about being so darn full of love for yourself is that you will have gobs of overflowing love to share with others. Considering that there are so many love-starved people out there, this is a good thing. Plus, the more love you give, the more you receive in return. That means more love for the entire world. Imagine, just like we talked about at the beginning of our journey, a world that really is full of love!

My friend SARK (Susan Ariel Rainbow Kennedy), a bestselling author and super-sister of self-love, says she lives as much as possible as a full cup of self-love, sharing the overflow with the world. And when she feels half-empty — which is every day — she fills herself back up from the inside, using her transformational practices and processes. The more she fills her cup with love for herself, the more she can serve others from the overflow, and she does. She is an ambassador of love. Susan, like me, is a walking, talking experiment in all the things she teaches. And, I have to admit, the self-love dares she takes make some of the self-love dares I've suggested seem as easy as brushing your teeth.

Susan practices "exquisite self-care." She's received hugs from complete strangers in grocery stores, and she's even stood up in the middle of the DMV and begun singing just to change her mood from sad (you know how depressing the DMV can be) to glad! She's my self-love-dare shero and a master at generating love for herself. And because she is so daring and unapologetic about generating love for herself, she can share so much with the world. Anyone who is a fan of SARK knows what I am talking about. Visit www.PlanetSARK.com, or hear the conversation on radical self-care that SARK and I had — it's part of the Self-Love Kit found at www.ChooseSelfLove.com.

Love overflow is possible for every woman and girl on this planet. I know because I have experienced it myself and witnessed it again and again in women around the world. When you make it your practice and business to fill yourself up with love, using all of the dares and adventures I have shared with you, you become able to give and receive almost infinite amounts of love. You become able to better serve the world and all the people in it. You become a better friend, sister, partner, and person. And you gain the power to generate love anytime you need it. You don't have to wait to receive love from your partner. And you don't have to rely on any specific person to give it to you. You have the power to create love at the snap of your fingers, and that is some serious love power. Imagine having the power to — anytime you feel lonely, afraid, or sad — generate love. So instead of reaching out in unhealthy ways and doing all those things you know only make you feel lonelier, sadder, and more afraid the next day, you flip the switch on your love generator, and super amounts of love flow into your hungry heart.

This final chapter provides you with a series of Daring Acts of Love that will activate your love-generating power so that you don't have to merely imagine having the power to feed your heart love when you need it. You can live in love, every day. And of course, the more you generate, the more overflow you have to give.

Generate Love for Yourself:
Be a Love Ambassador to Yourself

The following dares are specific "love prescriptions" for when your love tank is low. Think of them as love boosts whose purpose is to restore your self-love levels and feed your self-love branches. Use any one or all of these dares to generate the l-o-v-e you need in those moments when the loneliness, fear, sadness, exhaustion, or shame kicks in.

Daring Act of Love
Go out on an Adventure to Collect Love!

Take this dare for an *immediate* love boost. Collect evidence of love for fifteen minutes, thirty minutes, one hour, or an entire day by using all of your senses to find evidence of love everywhere. Take a love-collecting field trip during lunch or in the late afternoon. See, smell, taste, feel, and hear it. Literally breathe love in, take note of loving exchanges between others, taste love in your food, smell love in a flower, hear love in a song or in a compliment you receive, feel love when you take a moment to hug your dog or do anything else that opens your heart. And then actually collect the love. You must capture this evidence of love somewhere, either by writing it down, taking a picture of it, sharing it with your social network, or recording it on a voice recorder — whatever makes you happy. Here are some super ways to collect the evidence of love and boost your love levels.

♥ Pick your collection device of choice — a pocket-sized notebook, a digital device you can write on, Post-it Notes, or a camera you can snap pictures with.

♥ Be on the lookout for love everywhere — in nature, your interactions, the interactions of others, signs, objects, animals, food, literally anything you can see, taste, hear, smell, or feel.

♥ Look for love even in the challenging moments. In moments of stress, challenge yourself to look beyond what's difficult and find the love. Finding beauty, gratitude, and inspiration are great ways to do this.

♥ Take a picture with your heart. As you find this evidence, pause to experience the boost of love, noticing the love and storing the event away in your mind and heart as evidence that love exists everywhere, that you just have to look for it.

Daring Act of Love
Graffiti Yourself with Love

Take this dare when you need a love boost *within the next few hours*. You. Your body temple. A warm bath. Candles. Love-generating music. Red lip liner. Heart-shaped soap. Cozy and pretty pj's. Create a sacred and warm bathroom space, get naked, and take out the lip liner. Proceed to write words and draw symbols of love all over your body temple. Love mantras like "I love you," "I am beautiful," "You are imperfectly perfect," and "Thank you." Love symbols like hearts, wings, and smiley faces. Treat this as a spiritual communication between you and your temple, and let her show you the words and symbols she needs you to see. When you're completely covered, and I mean completely, get into the bath and soak in these words.

When ready, gently go over the love graffiti using the heart-shaped soap, not to rub the words off but to gently rub the words in. The lip liner will fade as you soap it, but make sure some remains even after you get out. (You can remove it the next day if you want, but you may decide to keep it on — daring!) Once you have touched each of the words and symbols and body parts and honored them, get out of the bath, get into your pretty pj's, and journal about your experience — or go to sleep with thoughts of you loving you, whatever your temple needs. Wake in the morning, and notice which words and symbols still remain.

Daring Act of Love
Take an "Impossible" Self-Love Sabbatical

Take this dare when you really need to fill your love tank *in the next few days.* This is for those times when you need a love life-line: you can feel that you need love, you know you need to fill up inside, but it doesn't seem possible because there is too much going on. You are in self-love-emergency land, and you need to hit that love-generating red-alert button right now and make the impossible possible. First step: look at your calendar, and in the next seventy-two hours — that's three days — find an entire day when you can clear your calendar. Doesn't matter what is scheduled — move it. If you can't do an entire day, start at sundown the day before and go to noon the next day. If you have to reschedule something, tell people you are taking an Impossible Self-Love Sabbatical. You can bet they won't know what that is, and so most won't ask but will just say okay. Those who do ask will be interested because they probably need one themselves, so you will inspire them!

And here's one great thing about this sabbatical: you can do it right from home — as long as anyone you live with knows you are on sabbatical. On this day, they are not allowed to ask you for anything. You can also check yourself into a nearby hotel for the night. When you make reservations on the day of or day before your stay, you can usually negotiate a great rate. I take my sabbaticals at a resort ten minutes from my house. If you have kids, this may require more than three days' planning, and you will need support, so ask for it. Believe that others want to help you because you dare to love yourself enough to fill your love tank back up.

Share the Love: Be a Love Ambassador to Others

One of the best side effects of having an overflow of love is that you can share it with everybody and anybody at any time. You can be totally spontaneous when giving others love boosts and kick-starting their love generators. You can also plan and create love-generating experiences that leave people full up with love for days, weeks, and even years. Filling others' tanks with love has the power to create more love, raising their love set-points to new levels. What follows are some of my favorite Daring Acts of Love that involve activating love for others — from strangers to your soul family. Do you dare to share the love?

Daring Act of Love
Give Flower-Power Love to Strangers

Be a Krishna devotee for the day. No, you don't have to shave your head or trade in your designer jeans. This is just about you being daring enough to light up a person's day with one of the most powerful and affordable love generators in the entire world — flowers! Rutgers University did a study that proved receiving

a flower creates the same amount of joy as when people interact with a baby or a puppy or kitten. Their hearts open and love
comes flowing in. You too have the power to open people's
hearts!

Stop by the flower shop and pick a up few stems of a
happy-making flower — sunflower, gerbera daisy, hydran-
gea — and go about your day distributing the flowers to
people at random when your heart feels moved. When you
give the flower, just say to the person, "I wish you a happy,
love-filled day!" I've done this dare on Sunday mornings at
brunch and given flowers out at the restaurant and neighboring establishments as I waited in line for my table. You can
also do it at the office and stop by people's offices and desks —
wow, will you make their day!

Daring Act of Love
Give Love Money

Pick your favorite number, and then go to the bank and get that
many dollar bills. Take each dollar bill and some colored pens or
markers and infuse the money with love by drawing symbols and
writing words of love on the dollar bills. Put these bills in your
wallet. Then throughout the week, when you are in a store and
the cashier looks like she needs some love, pay using one or two
of your love-money bills along with other cash — put it on top,
and watch what she does. If she notices, take that moment to tell
her it's love money, and explain that she has just received some

love! When you see a homeless person, instead of giving him a bill and just marching on, pause, give him some love money, and say, "May this dollar bill of love bring you much love." This is called a "love blessing," and as a Love Ambassador who has the power to generate love, you are fully authorized to give such blessings.

Daring Act of Love
Celebrate Bizarre Holidays for Good Reason

Surprise the people you love with flowers or love-infused gifts in unexpected places and in unanticipated ways, tapping into the love-generating power of flowers and special somethings without falling into the trap of expectation and routine. Sure, there are the birthdays, anniversaries, and traditional holidays, when people expect to receive a bunch of pretty stems. But you are much more original than that. One superpowered way to generate and share love is to show people that they are special to you, that your relationship matters. Do an Internet search for the terms *weird holidays*, *zany holidays*, and *outrageous holidays*, and see what's coming up this month that fits with a person in your life you want to express love for. On that holiday, show up at his or her doorstep or office with flowers or a special personal gift, or, if necessary, have your florist deliver flowers with a personal note from you. Here are a few of my favorites:

April 2, International Pillow Fight Day: Flowers, a pillow fight, and lots of fun!

May 15, National Pizza Day: If you like pizza, what a great excuse for a date, or a great time for bonding with a friend or your mother, daughter, or sister. Pizza and flowers. Divine.

November 29, National Forgiveness Day: Give your special person flowers and a love letter and lovingly say, "I'd love to ask for forgiveness for anything I've ever done that's hurt you. I love you. Clean slate?"

Daring Act of Love
Be a Super-Love-Generator and Throw a Self-Love Party

Every year on or around February 13, Love Ambassadors from around the world light up and throw self-love parties and events with groups of people they love. Mothers band together to create love-filled self-discovery experiences for their young daughters, generations of women gather to watch heart-provoking movies and open up new conversation and connection, girlfriends gather for dance parties and the writing of love letters, and coaches, yoga instructors, community leaders, and teachers of all kinds connect to throw self-love soirees and self-love playshops. Around this time of year, I am usually traveling to different cities hosting big love boosts in the form of Madly in Love with ME events. It's a grand expression of how much love can be generated where two or more people gather with the intention to create love through the magical experience of self-love. Now that you have made it to the final part of our adventure together in this book, you are officially invited to join us as a Love Ambassador! And you are invited to join us every February 13 forever. We'd love to have you with us on this adventure to light the world up with love. You can join us at www.SelfLoveAmbassador.com. Each year we make available to all Love Ambassadors a full Madly in Love with ME party kit with all kinds of goodies to help you throw and host your own love-powered event — plus the chance to join with a community of people around the world doing the same.

More Love Generators for Love Ambassadors

Now, February 13 comes only once a year, and if it's already come and gone for the year when you read this, I surely don't want you to wait until next year to start generating love in a big way. So I've included two of my favorite ways to gather people for a love-filled experience that will keep them humming with love for weeks, maybe even months. There are many more, and every year we add still more as the movement grows, but for now try one (or all) of these with the groups of people you love.

Dinner, Movie, and LOVE!

A woman's power comes from sitting together with other women, sharing from the heart, witnessing the stories of the other women, and realizing that she is not alone — that we *all* have had so many of the same experiences. For many women and girls, having that kind of intimate conversation can be a little intimidating. Even among those who have learned to love sitting in a circle with women sharing from the heart, conversation that lacks a juicy common focus often does not go deep enough. It has to go deep so that truth can be shared, women can feel seen, and heartfelt connection can be made — the kind of connection that has the power to create a lasting shift. And when women come together in a powerful, heart-opened way, shift happens!

One February, I experienced the power of sitting in a room with five hundred women watching powerful images and stories of women onscreen and then having what I call "real and wise girl talk" afterward. They opened up, shared their hearts, talked about what wasn't working, and empowered one another to make changes individually and collectively. I've also experienced this same power with five women in a room, especially when different generations were present. So no matter how few or how many, gather the girls of all ages! Some suggested movies:

Iron-Jawed Angels, with Hilary Swank
Elizabeth and *Elizabeth, the Golden Age*, with Cate Blanchett
Miss Representation, by Jennifer Newsom
Killing Us Softly, by Jean Kilbourne
Divine Secrets of the Ya-Ya Sisterhood, with Sandra Bullock

Love Letters to Ourselves

Get your friends together and ask them to write love letters to themselves in one of the following three ways:

Remember yourself as a younger version of you. **Pick an age like ten or fifteen — or twenty at the latest — and write a letter to the girl you were at that age. Tell her about your life today — about what you've learned and the wisdom you now have. Tell her what you would have wanted her to know back then — as if you can bestow that wisdom on her. Describe** all the incarnations of the woman you have been since that time, and how you have grown and evolved (it may help in your writing to go back in five- to ten-year increments to remember who you have been in your life). Tell her about dreams you still have, some of which she may have had too. Promise her that you'll always care for her. Let her know she is loved.

Imagine yourself as an older, wiser you. Pick an age at least ten or twenty years older than you are today. Write a love letter to that woman, telling her all the things you love and admire about her. Remind her of why she is such a wise woman. Remind her of all that she has done and seen in her life. Remind her of the person she has chosen to be in this lifetime. Tell her about the impact she has made on your life and on the lives of others and the world. Express to her your love, and your devotion to her heart, her spirit, and her body. Feel her strength and remind her that she is beautiful and loved because of who she is in her soul. After you've read the letter back to yourself a few times (and to the group), seal the letter and store it. Write the age on the envelope that you will be in ten or twenty years, along with the year it will be. Open this letter then. Like your own love capsule!

Imagine yourself as your own best friend. Write the letter to yourself as if your best friend were writing it to you. If you were your own best friend, what would she want you to know? What does she know that you need to hear? What does she want you to remember, no matter what? And what does she think is just the coolest thing about you?

Once the letters are written, have every woman in the group read her letter to the others. Have her talk about what it was like to write to her younger self, older self, or herself as her own best friend.

As the members of the group share, have one person scribe, gathering all the collective wisdom. Then write it up or create something after the event that reflects that love and wisdom — a poem, a song, a poster. Send it to all who attended, and ask them to share it with their friends.

Tip: You can have your guests write these letters either before they come to your party or at your party. If they're going to write them at the party, be prepared with good love-letter-writing music and nice paper, even if it's just colored paper. Also, instead of asking guests to write all three love letters, you can share the three ways to write the love letter and let each guest decide how she wants to write it.

One of the best parts of being a Love Ambassador is that you get to both give and receive love. You demonstrate that it is possible to be a woman who completely loves herself in all the ways a woman must — by taking care of herself first, expressing herself completely, adoring and appreciating herself daily, requiring unconditional respect and love in all relationships, and so much more — while still taking care of what and who she loves (and, honestly, even better than she did before she chose to love herself well).

To receive the full Love Ambassador Kit with more love-generating acts that you can share, go to www.SelfLoveAmbassador.com.

I invite you to join a legion of Love Ambassadors around the world as we stand together, united, simply by giving and receiving the love every human being on this planet needs in order to thrive. Love is free. Love is everywhere. Love is yours to give and receive. Go forth and share the love!

A Love Letter for You

Dear beautiful, magical, powerful soul,

Wherever you are in the world in this moment, it is my deepest desire for you to realize the power of love you possess — for you to remember how to find, feel, and generate love without needing anything other than what you already have inside you. I invite you to open up the magical world of self-love, to continue your exploration of the beautiful, bountiful tree of self-love, which I know you will continue to cultivate as you grow unconditional love and respect for yourself, year after year. There really is nothing more powerful, beautiful, or free than a woman who truly loves herself. And you, my love, are powerful, beautiful, and free. As you stand tall and reclaim self-love as your birthright, own your power to generate love whenever you need it, and serve the world by sharing the overflow of the love that beams out of you, this world *will* shift. And together we will create a world in which no child, no woman, and no man has to *imagine* a world of self-love. They will be *living* in love instead.

I look forward to seeing you on the playground of love as you dare to be, love, and live the miracle and magic that are your unique divine imprint of love. Fall more in love with yourself every day for the rest of your life. And in the process, you will inspire us all to do the same. Hail to you, woman who dares to love herself, Love Ambassador to the world! You are a beacon of love. Keep shining!

With great heart,
Christine Arylo
Founder of Madly in Love with ME,
affectionately known as the Queen of Self-Love

Acknowledgments

People say it takes a tribe to raise a child; the same is true of this book. Without the guidance, unconditional love, and generous offerings of my soul tribe, *Madly in Love with ME* would have remained a burning desire in my heart instead of a star of love setting out to light up hearts around the world.

The first person my heart must acknowledge is my soul partner, Noah, who when I announced that I was leaving my cushy corporate job to inspire and teach women and girls to fall madly in love with themselves didn't think me mad but instead supported me 100 percent. None of this would be possible without his unwavering trust and willingness to invest in me and this mission. Thank you, Noah, for your never-ending belief in and love for me, and for putting up with all that comes with being married to an impassioned woman who loves her work. You have never complained, just loved.

To my soul sister and transformational artist Shiloh Sophia McCloud, who while sipping wine and eating chocolate on our New Year Retreat 2010 told me if I didn't write this book now, then I was never going to write it. In one weekend, with her artistic tutelage, I created a hand-illustrated booklet that became the foundation for this book. Thank you, Shiloh, for being a visionary's visionary and for giving your love and talents so generously.

Speaking of generosity, this book was written in the most beautiful places — California's wine country and coast — thanks to my soul sisters Kristine Carlson and Nan Crawford, who shared their homes with me so I could retreat from the city and find space near the ocean and the vines. Your spaces held space for me to write this book in beauty with the divine. I am forever grateful.

To Amy Ahlers, my self-love sister and the best business partner a girl could ask for, thank you for always leaning into love in our partnership — and for leaning in extra so I could have space to write this book. Your support has been like love medicine.

To my beloved four-legged soul companion, Nanook, whose unconditional love gave me the strength to keep trusting in love, even after she left this earth a month before I began writing.

To other members of my soul tribe who stuck with me like love glue — Catherine Reser, Tarja Sovay, Michele Livingston, Christine Hassler, Shannon Thompson, Debra Kocher, Rhonda Britten, Indigo Fontaine, and Anne Wagner — thank you for being so fairy-tastic, so full of love!

To all my self-love sisters and brothers who have been there to witness and cheer me on through this wild ride and for supporting me in getting this body of my Great Work into the world — with a special shout-out to my Femmamind, Karen, Amy, Kris and Carol, my rockstar Mastermind Mike, Lissa, Amy and Steve, the team at New World Library, and Marci Shimoff for dubbing me the Queen of Self-Love. And to the countless people who have given their time and energy to this self-love movement, with a special appreciation to Laurie Jacobsen Jones, and a big hug to all the Self-Love Ambassadors. Go, Team Love!!

Last, with eternal gratitude I thank all my spiritual teachers — both formal and informal — who assisted me in finding my way back to the place my soul began, enveloped in unconditional love for myself and embraced by unwavering love from the divine, with a very special heart-full bow to Ariel Spilsbury, in service to the one heart.

Notes

Page xviii, *This fact is backed up by a study*: Nancy Gibbs, "The State of the American Woman: What Women Want Now," Time, October 14, 2009, www.time.com/time/specials/packages/article/0,28804,1930277_1930145_1930309-1,00.html.

Page 30, *Narcissistic personality disorder*: "Narcissistic Personality Disorder: Definition," n.d., Mayo Clinic website, www.mayoclinic.com/health/narcissistic-personality-disorder/DS00652.

Page 31, *You yourself as much as anybody*: Arnie Kozak, *The Everything Buddhism Book* (Avon, MA: Adams Media, 2011), 168.

Page 31, *I love myself...I love you*: Deepak Chopra and Demi Moore, *A Gift of Love: Deepak & Friends Present Music Inspired by the Love Poems of Rumi*, track 6, "Do You Love Me?" (Rasa Music, 1998).

Page 31, *No matter how much we give love*: Louise L. Hay, "Drawing from the Well of Self-Love," *Handbook for the Heart*, ed. Richard Carlson and Benjamin Shield (New York: Little Brown, 1996), 117.

Page 31, *If enough of us embrace love*: Deepak Chopra, "Heart Sounds," *Handbook for the Heart*, ed. Richard Carlson and Benjamin Shield (New York: Little Brown, 1996), 13.

Page 31, *I have an everyday religion*: William Safire, *Words of Wisdom* (New York: Simon & Schuster, 1990), 345.

Page 300, *Wisdom requests a pause*: Alice Walker, *We Are the Ones We've Been Waiting For* (New York: New Press, 2007), 69.

About the Author

Christine Arylo is a transformational teacher and an internationally recognized speaker and author. After earning an MBA from Kellogg and climbing the corporate ladder for fifteen years, she chose to devote her life to creating a new reality for women and girls, one based on self-love and true feminine power instead of the relentless pursuit of having to be, do, and have it all.

A recovering achievement junkie and doing addict, Christine left her cushy executive lifestyle in 2006 to found an international self-love movement, author the go-to book on love and relationships *Choosing ME before WE*, cofound a virtual self-love school for women, Inner Mean Girl Reform School™, and mentor other women. Her dedication has earned her the affectionate title "the Queen of Self-Love." Christine has been featured on CBS, ABC, FOX, WGN, E!, the *Huffington Post*, Beliefnet, the Daily Love, radio shows, and stages around the world, as well as at spas and conferences. She lives in Northern California with her soul partner, Noah.

To find out more about Christine, including how to receive her weekly Love Letters, go to www.ChristineArylo.com.

Throughout the year, Madly in Love with ME offers events, workshops, and self-love retreats around the world and online, as well as a growing collection of self-love accoutrements designed to remind you to love yourself every day. To find out more and join this movement, go to www.MadlyinLovewithME.com.

Each year on the international day of self-love, February 13, Love Ambassadors from around the world consciously choose to recommit to their relationship with themselves by making a self-love promise for that entire year. Love Ambassadors host parties and gatherings big and small to encourage others to make the same commitment. We invite you to join us at www.SelfLoveAmbassadors.com.